CHINA MISPERCEIVED

ALSO BY STEVEN W. MOSHER

Broken Earth: The Rural Chinese (1983)
Journey to the Forbidden China (1985)

CHINA
MISPERCEIVED

American Illusions
and Chinese Reality

STEVEN W. MOSHER

A New Republic Book

BasicBooks
A Division of HarperCollins*Publishers*

Library of Congress Cataloging-in-Publication Data
Mosher, Steven W. ~e s T l-e⁊, 1948~
    China misperceived : American illusions and Chinese
reality / Steven W. Mosher.
        p.   cm.
    Includes bibliographical references and index.
    ISBN 0-465-01097-0 : $22.95
    1. United States—Relations—China.   2. China—
Relations—United States.   3. China—Foreign public
opinion, American.   4. China—Politics and government—
1949–   I. Title.
E183.8.C5M63   1990   90-80246
951.05'9—dc20   CIP

Contents

❧❧❧

Acknowledgments

This book owes its inspiration to a conversation with William F. Buckley about China. Someone should take a closer look, he suggested, at the decidedly gentle treatment accorded Mao's China by Nixon's press corps in 1972. This odd episode in American journalism had long intrigued me as well. Dozens of America's top journalists, so sure-footed on their own turf, had fallen all over themselves praising one of the most despotic regimes ever known to man. I decided to take up Buckley's challenge.

The root cause of the journalists' misperceptions turned out to be neither media bias nor mass delusion. The positive images of China popularized by the correspondents may have been reinforced by eight days of guided tours in February, 1972, but they did not originate there. Richard Nixon and the China watchers, not to mention the Beijing regime itself, might have been working for years to mask the cruelty and violence of the Cultural Revolution, but the kind and sympathetic images of China they deployed in this effort were not, it soon became apparent, solely of their own making. American perceptions of China had been oscillating between poles of attraction and repulsion for decades. It was necessary to trace this larger cycle of hostility-admiration-disenchantment-benevolence.

The tragedy of the Tiananmen Massacre occurred as I was writing the last chapters of this book. It exposed irreconcilable differences between the Beijing regime and the Chinese people, and suggested a way to resolve, once and for always, the longstanding dualism in America's attitudes toward China.

Support for the initial period of research for this book was provided by the Historical Research Foundation, and was later supplemented by a fellowship from the Bradley Foundation. I am grateful to both. Most of the actual writing was done in residence at the Academic Relations Department of the Heritage Foundation in Washington, D.C., where I spent the 1988–89 academic year as a Bradley Resident Scholar. My greatest debt is to the Claremont Institute, which has been my academic home since 1986, and to its president, Dr. Larry Arnn, whose encouragement of this project from its inception was critical to its completion.

Conversations with colleagues enabled me to put a sharper point on my arguments, though I hasten to add that they did not always agree with my conclusions, for which I alone am responsible. Those who served as sounding boards included Chris Flannery, Charles Heatherly, Tom West, Gary Bullert, Rafal Krawczyk, Ben Alexander, Marvin Olasky, John S. Aird, Juergen Domes, Dan Palm, Brian Kennedy, Doug Jeffrey, and Charles Kessler. I am grateful to William F. Buckley, Miriam London, Orville Schell, and Richard Thornton for kindly providing copies of their columns and articles on China. Charles Johnson, an inveterate wanderer through secondhand bookstores and the Dewey decimal shelves of libraries, came up with many useful items. John West, until recently managing editor of Public Research, Syndicated, provided many helpful observations about the journalism field in general. Ed Peffer generously gave me his collection of books on China from the fifties, of which *An Enemy Within* proved especially germane. John Copper drew my attention to the post–Tiananmen Massacre Gallup poll data cited in Chapter 10.

A number of people helped with the manuscript in various stages of preparation. Mark Pietrzyk, my research assistant at the Heritage Foundation, helped to locate and sift through much material from the fifties and sixties at the Library of Congress. Leah Ramalingam, who serves as the administrative assistant of the Asian Studies Center of the Claremont Institute, was invaluable in tracking down obscure references in the library and in typing many chapters of the manuscript. Bill Newlin of Basic Books was everything an editor should be, giving constant encouragement and trenchant suggestions, and I wish him well in his newly chosen vocation of China watcher.

I am indebted, most of all, to my wife, Vera, whose boundless enthusiasm for this project spurred me to write late into the night, while Julie, Stevie, Matthew, and Hannah slept, until the book was finished.

Beyond the bland facade of China's great open cities and the green abundance of its showplace communes lies a vast country *in obscuro*—a China through the looking glass. In this, some say imaginary, country, people do not converse in *People's Daily* platitudes, but use a distractingly earthy language, enriched with sly puns and ancient proverbs; young men sing melancholy songs and brood over lovers and lost illusions; sons and daughters esteem their families above the Party; there are thieves, pickpockets, and prostitutes; village cadres keep "one eye open and one eye shut" to sideline business activities; women quarrel hysterically over their woks in communal kitchens; speculators slip in and out of towns buying and selling ration coupons; underground factories operate; farmers lavish care on their private plots while neglecting the collective lands; and massive numbers of the Chinese peasantry, immemorially patient and industrious, labor daily under hardship and deprivation for three meals of rice gruel and sweet potatoes a day.

—Miriam London and Ivan D. London
"The Other China, Hunger: Part 1:
The Three Red Flags of Death"

Prologue
Nixon's Visit:
The Chinese Shadow Game

—————————— ❦❦❦ ——————————

On 21 February 1972 at 11:30 A.M., the *Spirit of '76* rolled to a stop on the tarmac at the Capital Airport near Beijing, China. On board was the second half of the largest, and arguably the most important, foreign delegation ever to visit the People's Republic of China. The President of the United States, Richard Nixon, accompanied by his national security advisor, Henry Kissinger, his secretary of state, William Rogers, and several dozen White House and State Department senior staffers, disembarked to be greeted by Chinese premier Zhou Enlai. The nonofficial half of the American delegation was already on the field, having arrived a day earlier in its own 707. It consisted of some eighty-seven television and print journalists representing the cream of the American media, including Walter Cronkite, Barbara Walters, and Dan Rather, and the columnists William F. Buckley and Theodore H. White. During the next week these two groups, the media and the White House, so often at loggerheads during the Nixon presidency, found themselves collaborating in an odd and unprecedented endeavor: cementing a shift in domestic opinion toward a Chinese Communist regime that many Americans still numbered among their nation's bitterest enemies.

By early 1972, the Yellow Peril, the prime geopolitical menace of Asia in the 1950s, was rapidly receding on the American threat horizon. The human wave attacks of the Korean War had not been replicated in the Vietnam conflict, where the Chinese, while providing

1

aid, arms, and worker battalions to the North, stopped short of committing combat troops. The indefatigable aggressor of Asia was well on the way to being transformed, in the American mind, into a New China of peaceful construction, socialist civilization, and ideals that appealed to the egalitarian strain in American thought. A renewed enchantment with China burst forth on all fronts. Window shoppers found fashionable Chinese gowns on display in the windows of Saks while other shops displayed Mao jackets and the padded cotton tunics worn by Chinese peasants. Modern Marco Polos returned from Beijing to write wondrous tales about life in pastoral communes and worker-run factories. And Maryknoll seminarians concluded from their study of Mao's Little Red Book that China was close to achieving a truly selfless society, a secular version of St. Augustine's City of God. Even less-captivated Americans were impressed by China's discipline, austerity, and public morality.

If reshaping popular images of China struck many journalists as long overdue and politically desirable (and we shall see that it did), it was for Nixon a political necessity. By his visit to China in an election year, he was engaging in political theater on a grand scale. But the cast of 800 million and the exotic settings that had been arranged by Kissinger would avail him naught if his protagonists, Chairman Mao and Premier Zhou, stepped outside their scripted roles. Any repetition of the anti-American rhetoric of the recent past, and support for his mission would vanish.[1] Any declarations of aggressive or expansionist intent would wreak havoc with his reelection plans. But convincing Americans, with the help of the Chinese leadership, that China was no longer an implacable foe was only half of Nixon's problem. The strong moralistic strain in American foreign policy would not permit a U.S.-China rapprochement based on cold-blooded calculations of national interest alone. The unalloyed tyranny that the People's Republic of China had become during the Cultural Revolution had to be gilded.

The visit did not begin auspiciously. Gathered in front of a phalanx of soldiers, the reception committee was smaller than the waiting American press corps. Nixon emerged from his plane clapping his hands—the gesture of a man who has been told that in China the polite visitor returns applause—and awkwardly stopped when he saw that no one was applauding. Premier Zhou greeted the president after a fashion that was more correct than cordial, and the two briefly trooped the line, Nixon's party straggling behind. Worse yet, the route from the airport to Beijing was deserted, and the police could be seen at a distance of 150 yards or so keeping away the curious. To the accompanying press corps the absence of a crowd seemed a deliberate slight, since Beijing routinely assembled crowds for visiting dignitaries. A cheering claque of more than five hundred thousand had enthusiastically greeted Emperor Haile Selassie in recent weeks, yet now the streets were empty.

Whatever private thoughts Nixon harbored about the country in which he had just landed, the cool reception he had received, or the man with whom he would be negotiating, he kept them to himself, subordinating all to the hope of scoring a resounding foreign policy success. Nixon, the old cold warrior, may have gone to China "without illusions," as he claimed a few weeks before his journey, but he arrived burdened with the need to create an illusion of his own about China and its leaders.

This burden grew measurably lighter after Nixon, accompanied by Kissinger, was unexpectedly whisked away to a private meeting with Chairman Mao that afternoon. Though the president would not divulge exactly what had passed between them, the mere fact that a meeting had occurred convinced the accompanying reporters that his visit had the chairman's blessing and would no doubt succeed. Both Nixon and Zhou, who had also been at the meeting, were transformed.

That evening, at the welcoming banquet in the Great Hall of the People, Nixon was aglow with cordiality, and his toast was a masterpiece of conciliation, intended as much for his audience back home as for the Chinese. "There is no reason for us to be enemies," he proposed, gliding over the fact that America and China were supporting opposite sides in the Vietnam War. "[N]either of us seeks to stretch out our hands and rule the world." Invoking the founding myth of the Chinese Communist party, he proposed that the two countries should "start a long march together." He called down the benediction of the Founding Father himself on these efforts to "build a new world," reciting a poem by Chairman Mao:

So many deeds cry out to be done, and always urgently. The world rolls on. Time passes. Ten thousand years are too long. Seize the day, seize the hour![2]

Concluding his toast, the Leader of the Free World asked everyone present to join him in "raising your glasses to Chairman Mao, to Prime Minister Zhou, and to the friendship of the Chinese and American people." Nixon then proceeded from table to table and, like a groom at a Chinese wedding required by custom to toast all the guests individually, clinked his glass with each Chinese official at the banquet. By the count of one bemused reporter he personally saluted in this fashion more than seventy high-ranking Communist officials in the cause of Chinese-American friendship. All in all, it was a singular performance from a man whose public persona was the exemplar of a hard-line anti-Communist. But if Nixon's dinner party behavior seemed, well, slightly out of character, his attendance of a "revolutionary opera" the following night and his reaction afterward were nothing short of surreal.

The revolutionary opera was the brainchild of Mao's wife, Jiang Qing, who became China's *de facto* cultural czar during the Cultural Revolution. It was Mao's dictum that all art should serve the state, and she had applied herself to that task with notable ruthlessness. One of her first acts was to ban *all* traditional operas as licentious, feudal, and reactionary. In their place she installed half a dozen so-called "Revolutionary Model operas on contemporary themes," based on the prerevolutionary propaganda skits that Red Army troupes used to mobilize peasant support for the Communist cause during the Chinese civil war. These Maoist morality tales, taken together, are surely the most relentlessly propagandistic and brazenly militaristic works ever to be trod upon the boards. Simon Leys scathingly described them as "feeble Punch and Judy shows, where the only 'revolutionary' daring is to maneuver on stage, to languorous saxophonic Khachaturian-like music, platoons of the People's Liberation Army complete with banners and wooden rifles."[3]

The play Jiang Qing selected for the president's edification was *The Red Detachment of Women*. The heroine is a poor peasant's daughter, so cruelly mistreated by Despotic Landlord and his henchmen that she runs off and joins the Red Army. "Under the banner of Mao Zedong," and with "the support of the broad revolutionary masses," her platoon of Communist amazons wins victory after bloody victory. Finally, the day of liberation dawns, and the People's Republic of China is established. In the climactic scene of the play, she returns to her native village to settle old scores. With guns popping, machine guns chattering, and grenades bursting in the air, she strikes Despotic Landlord dead. It was a crude and simple tale, dedicated to the proposition that all who support violent revolution are paragons of proletarian virtue while all who oppose it are unredeemable devil's spawn. Lest any interpret the play in narrow, nationalistic terms, the official synopsis pointed out that the valiant and sanguine warriors of the Red Army were struggling "for the freedom of all mankind."

Now Richard Nixon, who had made no secret of his aversion to class warfare, would have ordinarily had some difficulty coming to terms with this message. A few months before, for example, he had described some domestic advocates of revolution, the Students for a Democratic Society (SDS), as "campus bums." In another recent speech he had beckoned mankind to join him in establishing "a generation of peace." Yet here he was seated next to Madam Mao, revolutionary role model for the SDS, vigorously applauding each new victory of the proletariat. Even the show's bloody finale did not drive the smile from his face, and afterward he was quick to congratulate its patroness.

Nixon may have felt that diplomatic courtesy dictated his presence at this performance, as well as a courteous comment or two upon its completion (although it is doubtful that the use of some face-saving formula—a slight indisposition, say—would have offended his Chinese hosts, given their grasp of the ideological conflicts involved). In his determination to ingratiate himself with China's leaders and reshape American public opinion, however, Nixon went whole hog. Asked by a reporter the following day if he was finding the afterhours events entertaining, Nixon practically burst into song. "Fantastic!" he warbled. "I thought the ballet was great. . . . Then, too, the ballet was, of course, as we all know, it had its message and that was one of its purposes, but also, while it was a powerful message and intended for that, it was also very dramatic—excellent theater and excellent dancing and music, and really superb acting. I was very impressed. I have seen ballets all over the world, including the Soviet Union and the United States. This is certainly the equal of any ballet I have seen. . . . (A)nother thing was the vivid effect when they had the rifle fire, having the gunpowder smoke float back into the audience so we could smell it. You had a feel of realism that was quite vivid."[4] President Nixon's claim to the contrary, he was not known as a habitué of the opera, and it is possible that he truly found the wooden performance he had witnessed enchanting. The real message in the bottle, however, was his casual dismissal of the play's propaganda content. "I did not take offense at the opera's blatantly Marxist message," he winked at the watching Chinese, "and you shouldn't either," he nodded to listening Americans.[5]

The remainder of the week unfolded in like fashion. The president spent most of his time closeted with Premier Zhou and Kissinger. He emerged from his isolation only for the occasional cameo appearance—a tour of the Great Wall, a visit to the Forbidden City, a jaunt down to Hangzhou, a farewell banquet in Shanghai—and used these occasions to praise China's past and utter pleasantries about China's present. Just as Premier Zhou published pictures of a smiling Chairman Mao greeting President Nixon in the *People's Daily* to reassure the Chinese people that the visit of the world's Number One Capitalist Roader had the blessing of the Chairman, so Nixon seized upon his opportunities in front of the camera to utter sound bites of reassurance to domestic audiences that the Chinese Communists weren't such bad fellows after all.

The Chinese proved to be as concerned as Nixon, and more adept than he, about projecting a benign image to watching Americans. "From its inception," *Newsweek* remarked approvingly, "the visit was orchestrated by the Chinese with a unique mixture of elegance and simplicity, propriety and warmth."[6] The emphasis here should be on the word *orchestrated*. When the presidential party toured the gardens at the Ming Tombs, burial place for thirteen Ming Dynasty emperors, for example, they encountered one group after another of "happy" Chinese citizens *en tableau:* smiling children with rouged faces skipping rope, giggling teenagers playing gin rummy, and happy cadres making a great show of listening to transistor radios. Similar set pieces decorated the Great Wall and the entrance to the Forbidden City. If Nixon was aware of the meticulous care with which the

Chinese had choreographed each of his outings and other activities, he gave no sign of it, and the media mentioned these efforts only to praise them. "As if to emphasize that they . . . wanted more communication between peoples, the Chinese staged a small 'spontaneous' gathering of citizens at the site of the fabled Ming Tombs," was how *Newsweek* calmly described these Potemkin villagers.[7]

It was in this same all-forgiving spirit that Nixon lifted his glass one last time to his "Chinese friends," as he thrice referred to them, at the farewell banquet given by the Shanghai Municipal Revolutionary Committee. From his final remarks (he was to leave for home in a few hours) the press singled out as extravagant and self-serving his claim that his brief sojourn in China had been "the week that changed the world." Overlooked were several other, hardly less extravagant claims about the China he had seen. "We have, today, seen the progress of modern times," Nixon said, referring to their visit to the Shanghai Industrial Exhibition. "We have seen the matchless wonder of ancient times. We have seen also the beauty of the countryside, the vibrancy of a great city, Shanghai."[8] Professed at a time when "progress of modern times" had ground to a halt because of the Cultural Revolution's attacks on education and its disruption of industry, when China's "matchless wonders" had been largely destroyed by rampaging Red Guards, and when the "great city" of Shanghai had been reduced to a husk of its former vibrant self—these claims are nothing short of fantastic. Yet the media did not find them objectionable, or even remarkable: They had been crediting the "New China" with similar advances all week.

During Nixon's one-week visit the eighty-seven-member press corps produced a small blizzard of television, newspaper, and magazine accounts of life in revolutionary China, almost all favorable. They also bore a strong family resemblance to one another, a testament to strict Chinese control over access. They were in China but were not free to explore China. Everything was off-limits except a carefully vetted list of twenty-seven outings. Upon request, a reporter would be taken to see the Hua Xi Li Housing Project, or Beijing University, or the Lougoujiao Commune in suburban Beijing. What these and the other two dozen organizations on the list had in common was that they were all showcases, stocked with well-rehearsed officials and model peasants or workers. The result was that each

7

reporter's account of his visit to, say, the ever-popular Lougoujiao Commune resembled every other account.

Those who are familiar with the no-holds-barred attitude of reporters may be surprised to learn that these restrictions did not chafe at their professional sensibilities. Almost everyone in the American contingent was disarmed by the extraordinary politeness and charm of Chinese officials. In particular, those who had experienced the heavy-handedness of the Russians and East Europeans were so soothed by the stylish Chinese way of managing barbarians that they were slow to realize how closely they were tethered. With officials gracefully offering a *choice* of twenty-seven different destinations, how could they fail to feel a sense of expansiveness?

The convergence in reporters' dispatches that resulted went far beyond superficialities of local color. Most journalists were of one mind about larger issues as well: the beneficial impact of the Cultural Revolution on the institutions of society and on public mores; the eradication of human vices such as crime, drug addiction, and prostitution, with its attendant scourge of venereal disease; the creation of a new, selfless Maoist man; the success of the rural communes in improving peasant lives; and the material achievements of the revolution that (in their collective view) had elevated China to the status of world power.

Perhaps the most influential of the print journalists to accompany Nixon was Theodore H. White. Widely known for his "Making of the President" series, he had cut his journalistic teeth in China, having served as the *Time* correspondent in China for several years in the mid-forties. *Thunder Out of China*, the book that resulted, was a mixture of scathing denunciation of the Ins (the Nationalist government) and enthusiastic cheerleading for the Outs (the Chinese Communist party). Back in China for the first time since the revolution, White was on assignment for *Life* magazine. But his first and most attentive audience consisted of his companion journalists, who were anxious to hear the verdict of an Old China Hand on the New China. They did not have long to wait.

White began his deliberations on the flight over, at one point holding up to ridicule a press clipping reporting that 34 million people had been killed since the advent of communism in China.[9] His suspicion of statistics vanished once on the ground, where he was bombarded with production figures on everything from tons of steel and coal to pounds of cabbage and radishes per *mou* (about one-sixth of an acre), "all of them rising." "For Chinese, statistics are the poetry of politics," he rhapsodizes, apparently unaware that he had stumbled upon the truth.[10] The numbers game played by Chinese officials had much more to do with the art of political survival than with the science of statistics. Woe to the official whose figures on steel or spinach, bicycles or barefoot doctors did not show hefty annual increases beginning with Year One of the Cultural Revolution, especially if they had been assigned to work the foreign guest circuit.

If the possibility of Chinese officials' cooking the books occurred to White, he does not mention it. The skeptical, hard-nosed reporter who had relentlessly tracked half a dozen candidates from the hustings to the White House seemed to have dedicated his visit to taking Maoism at face value. The sham statistics "add[ed] up to a simple fact: power. . . . There is muscle here," he insisted, "a thrust, a rhythm of growth, a complex of a strength which is by now one of the world's primordial facts."[11] White had reached his first conclusion: The revolution was a resounding material success. During his twenty-five years out of the country, China had become one of the world's economic giants.

The Communist leadership had made striking improvements in human virtue as well, White maintained, "mold[ing] the minds of illiterate peasants, calling them to dignity, writing sharp new ideas on minds erased of thought by centuries of oppression and servility. On these blank minds they wrote the idea of the collective, the common will, the nobility of work, sacrifice and death for the common cause."[12] Among those who had had their minds thus rewritten were pedicab drivers. Unlike the venal rickshaw man of Old China, White's driver on a trip around Peking neither touted for prostitutes nor accepted tips. The cynic might view this as a case of fear paralyzing greed, since the punishment for accepting such ill-gotten gains was severe. White saw it as another jewel in the crown of the New Maoist Man.

No revolutionary achievement loomed larger in White's mind than the Maoist commune, which he perceived as the salvation of the "oppressed" Chinese peasantry. "Prewar Chinese villages were always in a state of crumbling," he assured his readers. "[They had] holes in the roofs, tiles gone from the rafters, gaps in the adobe walls, pigs, chickens, oxen in the family courtyards."[13] Since White did not arrive in China until 1941, by which time hostilities with Japan were entering their fifth year, it is not surprising that he was jarred by the destruction and desolation of wartime China. But this was not "pre-war" China, of which he had no personal acquaintance.

Using his memories of wartime China as a yardstick, White found that Lougoujiao Commune, the popular rural showcase, more than measured up. He was particularly impressed by the houses ("solidly built, with no pigs, chickens or animals in the courtyard"), and the country store ("a shopping center" with goods "decisively more abundant than in rural France or southern Italy").[14] What White doesn't tell us, probably because he does not know, is that the private rearing of animals was forbidden during the Cultural Revolution as a "capitalist weed," and that collectively run pigsties and chicken coops made up only a fraction of the difference. Rural incomes plummeted, putting almost all of the goods available in the state store out of reach, even if they had been for sale. In fact most of the stock was for display only, especially in communes designated for foreign guests, and much of the rest was rationed. Had White not been so eager to validate the central myth of the revolution, that the peasants had benefitted mightily from its bloodshed, he might have realized that there were worse things than having to keep pigs, chickens, and oxen in the family courtyard—namely, being forbidden to keep farm animals at all.

If there was anything that troubled White about the New China, it was the overpowering presence of the Chairman of the Chinese Communist party. He clearly found it distasteful that the Great Helmsman's books dominated every bookshelf, that his slogans smothered every available exterior wall, and that his visage commanded every private and public altar. Yet in the face of the most elaborate cult of personality since Joseph Stalin's, White could not bring himself to utter that disparaging phrase. "There is no easy way of understanding [Mao's role in Chinese society]," he declares with serpentine ambiguity, "this is no classic tyranny or dictatorship."[15] He admits that Maoist ideology leaves "no escape, no crevice for private thought," but has no use for the word "totalitarian"; he writes that the Cultural Revolution has "eliminated" and "erased" many in the leadership, but stops short of calling this political emetic a "purge"; and, the most remarkable omission of all, he publishes a six-thousand-word article about a self-declared people's republic ruled by a party whose patron saints are Marx, Engels, Lenin, and Stalin, but never once refers to it as Communist. The most charitable explanation for these lacunae—that White was worried about offending Chinese sensibilities—doesn't wash: The Maoists in control of China at the time gloried in their ideological purity. Rather, the answer seems to lie with White himself.

In the words of William F. Buckley, who sat next to White on the flight over, his liberal fellow journalist was "ecstatic at the prospect of . . . justifying his early optimism about the vector of Chinese Communism."[16] Once in China, White was an easy mark for encounters, the more striking the better, that would affirm his long-held beliefs. One man refused a tip, and all Chinese became New Socialist Men; a few sets of phony statistics, and China became an economic power; pigs no longer root in the courtyards of Lougoujiao villagers, and collective agriculture was a stunning success. White proved unable or unwilling to make a distinction between that which he had been encouraged to see and that which had been hidden from view. No generalization was too broad, no conclusion too sweeping, in the collage of socialist progress that he constructed.

As White's ideological opposite, William F. Buckley brought a different set of presuppositions to bear on the People's Republic of China. A staunch anti-Communist, he had been dismayed by the defeat of the Nationalists at the hands of the Chinese Communist party. Unlike White, he had spoken out frequently and forcefully when the revolution had devoured first its enemies and then its own, convinced that the only "great achievement" of the "New China" was the enslavement of the Chinese people. Again unlike White, he believed that Nixon's overture to China was not only not in the best interests of the United States, it was positively immoral given the enormity of the crimes of those with whom Nixon would be meeting. Consider, for instance, his description of Nixon's unexpected round-robin toasting of "two dozen . . . old generals, commissars, politicians" of the "largest totalitarian country in the history of the world":

11

Kindly make no mistake about the moral courage this required. It is unreasonable to suppose that anywhere in history have a few dozen men congregated who have been responsible for greater human mayhem than the hosts at this gathering and their spiritual colleagues, instruments all of Mao Zedong. The effect was as if Sir Hartley Shawcross had suddenly risen from the prosecutor's stand at Nuremberg and descended to embrace Goering and Goebbels and Doenitz and Hess, begging them to join with him in the making of a better world. Never mind the difference, that the latter were convicted butchers, aggressors, and genocide-makers, and the former, by the narrowest quirk of the Cultural Revolution, are not: all that that difference reminds us of is that history is indeed the polemics of the victor.[17]

Buckley's reaction to a visit to Beijing University—one of the twenty-seven guided tours available—was a similar mixture of wit and venom:

[This visit was] probably the most shattering single experience of the journey because one had the sense of participating in a show trial. Our host was the active head of the university, who got his advanced degree in physics from the University of Chicago in 1926, which solved the language problem, right? Wrong. The poor derelict, whose English had been previously ascertained to have been as good as Eric Sevareid's, spoke through an interpreter. Because the room was full of Red Guard thugs, and it was obvious that they desired to hear his answers so that, if necessary, they could later on correct him for ideological irregularities.

Cautiously, during the question period, we probed the circumstances of his and his university's humiliation, without of course exactly letting on. We knew that he knew that we knew that he was reduced to puppetry. . . . Someone asked him what had been the errors of Beijing University before the Great Proletarian Cultural Revolution caught up with them, and he replied that the errors, partly his own responsibility, had been to imitate Russian universities by forgetting the imperative of proletarian politics and lending itself instead to the cultivation of an academic elite. Translated, that means Beijing U sought excellence. How had he learned the exact nature of his delinquencies? A "Mao Thought Propaganda Team" came to the university in the fall of 1968 and stayed on a whole year. After they left, the governing of the university was turned over to a "revolutionary council," of which this wretched man had become the spokesman, surrounded by brachycephalic peasants who, knowing only how to praise the thoughts of Chairman Mao, need know aught else, in order to correct the venerable professor.

We puzzle that our hosts should have proudly invited us to view contemporary Chinese Communist academic life. One recalls Evelyn Waugh's Azania, where the young black prince, incompletely educated in Western habits, gave a state banquet to two very British ladies come to inspect the local situation in behalf of the Royal Society for the Prevention of Cruelty to Animals. In his toast, the prince solemnly averred that, in Azania, they worked industriously to devise means of being cruel to animals, that they had not yet achieved English standards, but that they were every day making progress.[18]

In contrast to Buckley's vigorous criticism of the Maoist university and the ongoing persecution of intellectuals, White manifests a lame ambivalence:

"One tries to pick up conversations with professors, but finds it difficult. It is as if they had been lobotomized, as if China's past were erased. Before the Cultural Revolution, scholars here [at Beijing University] taught no less than ten courses in history to cover China's chronicle of 3,000 years. Now only three courses are given. One covers the span from primitive past to the Opium War of 1840; another covers the years of humiliation by the West between that date and the May 4th movement of 1919; the third is simply the history of the Communist party to date. History, sociology and social sciences are unnecessary in China any longer. . . . Science is, apparently, well taught. But what there is to know of man and his problems—all this is encompassed in the thinking of Mao; and the university, as all China, vibrates to it, tries to act on it."[19]

The visions of China contained in the dispatches of White and Buckley could not have been more dissimilar. White hints at the moral superiority of the communist order; Buckley speaks of its heavy toll in human suffering. White heralds the great achievements of the revolution; Buckley speaks of the regimentation of the human spirit. White apologizes for the Cultural Revolution; Buckley calls it a disaster. If White's rosy optimism about the revolution led him to extrapolate from model communes and factories to all of China, then Buckley's robust skepticism collapsed Nixon's visit to a cardboard facade. "Totalitarian societies are very good at hiding things like concentration camps, Liu Shaoqis, and material misery," he noted at one point, referring to China's one-time "Chairman of the People's Republic," who had mysteriously vanished at the height of the Cultural Revolution some years before.[20] Yet while Buckley's iconoclasm, combined with a general knowledge of Communist history and tactics, served him far better than White's credulousness, these only partly compensated for the lack of hard data. In retrospect, even he erred on the side of optimism.

The Red Guards had disappeared by 1972, and the correspondents, Buckley included, assumed that the Cultural Revolution was over. In fact, it was to last four more years. Though rejecting the notion of China as a nascent superpower advanced by White, Buckley agreed that its economic progress had been impressive. In fact, China's economy was a shambles, a victim not only of the waste, fraud, and inefficiency of central planning, but also of the chaos and lack of incentive produced by the Cultural Revolution and its leveling schemes.

Far and away the most critical issue confronting the press was the degree to which each correspondent thought that he or she was being actively deceived about conditions in China, for on that evaluation hinged one's entire reaction to the China experience. Though Buckley was convinced that Nixon's visit had been carefully choreographed, skepticism alone could not tell him how incredibly elaborate the preparations had been. Fully three months before the arrival of the president, a set of official party documents had been circulated throughout China to inform the masses that the decade-long policy of targeting "American Imperialism" as China's number one enemy was about to be scrapped. As the visit drew nearer, each of the provinces and cities that Nixon or the press were expected to visit launched massive public education and clean-up campaigns. The dissident author Chen Jo-hsi, in her artfully written story "Nixon's Press Corps," recounts the instructions received by students and faculty at a Nanjing university:

The eighty-man press group traveling with Nixon may pass through Nanjing tomorrow for a one-day visit, [the party officials said] so we must be ready. Today we will suspend all normal activities in order to have a general clean-up and to tidy up the lawns. All laboratory equipment must be cleaned up and labeled in both Chinese and English; if necessary, get some help from the Foreign Languages Section. We believe that the reporters will be in Nanjing for the day only, so the possibility of a visit to our school is very remote. But as Chairman Mao has taught us, "Do not fight unprepared battles." . . . It is of the utmost importance for us to grasp the characteristics of these reporters. They have their "three excesses"—an excess of running around, an excess of questions, and an excess of picture taking. But we have our ways of dealing with them. . . . Don't go milling about on the streets tomorrow unless you have something important to do! There are some who must pay special attention to this, who must behave themselves and refrain from any untoward conduct![21]

On the chance that they might nevertheless run into these inquisitive foreigners, lists of sample questions that the correspondents might ask were distributed, "so that," as Chen put it, "everyone could practice giving appropriate answers."[22]

In fairness to Buckley, the raft of favorable reports about China by selected journalists, scholars, and public figures allowed to visit that country in 1970–71 had created a current of favorable opinion that was difficult to resist. Had he suggested that the country was mobilized to put its best foot forward, that political prisoners were being tortured, and that dissent was only suppressed by the Maoist Terror, he would have been dismissed as a paranoid crank. To have given such positions respectability would have taken someone with the moral authority of a Solzhenitsyn, reporting at great personal risk from within China.

A few publications initially eschewed what I have characterized as the White and the Buckley views and pledged themselves to an effort to find a nonexistent "middle ground." *Newsweek,* for example, editorialized that China fit "neither the old cliches nor the new stereotypes," that it was "neither a frenzied red anthill nor an egalitarian utopia." Yet the report that followed was almost as riddled with false claims as were the "enthusiastic accounts of modern visitors" that it had initially criticized.[23]

Time would gradually reveal which view was closer to the truth, but there was no doubt which one came to dominate the minds of Americans. By the time the *Spirit of '76* lifted off for home, images of China had been radically altered. Nixon's days in China may not have been, in his extravagant phrase, "the week that changed the world," but they did cement a new set of American attitudes toward China and the Chinese. The transformation was highlighted by a Gallup Poll in which those surveyed were given a short list of adjectives and were asked to choose those that best described the Chinese. In 1966, with the exception of the word "hard-working," respondents placed only pejorative terms—"ignorant," "warlike," "sly," and "treacherous"—at the top of the list. By the time Nixon concluded his visit, the five most frequently selected adjectives were "hard-working," "intelligent," "artistic," "progressive," and "practical."[24]

These new images of China were not originated by Nixon, although they were essential to the success of his visit. Nor were they the creation of the American media, although they provided much grist for the reportorial mill and were welcomed by some as a vindication of socialism. The proximate source of these images was the writings, musings, and speculations of an informal coalition of disaffected intellectuals, liberal scholars, and foreign policy experts, including Edgar Snow, Ross Terrill, Henry Kissinger, John Gurley, and John K. Fairbank. The ultimate source was China itself. Beijing's ceaseless self-promotion of its socialist experiment had paid generous foreign policy dividends, as many assumed rather than debated the success of Maoism. The fawning reports that China's new rulers had orchestrated about the PRC had so muddied the waters that it was impossible for even a William F. Buckley to grope his way to the truth.

"If Mao Zedong had 'free elections' in Mainland China tomorrow," he wrote before his trip to that country, "it is altogether possible that he would achieve 99 percent of the vote even if immunity were granted to dissenters. The reason for this is apparent from the reports on China that have come flooding in since the authorities there raised the curtain to a few athletes and journalists last spring. China seems to have killed or otherwise disposed of the incremental objector, so as to have achieved a society of the perfectly misled. No doubt it is true, as a Bolshevik hack once blurted out, that when all the world is covered in asphalt, one day a crack will appear, and through that crack, a blade of grass will grow. There no doubt stirs, in a Chinese breast or two, the seed of defiance: but it is not the kind of thing that any longer threatens the regime. It is as safe from being taken over by people who desire liberalism, as the American Legion is safe from being taken over by Communists."[25] Thus, in the end, even William F. Buckley reluctantly endorsed the quintessential myth of the People's Republic, namely, that the Cultural Revolution had successfully molded a new Maoist man. The theory that human nature could be radically transformed would be dealt a final, unequivocal blow in 1989, when millions of Chinese would be seen in the streets of Beijing demanding a society based not upon a radical egalitarianism, but upon a respect for individual human dignity and rights. Yet at the time of Nixon's visit few doubted that this central objective of Mao's Revolution had been substantially achieved. In the cheerful, patient, industrious and, above all, orthodox Chinese they met, the correspondents discerned the collective face of fraternity and equality.

1
Introduction:
The Culture Brokers

————————— ❧❧❧ —————————

In 1958, a China journalist turned scholar named Harold Isaacs published a thoughtful examination of changing American perceptions of China entitled *Scratches on Our Minds*. He postulated two images of China, one benign and one malignant, which had in his view been competing for primacy in the Western mind for centuries. Isaacs' vivid description of these two extremes is worth quoting in its entirety:

> The name of Marco Polo is scratched onto the mind of almost every American school child. Attached to it are powerful images of China's ancient greatness, civilization, art, hoary wisdom. With it in time comes a heavy cluster of admirable qualities widely attributed to the Chinese as people: high intelligence, persistent industry, filial piety, peaceableness, stoicism. These were attributes identified in our own generation with the people of Pearl S. Buck's novels, solid, simple, courageous folk staunchly coping with the blows of fate and adverse circumstances.
>
> Genghis Khan and his Mongol hordes are the non-Chinese ancestors of quite another set of images also strongly associated with the Chinese: cruelty, barbarism, inhumanity; a faceless, impenetrable, overwhelming mass, irresistible if once loosed. Along this way we discover the devious and difficult heathen, the killers of girl infants, the binders of women's feet, the torturers of a thousand cuts, the headsmen, the Boxer Rebellion and the Yellow Peril, the nerveless indifference to pain, death, or to human disaster, the whole set of lurid, strange, and fearful images clustered around the notion of the awakening giant and brought vividly to life

18

again by Mao Zedong's "human sea" seen flooding down across the Yalu, massed barbarians now armed not with broadswords but with artillery, tanks, and jet planes.[1]

Each set of images has been ready to displace the other as historical circumstances permit. At the time of the American Founding, respectful views of Chinese civilization were common, absorbed from Enlightenment philosophers such as Leibniz and Voltaire who thought they saw in China the rule of right reason. As more came to be known about China's despotic government, these favorable impressions declined, vanishing altogether after China was defeated in the first and second Opium Wars, forced to cede territory to the European powers and grant extraterritorial privileges to their citizens. Among other things, these concessions gave impetus to the American missionary enterprise, whose practitioners set out to save the "benighted heathens" from superstition and backwardness. From open contempt, the attitudes of missionaries had moderated to a patronizing benevolence by the beginning of the twentieth century, as they broadened their scope from the individual soul to the salvation of the entire society.

The Japanese invasion overturned these old attitudes abruptly, as reports of the valiant resistance offered by the outgunned Chinese to their would-be conquerors was applauded by admiring Americans, especially in the wake of the surprise attack on Pearl Harbor. This sentiment ebbed in turn as reports of military ineffectiveness, civil strife, and governmental corruption mounted. By the end of the war the American public had come to view their erstwhile allies with a jaundiced eye. Disenchantment soured into active hostility when the Chinese Communist party emerged victorious from the civil war, forcing the Nationalists into exile on the island of Taiwan and forging an alliance with the Soviet Union. This antipathy was exacerbated by the Red Army's unexpected assault on American troops in Korea and the Quemoy-Matsu crisis several years later, and was carried forward into the sixties by the violence of the Cultural Revolution.

After Nixon quietly set out upon his long march to China in 1969, the pendulum began once more to swing in the other direction. Scores of American travelers reverently toured the People's Republic in 1970–72, returning to portray a truly heroic New China, a portrayal given further credence by the rash of articles that surrounded Nixon's visit. With more sustained contact in the late seventies, the political excesses of the Cultural Revolution (not to mention the petty deceptions practiced on visiting foreigners) became more widely known, and disillusionment set in once again. Although Americans recognized that the Communist government was largely to blame, they could not long remain indifferent to the newly revealed face of poverty and underdevelopment in China. The desire of the Chinese people to improve their lives and modernize their country struck a sympathetic chord. Despite strenuous efforts by both governments to create the impression that this time China and the United States were coming together as equals, the old patron-client relationship was reestablishing itself on several levels—cultural, educational, and economic. Where once America had seemed intent on saving China through transcendent religion, now it was bent on rescuing China from dire poverty by transcendent capitalism.

On 4 June 1989 China's leaders violently rejected America's tutelage. To Americans who had been romantically caught up in the student demonstrations for democracy, their brutal suppression was devastating. Once again the peaceful and courageous Chinese people were being oppressed by the cruel hordes of an alien ideology. The old image of the People's Republic as an evil empire came unbidden to the American mind.

Based on his review of perceptions of China through the mid-1950s, Isaacs suggests that "a certain chronology establishes itself, and if we were to list it crudely, like an exercise in a history book, it would look something like this:

1. The Age of Respect (Eighteenth Century)
2. The Age of Contempt (1840–1905)
3. The Age of Benevolence (1905–1937)
4. The Age of Admiration (1937–1944)
5. The Age of Disenchantment (1944–1949)
6. The Age of Hostility (1949–   )[2]

A similar chronology also suggests itself for the period from 1949:

1. The Age of Hostility (1949–1972)
2. The Second Age of Admiration (1972–1977)
3. The Second Age of Disenchantment (1977–1980)
4. The Second Age of Benevolence (1980–1989)

Even less than Isaacs' Ages does this periodization capture within its neat chronological boundaries the sum of America's recent emotions about China. Each of the attitudes that predominated for a time—hostility, admiration, and benevolence—has a core constituency, individuals whose image of China is unblurred by doubt and unshaken by conflicting information. During the Age of Hostility leftist Sinophiles continued to weave fancies about the People's Republic that were all the more elaborate for being unconstrained by any contact with Chinese reality. Although there is now a widespread perception that China is going capitalist, anti-Communists never tire of pointing out that the basic structure of government has not changed, a position mightily reinforced by the Tiananmen massacre. For the foreseeable future, regardless of which sentiment happens to predominate in the popular mind, all will live on.

THE CULTURE BROKERS

These several attitudes, though held by tens of millions of Americans, stem ultimately from a relatively small, diverse band of cultural brokers who spent time in China and returned to impress their findings on a substantial audience. With its many poles of attraction, China has been a magnet for missionaries, journalists, diplomats, bohemians, tourists, adventurers, dilettantes, scholars, New Agers, and Marxist revolutionary activists. These travelers, and their writings, represent the conduits by which information about China was transmitted to the United States. Sometimes this transmission was immediate and profuse, as with journalists whose dispatches reached millions. Sometimes it was diluted by time and limited in impact, as with a book by an academic published years after his or her encounter with China. But all in all, a surprising number of visitors to China wrote about their experience, and their writings reached many Americans, including important individuals within the political, academic, and media elite.

As may be evident by now, the purpose of this book is not merely to chronicle, à la Isaacs, America's alternating attraction to and repulsion for China, but also to distinguish truth from fiction in what has been written about China. Clearly unbalanced, this body of literature ranges from sycophantic "success stories" by Maoist (and latterly Dengist) admirers to the gamely critical anti-Maoist "dirty linen" collections. An informed account of American perceptions and misperceptions of postrevolutionary China is essential to an understanding not only of China, but also of those cultural brokers who would interpret that country to us, particularly those whose notions of truth are utilitarian, relativistic, or romanticized.

This is an auspicious time to attempt what may be called a revisionist history of American thought about China. An older generation of scholars and journalists, accustomed to operating in a polarized atmosphere of hostility or admiration toward China, are in or near retirement. Their replacements, able to come to grips with the Chinese culture and people in a way impossible for many decades, are less likely to engage in ideological flights of fancy as a result. Most important, Chinese intellectuals, bypassing the Chinese state, Communist apologists, and cultural brokers alike, are beginning to speak directly and bluntly to the West about their country's recent history, providing an important reality check. While truly unbiased witnesses remain a rarity—those who become interested in China are, after all, self-selecting—it is becoming easier to recognize the testimony of interested parties for what it is, and to discount it.

The past four decades have produced an enormous outpouring of books, articles, and editorials on China. Rather than ford this great river at its mouth, a daunting task for even the most dedicated Sinologist, I have ventured upstream, above the point where the academic, journalistic, tourist, and other tributaries join together. There I have attempted to take soundings of each over the years as the river floods, recedes, and sometimes changes course, thereby measuring its contribution to the whole.

No tributary is more important than that which springs from the academy. Many scholarly works are, of course, written about obscure topics in soporific prose for minuscule audiences and can safely be ignored for my purposes. Even the rare seminal study has an impact that is often delayed and diffused, replicating slowly through the minds of students, colleagues, and readers over the years and only reaching a wider audience, if at all, as dismembered bits of information, ideas, and attitudes. But riding on the crest of this slow and largely invisible current is a lively froth of popular editorials, articles, and books that influences many readers, primarily on the strength of its borrowed scholarly authority. In the case of China it was academics, expressing themselves in popular forums rather than in scholarly works, who for the most part created the epistemological context against which journalists probed, diplomats evaluated, tourists apprehended, and the public perceived unfolding events in China.

Especially during the years when China isolated itself from the West, the public readily accepted the implicit claim of Sinological savants to be an authoritative voice on all things Chinese. The Ching historian, the Confucian scholar, or the Marxist economist who spoke out on issues unrelated to his specialty was met with deference. I will examine the writings of such academics as the Harvard University Professor John K. Fairbank, who during a long career came to be known as the "dean of Sinology"; Professor Ross Terrill, an Australian Sinologist who for many years made a career out of interpreting Maoism to the American reading public; Professor Pierre Ryckmans, who writes under the pseudonym Simon Leys; and others. Scholars who, despite cleaving more closely to their specialties, produced works for which they claimed a larger political and historical significance, will also be included. The historian Maurice Meisner (*Mao's China*) and the economist John Gurley (*China's Economy and the Maoist Strategy*) exemplify the kind of Maoist apologist who became common in the sixties and seventies, just as the political scientist Richard Walker and the Sinologist Karl Wittvogel represent an earlier, more critical approach to the Communist experiment in China. Though writing books intended primarily for the edification of their students and colleagues, these and other academics found themselves engaged with a larger audience as well.

Given the formidable amount of copy produced by the nation's press, my survey is limited to a few major and, I think, representative publications. I have taken weekly soundings from the mass circulation newsmagazines *Time* and *Newsweek*, and other regular soundings from the journals of opinion the *National Review,* the *New Republic,* and the *Nation*. During pivotal times when American attitudes toward China were shifting rapidly—for example, during Nixon's 1972 visit—I expanded the net to include the national daily press in Washington, D.C. and New York City. In practice this meant reading the dispatches of the China correspondents and editorials of the *Wall Street Journal,* the *New York Times,* the *Washington Post* and, in more recent years, the *Washington Times*. I also felt free to use articles from major regional newspapers like the *San Diego Union* or the *Los Angeles Times,* though I made no effort to review their coverage systematically. Prominent correspondents with a long-standing interest in China, such as Theodore H. White and Harrison E. Salisbury of the *New York Times,* exerted an influence well beyond the copy they produced over the years. White, for example, was a bellwether for many of his colleagues not only during Nixon's visit but also later, in 1983, when he repudiated his earlier favorable view of China.

I have been undeniably eclectic in including books by tourists, both because they have generally been a less substantive source of American impressions of China and because so few have broken new ground. With the advent of political tourism to China in the early seventies came the "China diary," an account of a two-week visit to the standard set of tourist stops following diary form. I have taken a closer look at Charlotte Salisbury's well-publicized *China Diary* which, along with Shirley MacLaine's bestseller, *You Can Get There from Here,* marked the high point of the genre, which declined in popularity as America learned more about China. Few of these early tourists stayed interested in China long enough to become objective observers of the Chinese scene. Among those who did is Orville Schell, whose biennial works about China chart a Pilgrim's Progress from political fancy to political fact. Since Schell's course has proven a popular trajectory for China watchers of the eighties, his writings are of some interest.

The writings of other groups, including diplomats, adventurers, Marxists, and missionaries, are much scantier than those by academics, correspondents, and tourists, and show a pronounced ebb and flow over the years. The early fifties saw a flash flood of accounts by expelled missionaries that vividly described the systematic destruction of the missionary enterprise by the Chinese Communist Party.

The Pagoda and the Cross, by Father John F. Donovan, and similar books contributed to American hostility toward China in those years. This source dried up in the later fifties as another genre, highly favorable accounts of Communist China by nonacademic Marxists, began to grow from a trickle into a sizable stream. Han Suyin, Jan Myrdal, and Jack Chen are among those who in the sixties and seventies contributed books glorifying Mao, exalting the Maoist commune, and praising the Maoist road to development. This crew was effectively silenced by China's abandonment of the Maoist way, and this stream quickly disappeared into the sands of reform. China's renewed openness to tourism has given adventurers, long forbidden from the Chinese hinterland, leave to wander off the beaten track. Unlike most earlier writings about China, their accounts are virtually apolitical and have contributed to the political decompression of sentiments about China in the eighties.

Until the student demonstrations of 1989, neither television nor movies had made a major contribution to the substance or accuracy of American perceptions of postwar China, and I make only brief mention of them. Hollywood has for the most part used China only as a backdrop—*The Last Emperor* was a rare exception—when it mentions it at all. The television networks fought for seats on Nixon's press plane and provided millions of Americans with their first glimpses of China in twenty years. Yet these huge viewing audiences proved impossible to sustain, even after the establishment of diplomatic relations allowed each of the networks to station a full-time correspondent in Beijing. Chinese cities are visually unexciting, and big, breaking news of the kind that winds up in evening news broadcasts is in short supply. Foreign TV correspondents, kept on short tether by the Chinese government, have difficulty producing segments that meet network news demands for drama or, in Reuven Frank's memorable phrase, that "display the attributes of fiction."[3] Even when, at considerable cost, the *Today* Show or the ABC evening news relocates to China for a week or so of broadcasts, the result only highlights the inability or unwillingness of the networks to penetrate beyond surface glamour to Chinese reality.

The exception, and it is an important one, to the general toothlessness of television where China is concerned was the coverage of the Beijing demonstrations of early 1989 and their violent suppression. As millions of Americans watched this made-for-TV drama, attitudes toward China changed overnight.

CURRICULUM VITAE

It often seems that the only practical effect of the scientific ideal of objectivity, lately adopted by social scientists and historians, is to inhibit such academics from discussing their own *Weltanschauung*. Neither group, of course, disputes the notion that one's view of the world is shaped by a particular set of both conscious and subconscious premises. Most social scientists, indeed, are willing to grant as an abstraction that both their perceptions of social action, and the theories of causation that these produce in response, flow directly from the assumptions that they bring to their study. But when the time comes to apply these concepts to their own writing, they retreat into a pretense of naïve objectivity. This is not to say that they are subjectively dishonest, only that they rarely discuss their own background, opinions, and premises, and almost never speculate how these might affect their perception of events. Yet it is safe to say that the observer who recognizes and declares his viewpoint up front is likely to produce a more unbiased account than someone whose own position goes unstated.

My own views on China's long—and not yet completed—evolution from feudal despotism through bureaucratic totalitarianism to modern democracy were formed during successive periods of residence and study in Hong Kong, the Republic of China on Taiwan, and the People's Republic of China. With the exception of two and a half years spent at Stanford University in the late seventies, I resided continuously in the Far East from early 1974 until late 1983, and have traveled there frequently since. This is only part of a longer period, at this writing approximately fifteen years, during which I have been largely occupied with Chinese society and Asian affairs.

The day in early December 1973 that China first captured my imagination stands out clearly in my memory. The USS *Hector*, on which I was serving as main propulsion assistant, had anchored in Hong Kong's Victoria Harbor for a four-day port call, and I had taken advantage of a day of liberty to travel to the Chinese border at Lo Wu, fifteen miles away. There was a viewpoint, reached by climbing a flight of steps, from which one could look down, past the eight-foot-high barbed wire fence that demarcated the border, into China. I don't know what I expected to see. China's entry into the Vietnam War had long been the subject of nervous speculation in the American military, which feared a reprise of the Korean War. The Cultural Revolution had impressed on my mind scenes of chaotic terror by rampaging Red Guards. Even favorable reports on the Maoist commune had suggested to me a serflike regimentation of groups of peasants working in the fields to the regular beat of a lion drum, and woe to those who fell behind.

I was unprepared for the peaceful, almost idyllic scene that greeted my gaze. On the other side of the fence, instead of a fortified border zone or even observation posts, there was a simple sweep of rice paddy. Brown with stubble now after the last harvest of the year, it stretched down in easy terraces to a village in the distance. The buildings in the village were long structures of red brick, capped with red tile roofs, but the regular entrances and chimneys told me that they were row houses, not dormitories. On this bright December morning the few people about in ones and twos appeared bound on their own business, not marching in work gangs. All in all, the vista below bore little resemblance to the Red China that I had been led to expect. But neither did it, I shortly realized, correspond to the modernizing, industrializing New China of Beijing's claims. Rather, it looked like a village out of time. This first encounter with the enigma of revolutionary China planted a seed of curiosity in my mind that was to germinate into one of the consuming interests of my life.

Two years later I was back in Hong Kong, having resigned my commission in the Navy and set course for a new career. I had decided to become a China hand, and for this I needed to equip myself with a knowledge of written and spoken Chinese. Mandarin Chinese, the official language, is a forbidding tongue, its complex intonations and ideographs taking years to master. Hong Kong, where 95 percent of the population speak the dialect of Cantonese as their first language and English as their second, is not the best place to learn it. That distinction belongs to Taiwan. My first few months were spent in a Chinese Tower of Babel, as I attended courses in Mandarin at the

New Asia College by day and struggled to communicate with the Cantonese family with whom I was boarding by night. Though this linguistic confusion was at first productive of little more than head-aches, it was ultimately to prove a blessing. Years later, when I lived in the Guangdong countryside, I was able to speak Mandarin (the language they preferred) to officials, and Cantonese (the only lan-guage they knew) to villagers.

Hong Kong's great advantage over Taiwan and Singapore, for my purposes, was its proximity to the People's Republic of China. Hong Kong was then, and remains today, a superb observation post from which to track events in the sprawling "Mainland" a few miles away. The art of China-watching was highly developed and required spe-cialized skills, going beyond an ability to speak and read Chinese.

Many of the watchers concentrated on party politics, analyzing events on the Mainland from the bits and pieces of real news that could be filtered out of the Marxist-Leninist jargon that abounded in the *People's Daily* and other organs of the official press. This was painstaking work. A change in the order of names in an official list of guests at a state reception could mean a reshuffle in the hierarchy, while a name's repeated omission might signal the onset of a purge. I found this too monkish a pursuit for my liking, preferring flesh-and-blood discussions with recent Chinese emigrants about daily life in the villages and towns they had left. These refugees were mainly economic migrants, not anti-Communists, but none were given to nostalgia about the life they had given up, and not a few painted an unflattering portrait of Communist rule.

All of us in Hong Kong who squinted across the border at China labored under a common handicap. No matter how many documents we read, how skilled we were at reading between the lines, or how many refugees we interviewed, the lack of direct contact was a barrier to proper understanding. It was difficult, though not impossible, to develop a feel for the country and its people at such a remove.

After entering the doctoral program at Stanford University in 1976, I discovered that this problem was compounded among Sinologists in the United States. Not only did they operate at a greater physical and cultural distance from Chinese reality than did Hong Kong–based China watchers, but even the best of them were most com-fortable discussing events at a level of abstraction that often obscured what was happening on the ground. Since the founding of the PRC in 1949, for instance, China had been repeatedly wracked by Maoist mass mobilization campaigns, which had numbered millions among their victims. One of my professors at Stanford had reified these biennial political convulsions of the body politic into an ideal cycle. Drawn on the blackboard it made a pretty schematic, much like the exhaust, intake, compression, and combustion stages of a four-cycle engine. Naturally, neither the schematic nor his description of it conveyed anything of the flesh-and-blood trauma that these repeated convulsions of the body politic caused. This intellectual veneer innocently but effectively veiled the true nature of these cycles of hate and repression.

If the human cost of Mao's restructuring of society did not come through, reports of his success did, loud and clear, in the idealistic accounts assigned as reading. On the recommendation of my advisor, I dutifully read Jan Myrdal's two books on Liu Ling village in North China, *Report from a Chinese Village* and *China: The Revolution Continued*.[4] The agricultural collective and the Thought of Mao Zedong had succeeded, in Myrdal's view, in changing "human nature." Not that this conclusion bothered me. In my ignorance I readily accepted Myrdal's scribblings as the actual state of affairs. I did find it a trifle odd, though, when my advisor later suggested, as a serious research project, a comparison of the two books, in which he thought he perceived a *difference in China's attitude towards foreigners.* I agreed that Myrdal, a good Swedish socialist, was treated with greater suspicion during his second visit to Liu Ling village, which took place during the xenophobic Cultural Revolution, than during his first, but I privately wondered whether this trivial point was worthy of serious scholarship. It was only much later that I came to view this proposal as an example of the extremes of scholarly pettifoggery to which the absence of reliable data about China drove even widely respected Sinologists.

Other scholars were even less prudent, taking their lack of contact with the People's Republic as a license for conjecture. The Stanford economics Professor John Gurley wrote that "The Chinese—all of them—now have what is in effect an insurance policy against pestilence, famine, and other disasters. In this respect, China has outperformed every underdeveloped country in the world; and, even with respect to the richest one, it would not be farfetched to claim that there has been less malnutrition due to maldistribution of food in China over the past twenty years than there has been in the United States."[5] We will see in later chapters just how accurate such far-reaching claims were, but at the time, these opinions were freely voiced by many in Sinology, the field to which I had apprenticed myself.

Not all American Sinologists were as incautious in their formulations as these scholars. But enough of them were. In the absence of contradictory information, I left Stanford favorably disposed towards the Communist revolution, which I believed had created a society that was—to repeat a few of the epithets then current—egalitarian, just, unselfish, and liberated.

My first stop was Taiwan, where I embarked upon my dissertation research, a comparative study of a fishing and a farming community. Shortly into my stay, however, an opportunity to go to China arose under the newly inaugurated U.S.-PRC scholarly exchange program. My research proposal to spend a year in a Chinese commune in Guangdong province had been accepted. After receiving a green light from Beijing, and making arrangements to take a year's leave from the doctoral program at Stanford, I traveled to China in September 1979, eager to experience rural life in the real China.

A year in a Chinese village proved an effective antidote to the opinions I had imbibed at Stanford, though it did not take effect overnight. It took me many months in the village to learn that the Communist revolution, though leading to advances in rural health care, education, welfare, and flood control, was beset by serious problems of its own making. The forced regimentation of social and economic life had created a new class of party bureaucrats, whose power greatly exceeded that of the prerevolutionary village elite. Inevitably, this concentration of power had bred corruption. Officials awarded themselves special privileges, held feasts when other villagers were going without fish or meat, and built themselves large homes with public monies. These officials, and their superiors, were also implicated in an array of ongoing human rights violations, from forced abortions and sterilizations in the population control program, to the arbitrary arrest and imprisonment of individuals in political campaigns. The case of Wei Jingsheng, the Democracy Wall dissident who was sentenced to fifteen years in prison on a bogus charge, brought home to me how defenseless the Chinese people were against arbitrary state action.

Even as the grim reality of collective life was emerging all around me, one party claim still seemed to hold true, namely, that the establishment of the "New China" had benefited the Chinese peasant. For those who believed that the lot of the peasants, who constitute over four-fifths of the Chinese population, had improved dramatically, much could be forgiven or even brushed aside as nonessential. Almost to the end of my stay I remained a captive of this—the paramount myth of the Chinese revolution.

It was an outburst by an old gravedigger that planted the seeds of doubt. He had been hired by a village family to dig up the casket of a relative for reburial. As he worked, I asked him how burial customs had changed during his life. He was silent for a while, then suddenly let out a curse. "Since the revolution things have been real bad. We have to eat 'black rice' [rice of low quality]. We have to wear cheap, rationed cloth. . . . Even the rice liquor is not as good as it used to be."[6] I was taken aback by his outburst, and not only because it was dangerous to criticize publicly Communist party rule. Here was a poor gravedigger, the very sort of downtrodden and dispossessed individual that the Communist revolution was supposed to have greatly aided. How could he be alienated?

This puzzling episode spurred me to reexamine the relationship between the revolution and the peasantry. During my last weeks in the countryside I systematically interviewed over one hundred villagers, hoping to outline the ups and downs of peasant life over the previous fifty years. I stayed close to their own categories of well-being, asking them to tell me when they had eaten well and when they had eaten poorly, when they had lived comfortably and when they had done without, when had been the best of times and when had been the worst.

To my surprise, those old enough to remember the 1920s and early 1930s recalled it as a "golden age" of unprecedented prosperity. This good life ended with the Japanese occupation, which cut off Guangdong from its foreign and domestic markets and which led eventually to mass starvation and emigration. Prosperity gradually returned after the Japanese withdrawal, but by early 1950 the People's Liberation Army had reached Guangdong. Thereafter, to the peasants' way of thinking, the quality of life gradually declined. By 1980, the year I was in the village, conditions were held to approximate those from 1949 to 1952, when the Communists had yet to implement their rural program of collectivization and market control. Though real, the advances in rural health care, education, welfare, and flood control so loudly touted by officials turned out to matter far less to the villagers than I had initially assumed. For the many families who had been forced to tighten their belts after they lost their farms and the freedom of the market, those advances were scant compensation indeed.

Although I realized that villagers from China's poorer, interior provinces might have a more positive view of the liberation, I felt equally certain that the experience of my Guangdong villagers was far from unique. "For the 400 million peasants of the South China heartland, the liberation has probably proved to be an empty, undigestible myth," I wrote in 1983.[7] This peasants' eye-view of the world was even then being confirmed by the actions of the Chinese Communist party, which had rejected collective agriculture and market control in favor of family farms and free exchange. My earlier willingness, which I shared with many China watchers, to accept the Maoist commune as the solution to all peasant problems became for me incredible.

Not only was my view of the achievements of communism in rural China considerably altered by the end of my research, I was also considerably more skeptical of socialism. Through my writings I became involved in the process of "disillusionment," which will form the basis of a later chapter. Only later did I realize how many other scholars in China at the time had experienced a similar reaction. Vera Schwarcz, for example, wrote that Wei Jingsheng's arrest and imprisonment helped her realize that "freedom of thought and speech and legal due process—all of which were being attacked [by the Party and government] as products of 'bourgeois' revolutions like the American Revolution and the French Revolution—were, for me, universal values. I believe these values to be more beneficial to people across time and culture than do the ideologues who condemned Wei Jingsheng's quest for a fifth modernization: democracy."[8]

Like Schwarcz, I hold as a tenet of faith that political rights should be universally enjoyed. They are not. Moreover, a look at their actual distribution reveals that economic freedom and political liberty go hand in hand. A full range of political, civil, and religious rights is enjoyed by the citizens of almost all capitalist countries. Those who reside in socialist states like China, especially those nations that severely limit private economic activity, usually enjoy little more than a pretense of basic rights. The indivisibility of liberty is an empirical fact.

I am equally persuaded that capitalism is also the greatest engine of economic growth known to man, outperforming all known variants of communism and socialism. It is not only for its endowment of liberty, but for its contribution to economic progress, that the promotion of democratic capitalism should be a fundamental aim of government. It is this view, which many would characterize as "conservative," that guides my perceptions of China's economic reforms and political struggles, and that is generally reflected in the articles I have published over the years.

I have striven to write an objective account of American perceptions of China. For many events this is easy. The Chinese Communist party did drive the Nationalists off the Mainland, Chinese troops did cross over the Yalu in the Korean War, Mao did launch a Cultural Revolution, the Gang of Four was arrested, Deng Xiaoping did launch a wave of far-reaching reforms, and PLA (People's Liberation Army) troops did massacre pro-democracy demonstrators. America's ongoing judgments of China were colored and recolored by this progression of events.

After a brief review of past images of China (chapter 2), I reconstruct the attitudes of American correspondents toward the Chinese Communist movement during the Second World War (chapter 3). Muted during the general hostility toward the "Red" China of the fifties and sixties (chapter 4), these favorable impressions returned to vogue during the early seventies (chapter 5). They were advanced by an informal but effective coalition of admiring China-watchers and conservative realpolitikers (chapters 6 and 7), and dominated American attitudes toward China until the late seventies. It was only after the Beijing regime began to reveal the unpleasantness of its

Maoist past that such attitudes evaporated (chapter 8) and were replaced by the appealing notion that China was "going our way"— that is, evolving into a democratic capitalistic state (chapter 9). Only with the Tiananmen massacre did Americans, including many China-watchers, come to understand fully the gulf that still divides ruler and ruled in China.

2

Past Images of China: From Marco Polo to Mao Zedong

Everything must be handled calmly. Do not entertain their requests. If you take special pains to control them rigidly and check them courteously, how far will these barbarians' cunning get them?

—Emperor Xianfeng
Qing Dynasty

ADMIRATION

Throughout the Middle Ages tales of "the mysterious East" spun by Marco Polo and other travelers fascinated the common folk of Europe, but it was not until the Enlightenment that Cathay captured the imagination of Western intellectuals. It was Jesuit missionaries who, after gaining access to China at the turn of the seventeenth century, provided the first detailed overview of China's political and social system. Members of this learned Catholic order had set for themselves the formidable task of converting the Confucian elite to Christianity. In the end, though, like the China hands of the twentieth century, it was not they who transformed China, but China which transformed them. They became missionaries in reverse, ardent Sinophiles who wrote loftily of the nobility of Confucian thought and the special virtues of the Chinese political order in a voluminous correspondence they carried on with colleagues and friends in the West. Their highly idealized, even romantic, accounts were widely circulated, convincing many who read them that China was a society to be emulated.[1]

By the eighteenth century the swelling ranks of admirers of the great empire of the East included some of the most important philosophers of the Enlightenment, such as Leibniz, Voltaire, Quesnay, and Turgot. Leibniz asserted the superiority of the Chinese in their social organization and governmental organization. Voltaire went even further, praising China as "particularly superior to all the nations of the universe," and as possessing a religion, Confucianism, that was "simple, wise, august, free from all superstition and all barbarity."[2] Quesnay, who became known as the Confucius of the West, admitted that China was a despotism but argued that the emperor was bound by a framework of natural law that ensured he behaved as benevolently toward his subjects as a father did toward his children. One of the chief figures among the physiocrats, l'Abbé Baudeau, concurred: "More than three hundred twenty million people live [in China] as wisely, happily and freely as men can ever be. They live under a most absolute but most just government, under the richest, the most powerful, the most humane and the most welfare-conscious monarch."[3] All admired the Chinese civil service system, in which officials were selected by a series of examinations open to all without regard to nobility of birth or bounty of inheritance.

It was no accident that, of all Europe, the French philosophes and physiocrats were most receptive to the reports of the Jesuits. At odds with the Catholic church, opposed to inherited privilege, these intellectuals were eager to reform the ancien régime along secular, egalitarian lines. In China they saw—or thought they saw—their most hopeful speculations realized: a country whose creed was rationalist in temper, owed nothing to revealed religion, and had produced a virtuous, meritocratic government and a prosperous, contented citizenry. The temptation to ignore or downplay those aspects of China—a country these armchair philosophers were acquainted with only at second hand—that did not fit this particular vision of societal perfection was irresistible.

While the French devoted themselves to admiring China from afar, the enterprising British were busily adapting the Chinese civil service system to their own needs. The practice of competitive examinations came to Britain via the East India Company, which first adopted the practice in its Indian outposts. Parliament drew upon this experience, as well as information about the working of the Chinese system, when it later established the British civil service system.[4] Later, when the United States instituted its own civil service examinations, they were modeled upon the system in place in the British Empire, and it was left to Emerson to remind us that we owed this important advance in governmental administration ultimately to the Chinese.[5]

Underlying American regard for the Chinese examination system was the total social mobility it was presumed to have created, ensuring that each new generation of officials would comprise a natural aristocracy of ability. Harold Isaacs puts the point with his customary eloquence: "American[s] reacted with identifying approval to the discovery in Chinese society of a mythology akin to [their] own, the idea that long, long ago, the Chinese system aimed to make it possible for the lowliest farmer's son to rise by individual merit to the side of the Heavenly Throne. This won marks for the Chinese among Americans, as we have noted, all the way back to Thomas Jefferson's time."[6] Though this may somewhat overstate the case, since the American democratic dream has always been to aspire to high elective office, rather than to a mere sinecure in a governmental bureaucracy, traditional Chinese society doubtless seemed to Americans who knew it closer to their own ideal of equality of opportunity than the other static, stratified societies in Europe and Asia.

The Age of Respect was brought to a close by increasing familiarity. By the time of the American Revolution, Yankee sailors were threading their way up the estuary of the Pearl River to the southern port of Guangzhou (Canton) in search of trade. These merchants and their consuls were interested not in abstract Confucian principles, but in establishing a workable, and profitable, trading relationship. Instead, they found themselves regarded by the Chinese regime as little better than bearers of tribute. They were isolated in their warehouses on Shamian Island adjacent to Guangzhou, restricted to trading with a government monopoly, the "hong" merchants, and otherwise limited to contact with only a few selected junior officials. Applications by European states to establish more equitable diplomatic and trade relations were repeatedly, if politely, rebuffed. All that King George III got in return for his request, which his emissary Lord Macartney phrased in the most respectful and propitious of terms, for the expansion of British trade outside Guangzhou and the exchange of ambassadors, was the following lofty mandate from the Qian Long Emperor:

You, O King, live beyond the confines of many seas; nevertheless, impelled by your humble desire to partake of the benefits of our civilization, you have dispatched a mission respectfully bearing your memorial. Your Envoy has crossed the seas and paid his respects at my Court on the anniversary of my birthday. To show your devotion, you have also sent offering of your country's produce.

I have perused your memorial; the earnest terms in which it is couched reveal a respectful humility on your part, which is highly praiseworthy. In consideration of the fact that your Ambassador and his Deputy have come a long way with your memorial and tribute, I have shown them high favour and have allowed them to be introduced into my presence. To manifest my indulgence, I have entertained them at a banquet and made them numerous gifts. . . .

Swaying the wide world, I have but one aim in view, namely, to maintain a perfect governance and to fulfill the duties of the State; strange and costly objects do not interest me. If I have commanded that the tribute offerings sent by you, O King, are to be accepted, this was solely in consideration for the spirit which prompted you to dispatch them from afar. Our dynasty's majestic virtue has penetrated into every country under Heaven, and Kings of all nations have offered their costly tribute by land and sea. As your Ambassador can see for himself, we possess all things. I set no value on objects strange or ingenious, and have no use for your country's manufactures. This then is my answer to your request to appoint a representative at my Court, a request contrary to our dynastic usage, which would only result in inconvenience to yourself. I have expounded my wishes in detail and have commanded your tribute Envoys to leave in peace on their homeward journey. It behooves you, O King, to respect my sentiments and to display even greater devotion and loyalty in the future, so that, by perpetual submission to our Throne, you may secure peace and prosperity for your country hereafter.[7]

Such episodes did nothing to endear the Chinese emperor or his mandarinate to the West, especially after reports of widespread corruption and political despotism convinced many that the posture of arrogant superiority that Chinese officialdom had adopted toward the outside world was as undeserved as it was offensive. Changing Western views of what constituted a good government played a large part in the collapse of China's political reputation. The success of democracy in America and Britain had, by the beginning of the nineteenth century, raised a new standard—the consent of the governed—by which governments were to be measured. To nineteenth-century political philosophers, the Qing emperors looked increasingly archaic, arbitrary, and oppressive. John Stuart Mill wrote disparagingly of the concentration of power in the hands of "one man of superhuman mental activity [who] manag[ed] the entire affairs of a mentally passive people."[8]

The West's earlier enthusiasm for China's Confucian system of government had been corroded by closer contact. As Creel writes, "Disillusionment became complete; the 'Chinese dream' was over. Never again in the West, since the end of the 18th century, has interest in China and esteem for that country risen so high."[9]

But this would not be the last time that intellectuals and others profoundly estranged from their age would idealize and romanticize China's system of government for their own, sometimes only half-conscious, purposes. During the twentieth century, waves of disillusionment would twice more bring American correspondents and academics to China's shores. They would be drawn first by the beacon of Yenan, the Communists' wartime capital, which they saw even from afar as lighting the way toward a better and more democratic China. Later, after the revolution, it was the New China of Chairman Mao that they, like Voltaire in the early eighteenth century, would hail as "particularly superior to all the nations of the universe."

CONTEMPT

Oriental despotism or no, well into the nineteenth century the Chinese Empire still commanded a certain respect in the West for its imposing size, vast population, and impressive wealth. The Opium War in 1840–42 punctured this pretense of power, revealing the "empire" to be a destitute and hollow shell. A small British expeditionary force routed the Manchu armies and armadas virtually at will, and the emperor was forced to accept commercial and diplomatic intercourse on Western terms of equality. The terms of the Treaty of Nanking testify to the abjectness of China's collapse before British arms: Its Manchu ruler was required to pay a heavy indemnity, to cede Hong Kong to the British crown, and to open five treaty ports to the West. Foreign consuls and traders installed themselves in the newly opened ports under the protection of extraterritoriality, while Western missionaries ventured out into the hinterland. The weaknesses revealed by the war and its aftermath were fatal to China's residual prestige as, in the words of Kenneth Latourette, "The impression spread through America and Europe that China was decadent, dying, fallen greatly from her glorious past."[10]

The Manchu dynasty was, in truth, moribund. It was suffering from all the symptoms of dynastic crises: a sclerotic imperial administration, a crippling loss of bureaucratic morale, and growing peasant discontent over rapacious local officials and ruinous tax rates. It would have succumbed as early as the 1850s to the Taiping rebels, whose flood of revolution nearly reached to the gates of the Forbidden City, had it not been artificially resuscitated by military aid from the Western powers. In the pursuit of a stable environment for trade, they would continue to prop up the dying dynasty for another eighty years, until the atrophied imperial administration was a caricature of its former self. Ironically enough, Western observers reserved their most scathing criticism for precisely those elements of Chinese government and society that suffered most from this artificial prolongation of Manchu decline.

Western diplomats, merchants and missionaries were united in their disdain for Chinese officialdom. The mandarin, his ancient Confucian virtues no match for the exigencies of dynastic corruption and foreign intervention, was the favorite target of Western criticism. An Englishman who worked for many years as a translator for the Chinese government, John Fryer, described the mandarins with whom he dealt "as more like children than men" in their habit of throwing temper tantrums and their utter lack of intellectual curiosity.[11] The well-known American missionary, S. Wells Williams, wrote in his influential *Middle Kingdom* in 1848 that a mandarin would never take the lead in introducing new things. W. A. P. Martin, an American educator who supervised the Guangxu Emperor's introduction to Western learning, was of the opinion that "truth is not a point of honor with the Chinese, and adroit lying is with them admitted to be one of the prime qualifications of a mandarin."[12] An even stronger blast at reactionary officialdom came from W. H. Medhurst, an English missionary, who wrote:

> It is not in the nature of the Chinese to imitate reform or carry it honestly and steadily out. Neither the ruler nor the ruled appreciate its necessity; and could they be enlightened sufficiently to perceive it, they do not possess the strength of character or fixity of purpose to follow implicitly the course pointed out.[13]

Western merchants and diplomats were quick to generalize such views, seeing all Chinese, not just the ruling class, as members of a hopelessly inferior people, useful only as a mass market for the products of their respective companies and countries. The attitude of missionaries was more complex, informed as it was by the Judeo-Christian view that all men are created in the image of God. However benighted the missionaries found China, however appalled they were by the moral deficiencies of the Chinese—and they found the practices of female infanticide, polygamy, footbinding, and prostitution especially vexing—they still believed that each Chinese person possessed an immortal soul worthy of attention and respect. These men of God would, and did, treat potential converts with less affection than pity, less admiration than scorn, but unlike the residents of the treaty ports they could not reject the godless completely without abandoning the purpose that had brought them to China in the first place.

By far the most articulate missionary commentator on Chinese society was Arthur Smith, who spent twenty-one years at North China mission stations. Smith published two widely influential books on the Chinese, *Chinese Characteristics,* which appeared in 1894, and *Village Life in China,* published in 1899 (and still in print today).[14] Both display frequent flashes of the exasperation that he and his fellow missionaries often felt for the obstinate, backward, and sometimes mendacious objects of their extended missionary endeavors. In his first book, an effort to sketch the national character of the Chinese people by describing their most striking traits, Smith dwells at chapter-length on such troubling characteristics as "The Disregard of Accuracy, The Disregard of Time, Flexible Inflexibility, Intellectual Turbidity, Contempt for Foreigners, The Talent for Misunderstanding, The Talent for Indirection, The Absence of Nerves, The Absence of Public Spirit, The Absence of Sympathy, Mutual Suspicion, and The Absence of Sincerity." His second book, *Village Life in China,* while without a doubt one of the best books on rural China ever written, is equally pointed in its criticism of the villagers' reluctance to adopt such innovations as hand pumps, their lack of village sanitation, and other shortcomings.

But Smith's appraisal of Chinese society, although mixed, is rarely uncharitable, and never degenerates into the kind of blind contempt for the Chinese often displayed by the residents of the treaty ports. His sometimes acidulous criticisms are invariably leavened with generous doses of humor, and he remains hopeful for the improvement of China's societal and familial problems. As Smith himself remarks in the foreword to *Village Life in China:* "These chapters are written from the standpoint of one who, by an extended experience in China, had come to feel a profound respect for the numerous admirable qualities of the Chinese, and to entertain for many of them a high personal esteem. An unexampled past lies behind this great race, and before it may lie a wonderful future. Ere that can be realized, however, there are many disabilities which must be removed. The longer one is acquainted with China, the more deeply is this necessity felt. Commerce, diplomacy, extension of political relations, and the growing contact with Occidental civilization have, all combined, proved totally inadequate to accomplish any such reformation as China needs."[15] Smith and his fellow missionaries were certain if enough Chinese could be convinced to, in the words of St. Paul, "put on the new man," China could be saved. Chairman Mao was to undertake a similar effort to reshape the soul and spirit of the Chinese people in the Cultural Revolution, though in the name of a lesser, more violent god.

BENEVOLENCE

In the end it was the relatively benevolent views of missionaries toward China and the Chinese, rather than the often contemptuous attitude of traders and officials, that came to dominate in the American mind during the last half of the nineteenth century. But first the remaining restrictions on missionary activity in the interior had to be abolished. This was accomplished by the Sino-French Treaty of Tianjin, ratified in 1860, which guaranteed the right of Catholic priests to proselytize anywhere in the Empire. Most-favored-nation clauses ensured that these privileges were soon extended to Protestant missionaries.

The missions to China were soon embarked on a cycle of continuous growth. Missionaries, especially those from Protestant denominations, actively campaigned for additional support from the churchgoing public, then the vast majority of the American population. Through articles, letters, and lectures given to denominational colleges during home leaves, they helped to popularize China among potential missionaries. Each new wave of missionaries continued the campaign, generating more support—and more missionaries. The number of Protestant missionaries began to double every eight years, growing from 189 in 1864, to 3,445 by 1905, of whom over 90 percent were Americans or British.[16] By the early twentieth century, China had become the major focus of American missionary efforts, which along with Christianity brought Western education and medicine to China. Given the millions of Americans whose regular donations helped to support churches, schools, and clinics there, it was not surprising that America had come to view China with an almost proprietary interest.

An element of sympathetic concern began to enter into America's foreign policy toward China, formerly governed solely by considerations of self-interest. One expression of the special responsibility that America had come to feel for the well-being of the Chinese was the Open Door policy, this country's first major diplomatic initiative outside of the Western Hemisphere. By the turn of the century China was prostrate, unable to defend itself against predatory attacks by the Great Powers. All wanted to carve out spheres of influence, and Russia and Japan appeared intent upon dismembering the ancient empire. At this critical juncture America intervened, taking upon itself the role of protector of China's territorial integrity. Secretary of State John Hays addressed two notes to the Great Powers in 1899–1900, stating the United States' intent to guarantee China's freedom and independence. As John K. Fairbank writes, "Viewed cynically, the doctrine of China's integrity was a device to prevent other powers, for example, Russia, from taking over areas of China and excluding us from them. But the independence of China has also appealed to Americans as a matter of political justice. . . . [I]t fitted the doctrine of the self-determination and sovereignty of weaker nations, which constituted one of our major political sentiments."[17] Equally important, it was consonant with the moral guardianship that America, by and through its missionary activity and other good works, had assumed over China. This element of altruism surfaced again after the Boxer Rebellion, an antiforeign movement that erupted in North China in the summer of 1900. The heavy indemnity that the Manchu regime was forced to pay to the Great Powers as a result was later set aside by the United States, which used its portion to provide scholarships to Chinese students to study in American universities.

Although the Ching dynasty was not to be overthrown for another eleven years, the Boxer Rebellion marked the collapse of central authority in China. Not until the establishment of the People's Republic of China in 1949 was a Chinese government again effectively to control the country. In the decades up to the 1937 Japanese invasion of China, foreigners in general, and missionaries in particular, enjoyed wide access. The mandarins had disappeared as a class, and what authority existed found it prudent to facilitate, or at least not openly oppose, Western commercial and missionary interests.

For their part, American missionaries had become more diffident about the merits of their own civilization, especially after the First World War. The widespread devastation wrought by that conflict was hard for any thoughtful American to reconcile with earlier notions of Western cultural and political superiority. Missionaries also came to tolerate, even to respect, cultural practices such as ancestor worship that their predecessors would have condemned as backward and heathenish. Influenced by the demands of the social gospel, they came to count success not only by the number of conversions, but also by the number of their good works.

At least some of those who had gone to China hoping to Christianize that civilization became in addition (or instead) conduits by which understanding, sympathetic, and even enthusiastic views of the Chinese and their civilization flowed back to the West. Earl Cressy, a prominent missionary educator, vividly described how such "reverse missionaries" were converted:

> He had come to the Far East with a message that he was on fire to give, but in the process of transmission the East had spoken its message to him. He had gone out to change the East and was returning, himself a changed man. . . . The conversion of the missionary by the Far East results in his being not only a missionary but an internationalist, an intermediary between the two great civilizations that inherit the earth. Abroad he represents a universal religion, and is himself an embodiment of the strivings of the West to attain its ideals of social justice and world brotherhood; at home he is constantly changing the attitude of the millions of his constituency . . . bringing to them something of his new breadth of vision, and helping them to a larger appreciation of the greatness and worth of the civilization of the Far East.[18]

By 1928, much of China had been unified under the leadership of Chiang Kai-shek and the Nationalist Party. Chiang's prestige was greatly enhanced a short time later, at least in the eyes of the missionary movement, when he married Wellesley graduate Soong Mei-ling and announced his conversion to Methodism. With China's new national government headed by a Christian couple and numerous graduates of mission schools and American universities in positions of influence, Protestant missionaries seemed to have succeeded where the Jesuits had failed. With the installation of a Christian regime, the conversion of all China seemed finally within reach.

With thousands of missionaries offering kinder and more sympathetic images of the Chinese government, these gradually impressed themselves on the West. But no one taught more Americans to appreciate better what Arthur Smith called "the numerous admirable qualities of the Chinese" people than the Nobel Prize–winning author Pearl S. Buck. The daughter of missionaries, she drew on her forty years of experience in China to write a series of bestselling novels and numerous works of nonfiction about that country and its people. Her most famous novel, *The Good Earth,* first published in 1931 and later made into a movie of the same name, reached tens of millions of readers and moviegoers in the United States alone. It told the story of the peasant Wang Lung and his wife O-lan, of their lifelong struggle to raise a family and farm the land against the brutalities of men and the harshness of nature. Through these and other characters, Buck was able to create in the imaginations of Americans a new stereotype of rural Chinese as a strong and attractive people of the soil, kind and generous toward the young, respectful toward the elderly, and dignified, even cheerful, in misfortune.

WARTIME ADMIRATION

The new images of the Chinese provided by Pearl Buck and others could not have come at a better time. When a few years later the Japanese escalated their piecemeal attacks to all-out war, it was not the nameless, faceless masses of China who took up arms against the invaders, but Buck's Noble Chinese Peasants. America's generally favorable view of the Chinese quickly deepened and broadened into an unreserved admiration as these soldiers, displaying the same dogged strength and tenacity with which they had withstood the adversities of nature, mounted what was seen as a heroic resistance to the Japanese war machine.

That the Chinese had little prospect of evicting the Japanese legions from their homeland, and none whatsoever of defeating the empire that had sent them, did not dampen America's new enthusiasm. Quite the opposite. It placed them in the category of those who gallantly fight against the odds, deserving of the special sympathy that Americans reserve for underdogs. After a century of flaccid acquiescence to foreign demands, China was now standing up to an invader, putting up a resistance whose hopelessness only added to its heroism.

The Japanese contributed mightily to this sympathy by their cruel, barbaric crushing of Chinese resistance, which included massacres of innocent civilians. The bloodiest atrocity committed by the Japanese army was the incident known as the Rape of Nanjing. After occupying Nanjing, the Nationalist capital, Japanese troops went on an orgy of rapine and slaughter. By the time they were finished several days later, some three hundred thousand Chinese noncombatants, including large numbers of women and children, had been beaten, stabbed, and shot to death. This incident and others like it aroused and angered numerous Americans, who quickly transferred their residual images of Chinese cruelty and mendacity to the Japanese. There they would remain until the Chinese Communists had come to power.

As the powerful forces of the invader occupied the coastal provinces and moved relentlessly inland, the outgunned Chinese were forced to retreat, leaving little behind except scorched earth. Workers dismantled their factories and carried them to safe inland refuges, university students and faculty members carried their books to new campuses hundreds of miles in the interior, and a new connection to the outside world, the Burma Road, was constructed by picks and shovel through a trackless wilderness. Through documentaries and news reels, cartoons and editorials, the heroism and suffering of the Chinese was experienced by Americans in an immediate and graphic way, and quickly grew to mythic proportions.

The entire American community in China, from missionaries and diplomats to traders and journalists, was united in condemning the Japanese invasion. Pearl Harbor gave Americans at home and abroad an additional reason to empathize with China's struggle, since we were now allies struggling against a common aggressor. The interval from 1937 to 1944 was, in the words of Harold Isaacs, the "only one in which wholly sympathetic images of the Chinese dominated the entire area of American-Chinese relations. Of all the ages through which these images have passed, this alone could be called the Age of Admiration. . . . After all the long ages of contempt and benevolence through which he had lived in American minds, the Chinese, largely unbeknownst to him, now enjoyed there his finest hour."[19]

Initially, all information coming out of China, from the reports of missionary partisans to the sympathetic dispatches of the correspondents, served to create the impression in the American mind that the Nationalists' fate was synonymous with that of China. But the war had made travel between China and the United States perilous, and the net result was that the missionary movement was no longer the primary source of information about China for Americans. That distinction went to the increasingly influential corps of American and foreign correspondents. Although missionaries, for the most part, were to support Chiang to the end, most journalists and diplomats gradually distanced themselves from the Nationalists as the war progressed. By war's end, as we will see in the next chapter, many had come to believe that China's salvation lay in a victory by the Communist forces of Mao Zedong.

3

The Age of Infatuation: American Journalists in China During the 1930s and 1940s

―――――― &&& ――――――

Men have never taken the world just as it comes. We need to explain the world to ourselves, and to do so, we have used stories—myths and fables— to record our experiences and shape our values. In most cultures, these narratives are tied together in what has been called a "super story." Religions are a super story. Ideologies can be a super story.

—Thomas Friedman
Quoted in "Howard Beach: The Use and Abuse of Race"

Between the Japanese invasion in 1937 and the Communist triumph in 1949, almost all of the foreign correspondents reporting from China came to see the conflict between the Nationalists and the Communists as a struggle between the forces of Reaction and those of Progress. The correspondents used this shared but unstated framework to give meaning and significance to the complex political and military events they were observing. What they considered "news," what they wrote about in their dispatches, were events that could be interpreted to fit the tacit standard of relevance imposed by this, their "super story."

Although these journalists were, for the most part, scrupulously precise in the writing of individual dispatches, they were less than objective in other respects. The exact role their reports played in delaying and diminishing U.S. aid to the Nationalists, and in otherwise enhancing the fortunes of the Chinese Communist party (CCP), is beyond the scope of this book. What I will show is that, with few exceptions, they solidly aligned themselves on the side of the Progressive Forces, saw U.S. support for the Nationalists as merely delaying their certain defeat, and won over to their point of view important segments of U.S. public opinion.

What makes this "super story" important to examine in detail is not only its substantial impact in the 1940s, but its later return to vogue. Muted during the general hostility toward the Chinese Communists of the fifties, the story reemerged as the dominant refrain of the rising chorus of admiration for the People's Republic in the late sixties and early seventies. Many of the guiding principles of this later age of admiration originate here, during the Chinese Civil War, born of an infatuation with the CCP and midwived by the techniques, from passive controls to active deceptions, that the party developed for dealing with foreigners visiting its capital, Yenan.

THE HANKOU GANG

In 1937, when the Japanese began their bloody war of conquest, an odd assortment of professional and amateur journalists began firing off dispatches from embattled China. The new recruits included leftists, scholars, Sinophiles, and a surprising number of footloose "adventurers" who seized the opportunity to file eyewitness accounts.[1] China never became a Big Story, even after the Japanese attack on Pearl Harbor made us allies of the Nationalist government, and many of these early stringers were able to stay on as correspondents through the Second World War and into the last phases of the Chinese Civil War. Their numbers were augmented in 1938 by Franco's victory in Spain, when China became the front line in the worldwide struggle against fascism. Tillman Durdin, the *New York Times* correspondent, recalled that:

At Hankou [which became the temporary Chinese capital after the fall of Nanjing and is now part of Wuhan] we had a large number of people who had had some experience of the Spanish Civil War and who had been in Moscow. They brought with them very worldly political points of view. They felt at home in China because she, too, was fighting a just war like the one they had been pushing, observing, and covering in Spain on the Republican side. They were also great believers in the Russian Revolution. So at Hankou, with their presence, we had become part of the world scene.[2]

This perspective on the press coverage of the Chinese Civil War is not new, but it has recently been given additional credence by several highly reliable, albeit unlikely, sources—the correspondents themselves. The occasion was a 1982 conference in Scottsdale, Arizona, on American journalism in China during the 1930s and 1940s. In attendance were virtually all of the surviving correspondents, some forty in all, whose names had graced the China dispatches on that period. Relaxing in the company of their long-lost fellows, these aging dons of the print media shared anecdote after revealing anecdote.[3]

"[L]ike counterparts in Europe and Washington, China reporters were a community," MacKinnon and Friesen, the authors of the conference volume that resulted, tell us. "They met frequently and avidly clipped each other's work. During the Chongqing period in fact they even lived together in a Kuomintang-run press hostel. Through such interaction, consensus was reached about legitimacy of sources. Together they decided what was news and what should be reported and how."[4]

The correspondents who came to China, a vast country whose civilization owed nothing to the West, found themselves culturally adrift. Few were able to learn enough Chinese to dispense with interpreters, or enough cultural history to understand the lifeways of 500 million Chinese. Even those whose tenure in China lasted many years rarely ventured beyond the Westernized shallows of Chinese society, and their limited number of Chinese acquaintances invariably included only those who had studied in the West and spoke their own tongue. The brutal reality of everyday life, of a people ground between the millstones of poverty and war, was apparent enough, but personally repellent. The opaqueness of Chinese politics, conducted through networks of personal relationships that foreigners could not hope to penetrate, was professionally frustrating. Of necessity they turned for companionship to others like themselves, coming to form what MacKinnon and Friesen call the "Hankou Gang"— a small foreign enclave buffered by special privileges from the exotic, elusive world around them. Each came to see the others not only as friends, but as their most appreciative audience and most reliable sources.

The correspondents fed on one another's perceptions like a snake devouring its own tail. In the end their views no more resembled Chinese reality than the bloated and fly-blown carcass of a dead animal resembles its still-living relative. In their view the Kuomintang (KMT) was a reactionary, autocratic force (privately they came to call it fascist) that not only stood in the way of China's victory over the Japanese invaders, but would inhibit China's postwar reconstruction and modernization. Only the Chinese Communist party could throw off the heavy mantle of China's feudal past and liberate the peasants. It had already done so in its North China stronghold, Yenan, where democracy was aborning.[5]

This was the super story that the correspondents concentrated on justifying, or at least not contradicting. At its core were the cults of personality that grew up around key CCP leaders. It was their perception of the integrity and honesty of these central figures that initially led the correspondents to conclude that CCP dominion was more democratic than KMT rule, and that CCP violations of personal freedoms and human rights, while serious, merited less attention and criticism than did those of the KMT.

Peggy Durdin, a freelance writer and wife of the New York Times correspondent Tillman Durdin, spoke for all the correspondents at Scottsdale when she observed that "there was nobody on the KMT side who could touch Zhou Enlai in persuasiveness or in intellectual charm, which was a fascinating kind of charm. Nor was there anybody on the KMT side who could touch his head of public relations, the soft, lovely, beautiful Gong Peng, who was the most impressive public relations figure I ever met."[6] Toward Mao Zedong, the master of Yenan, the correspondents and other Americans felt something approaching awe. John K. Emmerson, an American foreign service officer briefly in Yenan with the Dixie Mission, described Mao in his diary as having "a relentless will behind his eyes and high forehead. I decided I would not like to cross him. . . . He stood up and spoke— in the shadows his frame loomed up and his own shadow against the wall was tremendous. How far, I wonder, will that shadow be cast over future China?"[7] Such is the stuff of legend.

Zhou Enlai, as the senior member of the Chinese Communist party in day-to-day contact with foreign journalists, was the Communist whom the foreign correspondents knew best. With his histrionic ability and innate mastery of the social graces, Zhou was the diplomat extraordinaire. Tillman Durdin recalled that "Zhou Enlai would say, 'One of my top personalities in history is Thomas Jefferson,' and he would say, 'One of my aspirations is to go to the United States someday, and please come to Yenan and see us,' and that sort of thing. The attitude was one of courting American goodwill and good relations."[8] Zhou's running monologue about the civil war was mesmerizing—besides, for logistical reasons, being extremely difficult to disprove. Most of the Communist party was off-stage, scattered throughout the hinterlands of North China.

Zhou had a genius for generating sympathy for the CCP cause, and the extent to which hardened, cynical correspondents fell under the spell of his personality is startling. Even after forty years, the correspondents who gathered in Scottsdale still waxed rapturous when they spoke of the handsome Communist representative. "One after another, these skeptical precursors of Henry Kissinger confessed their 'captivation,' " writes James Thompson wonderingly. "Even when he told untruths or something less than the truth, [Zhou] commanded their admiration."[9] Caught in a lie, Zhou was usually able to deflect their skepticism with his urbane good humor or to neatly defuse their anger with a plea for understanding. Father Laszlo Ladany, for thirty years the editor of *China News Analysis*, precisely captured the chameleonlike qualities of Zhou's personality:

> Zhou Enlai was one of those men who never tell the truth and never tell a lie. For them there is no distinction between the two. The speaker says what is appropriate to the circumstances. Zhou Enlai was a perfect gentleman; he was also a perfect Communist.[10]

Henry Lieberman, in China reporting for the *New York Times* from 1945 to 1949, was "very captivated by Zhou, as so many other Americans were. . . . Zhou Enlai was one of the greatest people I've ever encountered because of his charm, his skills, his mental and dramatic ability. One of the most important things of all, I think, is that he was one of the world's greatest actors."[11]

Lieberman was so taken by Zhou that when he found out his idol had feet of clay, he felt personally betrayed. The incident occurred during the Nationalist-Communist truce talks that were taking place through the good offices of the United States. Lieberman recalled that "Chiang Kai-shek's treaty with the Russians said that Nationalist troops were empowered to recover all Chinese territory that had been occupied by the Soviet army. On the other hand, Zhou Enlai was arguing that two places in Inner Mongolia were held by 'The People's Forces' and should not go to the Nationalist government. These places were Zhifeng in Jehol Province and Dolonor in Chahar Province. . . . Phil Potter and I . . . got to Zhifeng and found Soviet troops there and also the 'People's Army,' both in the same place. . . . Our hero had lied to us, and we confronted [Zhou] with, 'How could you do this to us?' In effect, he shrugged his shoulders.[12]

"This was a terrible blow to me." Lieberman went on. "My hero had misled us. In retrospect, I wasn't really angry at Zhou, but it gave me a different insight into what was going on in China. They were playing hardball politics there, and I was a pawn. They looked upon me as somebody to be manipulated, and this put me on my guard."[13]

Now it is a common occurrence in our country that men who lust after power will distort words to gain their own ends. Even as a novice correspondent, Lieberman would hardly have been unaware of this central fact of politics. His anger upon learning that he had been deceived suggests that he had suspended the normal rules of journalistic incredulity where Zhou was concerned.

Arch Steele of the *New York Herald Tribune,* known as the dean of the China correspondents, expressed belated reservations about the excessive reliance of the foreign press on Communist sources: "Remember Chongqing in those days and how difficult it was to get the truth about anything, how futile it was to go to the Chinese Ministry of Information to get their superficial communiques. . . . Then you would go to a little cubbyhole on the side street in Chongqing that was occupied by the liaison officer of the Chinese Communists, who were then our allies, and hear from a charming person like Zhou Enlai an explanation of, say, the latest conflict between the Kuomintang forces and the People's Liberation Army in some remote area of the interior, giving in great detail the facts, as he reported them, of what was going on out there. It was very tempting indeed to give considerable prominence to the detailed version and very persuasive words that we got from Zhou and to more or less ignore . . . the Nationalists' communiques."[14]

The Nationalists' reluctance to publish detailed information about the ongoing civil war, which so hurt their credibility among copy-hungry correspondents, seems to have originated with Chiang Kai-shek himself. As China's ruling Confucian patriarch, he was deeply shamed by his inability to prevent armed clashes between warring factions of his extended "family." Fearing that not only he, but all China would lose face in the eyes of the world if these internal divisions were widely discussed and published abroad, he took the characteristic Chinese stand that *Jia chou bu wang wai yang*—a phrase whose nearest English equivalent is "Don't hang out your dirty laundry in public"—and sought to minimize the seriousness of the conflict between his troops and the Red Army. The policy of official reticence that he inaugurated was, over the long run, to prove disastrous to the Kuomintang, since it gave a more or less open field to Communist interpretations of events.[15]

When the KMT and CCP versions of events were in conflict, as they were more often than not, the reporters were predisposed to accept Zhou's elaborate rendition. To Western correspondents under the sway of his great charm and persuasiveness, his account of events was inherently believable. Moreover, it was chock full of the valuable "details" they needed to flesh out their reports. Even if they had wanted to check out these details, they lacked a timely means of doing so. Venturing into the Communist areas was difficult and time consuming. The temptation, for both personal and practical reasons, was simply to accept Zhou's account at face value.

In the end, they even came to rely on him for information about the Nationalists. According to Tillman Durdin, "Later, in the Chongqing days, the breach [between the KMT and the CCP] was such that Zhou would gladly fill correspondents in on all the dirt they wanted about the doings of Chiang's circle and the Kuomintang government in general."[16] Kuomintang efforts to expose the short-comings and machinations of the Communist movement, on the other hand, were ridiculed when they were not ignored. Brooks Atkinson of the *New York Times,* after arriving in Yenan, wrote a barbed piece lampooning the "fantastic stories" that circulated in Chongqing about the "depraved villainies" of the Communists. He professed astonishment that they all had "two eyes, two ears, two arms and two legs, like most human beings. They seemed no more ferocious than ordinary persons."[17]

Theodore White, in a letter to the Scottsdale conference, remarked on the "immeasurable influence on our thinking" of Zhou and his public relations expert, Gong Peng.[18] Steele pushed the matter further at the conference itself, asking the aging correspondents to reflect on the extent to which "people like Zhou, and particularly Zhou, manipulated the views of the correspondents in China and their coverage of Chinese events."[19] Had these comments and queries come from critics of the press, they would likely have been met with pro forma denials. Coming from two of their own, they were greeted with rueful silence. The only "answer" to Steele's question came from the forthright Peggy Durdin, who with her husband had continued on in Hong Kong after 1949 and who had over the years gained some understanding of the reasons that the correspondents had erred in their earlier China reporting. "Now I'm not saying that correspondents in particular run around getting captivated," Durdin commented about their collective relationship with Zhou, "but I think the whole fact of unconscious reaction to events because of the qualities of the people you get involved with is something we all have had to face."[20]

Thus did Zhou adroitly create a favorable impression of his movement, convincing the correspondents that the Chinese Communist party was essentially democratic and therefore constituted a legitimate governing force. These perceptions were reinforced by junkets to Yenan.

CAMELOT IN NORTH CHINA

The Yenan mystique began with the publication of Edgar Snow's *Red Star Over China* in 1938. As Isaacs reports, "The book made its deepest impression on increasingly worried and world-conscious liberal intellectuals. It began the creation in a great many American minds of the impression of the Chinese Communists as austere, dedicated patriots."[21]

In allowing Edgar Snow to become the first Western correspondent to visit them in their new base area in 1936, the Communists made an excellent choice. Snow had arrived in China in 1928, easily qualifying as an "Old China Hand" in the eyes of his younger colleagues, and wrote for respectable journals like the *Saturday Evening Post,* the *New York Herald Tribune,* and *Foreign Affairs.* Like many intellectuals in the 1930s and 1940s, he believed only socialism could produce and sustain true democracy. But since he was not a Communist, his sympathy for the Chinese Communist party could not be written off by his colleagues and others as mere ideological solidarity.

At the same time, there can be no doubt that Snow was a devout and dedicated socialist. In both the public press and in private letters, he fervently advocated putting "the control of the means of production in the hands of the people."[22] He wrote his family back home that he was concerned whether President Franklin D. Roosevelt's program of public works construction could be carried "to its logical conclusion, to socialism, without reactionary minority elements mobilizing for a last stand and staging a Franco or a Hitler or a Mussolini on us."[23] He was disdainful of capitalism, which he saw as leading inevitably to fascism.[24]

Snow himself was aware of the difficulty of reconciling his professional responsibilities with his personal sensibilities. As he wrote in 1932: "[T]o begin to have feelings about the country and its people may prove a good road to ruin for a foreign correspondent."[25] Far from being a hard-headed, objective reporter, Snow comes across in his early books as a sentimental radical, all too ready to stand shoulder-to-shoulder with fellow proponents of socialism. And, as his biographer, John Maxwell Hamilton, writes, "After eight years of searching, Snow found [in Yenan] a political movement that . . . harnessed people's energies for the common good."

Red Star over China was everything its sponsors could have hoped for. Snow's admiration of the collective ownership and communal life practiced in Yenan was stamped on every page. Even Hamilton remarks that the book was marked by much "romantic idealism and partisanship."[26] The mythologizing of Yenan had begun.

This process was delayed somewhat by the blockade that Chiang

Kai-shek imposed on the area, but after the KMT was forced back to Chongqing and the skirmishing between the Nationalist and Communist forces resumed, Yenan's star rose as dramatically as Chongqing's fell. According to James Thompson, "Once lodged in Chongqing, locked into a war of attrition (with the United Front in shambles), the press corps found little 'romance.' Nationalist propaganda was patently noncredible, while Nationalist censorship increasingly rankled. . . . Blockaded by Nationalist troops, Mao's capital at Yenan became for many frustrated Chongqing correspondents 'the Camelot of China.' "[27]

On 17 May 1944 four correspondents who wrote for American dailies were given permission by the KMT to visit Yenan. The establishment of the Dixie Mission two months later created a permanent American presence in Yenan. Two other correspondents, Theodore H. White and Brooks Atkinson, were allowed to visit late that same year. John K. Emmerson recalls in his memoirs of his State Department colleague John Service that "six days after his arrival, [he] had expressed determination not to be swept off his feet. Yet, finding nothing to criticize, he concluded that 'the spell of the Chinese Communists still seems to work.' . . . [H]e agreed with a correspondent who knew China that 'we have to come to the mountains of north Shensi, to find the most modern place in China.' "[28] Service reported that "to the skeptical, the general atmosphere at Yenan can be compared to that of a rather small sectarian college—or a religious summer conference. There is a bit of the smugness, the self-righteousness, and conscious fellowship."[29]

As for Emmerson, he compared Yenan to the revival meetings he had experienced as a youth "where the converts suddenly got religion," and admitted that he, too, had "succumbed to the spell." Even such a seemingly mundane thing as Yenan's crisp, temperate climate took on significance for American journalists and diplomats eager to escape Chongqing's hot, muggy summers and cold, foggy, muddy winters. In Emmerson's diary of the time, he wrote: "I am influenced by the cold air and the sunshine and the hills so near. . . . The Chinese food is delectable and we are quite comfortable. Nothing like Burma and C rations! After the venality of Peru, the somnolence of India, and the chaos of Chongqing, this is truly utopian. . . . This first day in the 'brave new China!' Down the sawdust trail march we!"[30]

It was not just the Yenan sunshine that entranced Emmerson and the others, but its entire ambience. This, of course, was hardly an accident of climate or geography. The Communist party was keenly aware of the enormous power of the Western media and expended great efforts manufacturing a comfortable yet controlled environment for its representatives. It was in Yenan that the CCP first perfected the array of techniques to handle short-term visitors—parachute journalists—which they later used to such effect during Nixon's visit.

Unlike the Nationalists, who except for press conferences and official communiqués mostly left the correspondents to their own devices, the Communists approached the task of managing the barbarians in their midst with great vigor. Ensuring that the correspondents had a sympathetic understanding of the party's position through endless meetings with high-ranking functionaries was only a beginning. Equally important was insulating them from any conflicting information. The goal was to present a unified—and "democratic"—face to the visitors.

A small, comfortable cocoon of friendliness and conviviality was immediately spun around new arrivals. They were met by English-speaking officials from the foreign affairs section, whose job was to serve as their escorts *cum* translators. There would be a dinner party that first night, often hosted by the inimitable Zhou, who frequently returned to Yenan for such occasions. Later in the evening, after many courses of food and much toasting, Chairman Mao would join the festivities. He would hold forth for hours, while scribbling correspondents secretly congratulated themselves on their good fortune, and incidentally absorbed the fact that Communist leaders did not appear to claim exalted status.

When they were allowed outside of Yenan, the emphasis was on control, and the way was first carefully prepared. Raymond De Jaegher, in his book *The Enemy Within,* recounts a visit by one American correspondent to the Communist base area of An Guo, one hundred miles south of Beijing, where his mission was located:

"Late in March 1938 I noticed that, overnight, anti-American, anti-British slogans, painted in big Chinese characters on the walls of the city, had been erased. Posters of a highly complimentary nature to the United States and Great Britain, and printed in English, had been put up all over An Guo. I soon learned the reason for this artful dodge. . . . The Communists had invited [an American] reporter [from the Associated Press] to this part of Hebei to show him how they were fighting the Japanese, and they were putting on a great show of activity for him. . . . When Mr. Hanson arrived at the mission in the afternoon he was accompanied by three or four Communist officers ostensibly acting as interpreters.

" 'I have been astonished,' he said [to De Jaegher], 'to see the wonderful spirit and energy of the guerrillas.'

"I agreed with him, but smiled too, and joined him in praising General Lu's regime. The officers seemed quite pleased with the way things were going."

" 'How do you find things here under the Red Army, Father?' Mr. Hanson asked me.

" 'Fine! Fine!' I answered enthusiastically.

" 'Do you believe the people are better off under the regime of the Red Army than they were before, when the Nationalist officials were running things?'

" 'Indubitably so,' I answered. 'They are infinitely better off.'

"He looked at me questioningly, but I just smiled and praised General Lu Zhengcao for the wonderful way he was caring for the people. . . . [I] invited Mr. Hanson to tour the mission compound with me. . . . The soldiers followed along for a while, and then, out of the corner of my eye, I saw we were out of earshot.

"I pointed in one direction and leaned toward Mr. Hanson, whispering quickly to him, 'Don't believe a word I've said. I was exaggerating purposely. I had to. The Communists were listening to us. I was sure that you'd understand that any excessive praise to Communists from me would mean the exact opposite! Privately now, I'll tell you the whole truth.'

"He appeared amazed. 'But you are a Catholic priest! I expected the full truth from you! Do you mean you lied to me when I asked you about the way things were going under the guerrilla army?'

" 'Of course I lied to you,' I answered, a shade impatiently. 'I am afraid. Would I have said anything else with General Lu's soldiers listening to every word between us? How long do you suppose I'd be around here if I told you what is true—that conditions are deplorable, the people are in despair? And that the Reds—and I said

Reds, not guerrillas—are simply exploiting this Japanese war to extend Communist power?'

"There wasn't time then to say any more because the soldiers caught up with us, and I went back to describing the architecture of the cathedral to Mr. Hanson."[31]

Well-fed and pampered, flattered by their easy access to top leaders, insulated from the dark side of one-party rule, many of the correspondents "suddenly got religion." The dispatches they sent in from the Communist capital rang with an almost evangelical fervor, as each seemingly tried to outdo the other in praising the new society the Communists were constructing. Guenther Stein of the *Christian Science Monitor* declared ecstatically that "the men and women pioneers of Yenan are truly new humans in spirit, thought and action," and that Yenan itself constituted "a brand new well integrated society, that has never been seen before anywhere."[32]

Whatever else this new society was, it was more democratic than Communist, in the eyes of many correspondents. Brooks Atkinson of the *New York Times* wrote after visiting Yenan that the political system was best described as "agrarian or peasant democracy, or as a farm labor party." The Chinese Communist party was Communist in name only, he concluded.[33] Harrison Forman of the *New York Herald Tribune* and *London Times* was so impressed by the continued tolerance of small-scale private enterprise in Yenan that he announced this was not communism "in Soviet Russia's definition of the term." Later, in his book, *Report from Red China,* he went even further, stating that the Chinese Communists did not practice communism at all, at least not in the Russian sense.[34] Apparently Theodore White also called them "agrarian liberals" in his dispatches, only to have that malapropism edited out by Whittaker Chambers, then Foreign Editor of *Time*.[35]

Lavish praise was heaped on Mao's "New Democracy," especially its policy of "three-thirds," in which Communist party members were limited to one-third of the seats on any local government committee. Israel Epstein's report on a committee meeting emphasized that the Communists were a minority and that the committee's deliberations were conducted with openness and vigor.[36] Guenther Stein described the democratic methods in use in the Border Region as "far-reaching," and the claims of the leaders that these would continue in use in the future as "thoroughly plausible."[37]

A ROSE BY ANY OTHER NAME

Who were these men who came back from Yenan in 1944 to write such fundamentally misleading things about the Communist movement? The historian William Tozer writes that "Epstein [was] probably either Communist or strongly pro-Communist, while Stein was undoubtedly very sympathetic to the Communist cause. Forman, [Theodore] White, and Atkinson were not pro-Communist, but may have been anti-Kuomintang." Only one, Maurice Votaw of the *Baltimore Sun,* was said to be pro-Kuomintang.[38]

When after the fall of China these correspondents were accused of misrepresenting the Chinese Communist party as "agrarian reformers," they replied that they had simply been bearing witness to Chinese reality. Yet even during the height of the civil war the Communists, although utterly determined to create a favorable impression of their movement, were not in the least evasive about their basic ideological convictions. When asked why they called themselves Communists, instead of something more palatable like "agrarian liberals," CCP leaders usually responded in straightforward fashion: "We are Communists . . . and shall always remain Communists."[39] Nor, for all their talk about "New Democracy," did they attempt to conceal from the correspondents that the economic and political policies then in force were merely a temporary response to current exigencies and would in time be abandoned for more communistic policies.

At least some of the correspondents were listening. "Were we reporters aware that the Chinese Communists were not agrarian democrats?" Phil Potter asked at the conference. "Yes, we were, throughout. . . . A newsman could hardly be unaware of the fact that, if you don't have a free press, you're not an agrarian democrat."[40]

One explanation of why these correspondents called a spade a garden trowel was offered up by A. T. Steele, who laid the blame at the feet of his narrow-minded compatriots. "[Anti-communism] made it very difficult sometimes to say favorable things about what we saw [in Yenan]," Steele recalled. "[It] made it difficult to deal with the question of the Chinese Communists. . . . We were reluctant to paint them as real Communists, though, because we knew that that would go against the American grain. If you took a favorable attitude toward the Communists, it would probably have created, in the eyes of the publisher, a feeling that the correspondent in question was maybe pro-Communist." How could the correspondents report the good things they were finding out about the Communists without appearing pro-Communist to an American reading public that was traditionally anti-Communist? "One possible stratagem," Steele suggested, "was to deny that the Chinese Communists were 'real Communists.' "[41]

This sleight of hand raises serious questions of ethics: How can a journalist, for whatever reason, consciously conceal a central truth about a highly controversial subject? Having once sacrificed this truth to political considerations, how can a journalist then be trusted to convey other "truths" accurately?

What Communist programs were so worthy of praise that some correspondents decided to suppress the name of the cause in which they were carried out? Journalists applauded land reform and reclamation, since these gave landless laborers in the countryside the means to support themselves. They looked with favor on the 25 percent reduction of rents on tenant-cultivated lands and the low and equitable tax rates of the Border Region government. They commended the Communist party and its army, large in comparison to the local population, for growing much of its own food and thus easing the strain on the economy. Above all, they were impressed by Mao's dictum that "all people should be well-fed and well-clad," and by its corollary, that everyone, leader and follower, soldier and civilian, worker and peasant, must live a frugal, even austere life.[42] In all of these policies the Communists were making a virtue out of necessity, since the Nationalist and Japanese blockades meant that the Border Region economy had to be self-sufficient in any case, but the rough equality that it produced in dress and living standards greatly stirred the correspondents.

Chinese Communist economic policies of the time were well within prevailing liberal currents. It was not hard to convince transplanted

New Dealers like Theodore White of the virtues of welfare, guaranteed employment, and income leveling. Having grown up in the time of the Great Depression, they believed that governments had a duty to intervene in the economy to correct the instabilities and injustices of capitalism, real and imagined, and perhaps abolish it altogether. Even the CCP's stated goal of total state ownership of the means of production did not give such correspondents pause, both because it did not seem imminent and because it differed only in degree, rather than in kind, from their own notions of a widely embracing role for government.

The Nationalist government was hardly a liberal democracy. The KMT in principle considered China to be in a period of democratic tutelage but in fact governed China with an increasingly heavy hand during the 1940s. Fighting a war on two fronts is not conducive to democracy. Yet to the end of the civil war, the KMT was still a more pluralistic organization than the rigidly hierarchical CCP.

The relative openness of the KMT political structure did not win any kudos from the correspondents, even though they greatly benefited thereby. They lived for years in Chongqing (a testament to KMT tolerance, given the kind of copy they were producing) but devoted precious few column-inches to the existence of opposition political parties, to efforts to hold popular elections in a country lacking a democratic tradition, and to the gradual extension of modern legal codes over a peasant society.

There was also a surprisingly vigorous Chinese press, at least in the Nationalist areas. Phil Potter, reporter for the *Baltimore Sun*, belatedly recalled in 1982 that "I was up in Kalgan, capital of a Communist border region government, and one thing that was pretty obvious to a newspaperman was the fact that in Communist China there was not a single newspaper other than their own party organ, whereas in Kuomintang China there was a comparatively free press. You had the *Ta Kung Pao* and you had many others, so that you got a sense of opposition to the Kuomintang government."[43]

Far from being an advantage, the "comparatively free press" of Nationalist China at the time proved a major handicap. Opposition newspapers, some covertly operated by the Communists, relentlessly attacked the Nationalists, exposing their faults and factions. American correspondents, eager to see fascism, and especially its Japanese variant, defeated, quickly lost patience with a party in apparent disarray. They failed to grasp the larger point, namely that the very existence of such dissension demonstrated that the KMT was hardly the "fascist" organization of their nightmares. "The idiocies, the mistakes, in the KMT area were pushed upon you every day," Peggy Durdin recollected. "You knew the battles between the factions, you knew the miseries and all the rest of it. On the revolutionary side we knew very little and certainly not the seamier side of the factional fights."[44] By restricting access to information, the CCP was able to to maintain an appearance of political unity and common military purpose.

Had the correspondents been allowed in Yenan for more than short visits, and had they been fluent in the Chinese language, they would at least have had a chance to penetrate the veil of secrecy that the Chinese Communist party had drawn about itself. The odds against their succeeding would still have been daunting, however, since the CCP was conspiratorial, with the rank and file duty bound to obey uncritically the Central Committee's line of the moment. As Mao Zedong put it in a 1938 speech to a plenary session of the party's Central Committee: "[W]e must affirm anew the discipline of the Party, namely: (1) The individual is subordinate to the organization; (2) the minority is subordinate to the majority; (3) the lower level is subordinate to the higher level; and (4) the entire leadership is subordinate to the Central Committee. Whoever violates these articles of discipline disrupts Party unity."[45] Good party members did not talk out of turn, especially to foreign reporters. The intraparty struggles, the purges, the executions, all of these things were conducted out of the public eye.

Reporters who attempted to broach the party facade of unity risked losing access to their most prized source, Zhou Enlai. Phil Potter was one of those who was cut cold. "I was with the group of nine correspondents who first got into Manchuria with the Russian army and wrote many, many stories about its stripping of Manchuria," Potter recounted. "I'd been covering the negotiations between Marshall and Zhou Enlai for months, and I'd gotten to know Zhou Enlai very well. When I got back to Chongqing, the first thing I wanted to do was see Zhou and get his attitude on the Russian stripping of Manchuria. He would not see me. I wrote that it was obvious that he was hostile to it; that there was in the Chinese Communist party a minor schism between those who had implicit faith in Russia and those more moderate in their regard for China's northern neighbor, and that Zhou was the leader of the latter faction. The next time I went to his office, I was told he wouldn't see me, and I never saw him again, except at news conferences, until I left China a few months later."[46] The lesson was clear. Correspondents who valued their relationship with Zhou would not comment on the party's sensitive relationship with the USSR or on its internal schisms, but would faithfully reflect the current party view in their dispatches. There was no equivalent cost to reporting on the factions and personality conflicts of the KMT, which made good, if somewhat arcane, copy.

From the monolithic face presented by the party members in Chongqing and Yenan, the reporters safely concluded that those who lived in the Communist Base Areas were of one mind. This artfully created confection of popular unanimity, comprised of equal doses of "New Democracy" and deceit, convinced the correspondents, insofar as they needed convincing, that the "agrarian liberals" were democrats at heart and therefore constituted a legitimate governing force.

One measure of how dominant this position was among not only the correspondents, but the China-watching community in general, was offered by John Flynn, onetime managing editor of the *New York Globe*. He personally examined all books on China published in the United States between 1943 and 1949, the critical years in which the civil war was fought and decided. He first identified those books that contained prescriptive analyses of the Chinese political situation, eliminating those that dealt solely with travel, art, culture, or personal memoirs of the war. There were twenty-nine such books in all. These he divided into books that weighted their evidence and special pleading toward the Chinese Communists, and those that did not. There were twenty-two titles in the former category, including books by the aforementioned Guenther Stein, Edgar Snow, Theodore White, Harrison Forman, Israel Epstein, John K. Fairbank, and several other correspondents. There were only seven books in the latter, of which only two were by correspondents.

GATEKEEPING

However many editorial eyebrows the books and dispatches of the foreign correspondents raised back in the United States, few sought to exercise any control. MacKinnon and Friesen concluded that "the level of censorship and gatekeeping with which the China correspondents contended seems to have fallen within a 'normal' range, especially considering wartime conditions. . . . Neither China- nor Europe-based reporters received many direct orders from their editors. On the surface they were pretty much on their own."[47]

Paramount among editors who did interfere was Whittaker Chambers, who became the foreign news editor at *Time* magazine in 1945. Although Chambers could not know the extent to which Chongqing correspondents had become beguiled by the Chinese Camelot and by that remarkable man Zhou Enlai—who more than anyone else had made it happen—he found Theodore White's dispatches disturbing: White not only relentlessly criticized Chiang and the KMT, he also approached the whole problem of communism with muffled oars. Perhaps White couldn't tell the difference between a Communist and an agrarian liberal, but Chambers certainly could. With a surety born of his twelve years as a member of the Communist party, he rewrote White's dispatches to reverse the anti-KMT, pro-CCP spin that he found there. Nor did he hesitate to rework those of other foreign correspondents, especially those of John Hershey, *Time*'s Moscow correspondent, which he described as "written from the viewpoint that the Soviet Union is a benevolent democracy of unaggressive intent."[48]

Forty years later, memories of this "editorial interference" still rankled. John Hershey, in a luncheon address to the Scottsdale conference, accused Chambers of imposing "a monotone of paranoia on *Time*'s foreign news." At the time he had cabled *Time* owner Henry Luce with a strident protest that passages from his Moscow dispatches were being "torn from context . . . and put into [the] new context of *Time*'s editorial bias [which was] greatly unfair [and] actually vicious."[49]

Henry Luce's response to this and other complaints left no doubt whose views he considered more consonant with the real world. "The posture of events in January, 1945, seems to have confirmed Editor

Chambers about as fully as a news-editor is ever confirmed," Luce circularized his correspondents. "I have just been told, in a highly confidential manner, that Stalin is, after all, a Communist. I am also somewhat less confidentially informed that the Pope is a Christian. Some will say: what does it matter in either case? And what does it matter that Hershey advises me that he, John Hershey, is a Democrat? Well, I cannot say for sure just what these pieces of information signify, but one must respect the data in each case. A good Foreign News Editor, while guarding against the prejudices arising from his own convictions, will not ignore the circumstance that the Pope is a Christian and Stalin a Communist and Hershey, God bless him, a Democrat."[50] Armed with this ringing endorsement, Chambers continued to replace the Hankou Gang's "super story" with his own, which was substantively supported by subsequent events.

One example of the editorial treatments that Chambers meted out to White's China dispatches is found in the 13 November 1944 issue of *Time*. The report on China begins in typical White fashion by attacking Nationalist China as being less interested in fighting Japan than in fighting the Communists. It approvingly quotes Brooks Atkinson's harsh denunciation of KMT policies and practices. Then the report abruptly reverses course, attacking the CCP for subverting Chinese unity against Japan and suggesting that it was Communist belligerence that made the continued blockade of Yenan necessary. "If Chiang relaxed the blockade, perhaps all of China would ultimately be lost to the democratic cause," *Time* argued. Chiang should not be pressured into forming a coalition government with the Communists, it concluded, because the eventual and inevitable result of power sharing would be a Red China allied with the Soviet Union.

Had other foreign editors pressed their "captivated" correspondents to look past the brilliant silk screen of Zhou's performance to the reality of the Chinese Communist party, reportage of the China situation would have dramatically improved. Had the correspondents themselves borne in mind that, in Luce's words, Stalin was a Communist and the Pope was a Christian, they would have reached different, and considerably more accurate, conclusions about the protagonists in the Chinese Civil War. But this would have required them to be guided by a different super story. And it would have required them to fear anti-Communists less and Communists more.

History has not been kind to those who, like A. T. Steele, thought that a Communist victory would "open the way to a new day in China." Steele and his colleagues (with a few exceptions) were neither crypto-Communists nor fellow travelers. But they were enamored of Chinese communism's chief spokesman, they were put off by the chaos that was Chongqing and, most of all, they were trapped in the amber of the paramount political myth of their generation: that government is best that governs most. This myth led them consistently to exaggerate CCP economic and military accomplishments, to minimize the party's tyranny and censorship, and to purport its democratic tendencies. Their own super story rendered them blind to the numerous portents of postrevolutionary disaster.

In the event, the establishment of the PRC in 1949 was the beginning of a thirty-year nightmare of purges and political campaigns, culminating in the Cultural Revolution, which caught up tens of millions of ordinary Chinese in the party's cruel nets. Yet the correspondents who met in Scottsdale in 1982 seemed oblivious to all that. The sufferings that Mao and his revolutionaries had inflicted on the Chinese people occasioned from them neither reflection nor remorse. Far from reexamining the super story that led them astray, they clung with myopic stubbornness to the antiquated view that Yenan had been the birthplace of something splendid and new, a Chinese Camelot. Instead of offering a collective mea culpa, they took turns preening themselves on the "pretty goddamn good job" they had done in reporting from China in the 1940s.

All this constitutes a rather bizarre omission, like recalling the cute lion cub you once reared without mentioning that it grew up to devour your children. As we will see, however, such omissions are characteristic of an entire school of China-watchers.

4

The Age of Hostility

❦❦❦

A revolution is not a dinner party, or writing an essay, or painting a picture, or doing embroidery; it cannot be so refined, so leisurely and gentle, so temperate, kind, courteous, restrained and magnanimous. . . . To put it bluntly, it is necessary to create terror for a while in every rural area.

—Mao Zedong
"Report on an Investigation of the Peasant Movement in Hunan"

By the time that Mao Zedong proclaimed the founding of the People's Republic of China on 1 October 1949, the views of those scholars and reporters who had admired Communist rule in Yenan were no longer as popular with Americans, who saw that the all-China version of a guerrilla base area had a definitely totalitarian air about it. Precisely three months earlier, Mao had dramatically cast aside the cloak of bourgeois democracy that he and his party had worn for much of the civil war and announced that the new national government they were about to establish was to be a dictatorship, or more precisely, a "people's democratic dictatorship." The "people" in this formula were an amalgam of four good classes: the peasants, the workers, the "petty bourgeoisie," and the "national bourgeoisie." Together (with a little help from the Chinese Communist party), they would exercise a "democratic dictatorship" whose first and most important task would be to liquidate bad or "antagonistic" classes, defined as "the running dogs of imperialism—the landlord class [and] the bureaucrat-bourgeoisie, as well as the representatives of those classes, the Kuomintang reactionaries and their accomplices." Eventually all class distinctions would be leveled, Mao promised, but first these two offending classes had to be "eliminated."

Mao was not coy about how this class war was to be prosecuted. "Our present task is to strengthen the people's state apparatus," he wrote. "The state apparatus, including the army, the police and the courts, is the instrument by which one class oppresses another. It is an instrument for the oppression of antagonistic classes." Eventually the state would "wither away," but first it had to be mightily strengthened.[1]

In contrast to these stern and explicit marching orders, Mao's comments on democracy and civil rights were brief and vague. "The people" would "enjoy the freedoms of speech, assembly, association," and would have the right to vote and "elect their own government." But on one condition: none of this was to interfere with the primary task of the new government, which was to exercise a dictatorship over the enemies of the people. It did not take a political philosopher to see that, even if the rights enumerated by Mao were inalienable, the right to membership in "the people" was not. Those who vigorously exercised their freedom of speech (or assembly, or association), or took seriously their right to "elect their own government," would run the risk of being declared "enemies of the people" by the secret police, who would then punish, imprison, or execute them with impunity.[2]

Mao's address caused shock waves in the United States, especially among those who had been convinced that the Chinese Communist party intended to plot a more humane and democratic course. Attacks on the Nationalists for violations of freedom of speech, assembly, and publication, taken by some as evidence of CCP commitment to those ideals, were now seen as "united-front" ploys aimed at rousing domestic and international public opinion against their enemies. It was generally agreed in the United States that the earlier talk of "agrarian reform" and "a period of democracy before moving to the next stage of socialism" had been inventions of the Chinese Communist party, touted both internally and abroad by its foreign apologists for purposes of propaganda. Both were thoroughly discredited in the eyes of Americans. The "people's democratic dictatorship" was widely viewed as nothing more than a none-too-subtle ideological cover for the political supremacy of the Chinese Communist party.[3]

The anguish felt by so many Americans at this discovery was etched not only in anger but in humiliation. It was not merely that they had been cleverly deceived by China's new political elite. More painful still was that the American model of civil society had been decisively rejected. America's upstart ward, or at least those who now controlled its destiny, had declared their fealty to a doctrine that was the antithesis of the American faith in freedom, democracy, and human rights.

This self-declared dictatorship, already well equipped for class warfare, was about to become more so. At its disposal were the secret police forces of the Communist party and the People's Liberation Army, both honed to a grim efficiency by fifteen years of reaping crops of counterrevolutionaries within the liberated areas. With China under de facto military rule from 1949 to 1954, both were to be used extensively against the civilian population. An internal security apparatus was also germinating within the newly established central government administration under the jurisdiction of the Ministry of Public Security. Called the "Public Security Forces," the tentacles of this secret police agency soon penetrated every urban district and rural township in the country. The instruments of institutionalized violence were in place.

THE TERROR

The Terror—no other term will do—that began in 1950 was to last for three years and cost several million lives before it ended. It originated in two distinct political campaigns, each a ruthless effort to crush a particular class. The land reform, while nominally an effort to reapportion the land to poor and lower-middle-class peasants, was actually intended to destroy the old rural elite, replacing it with a new rural power structure dominated by those who had received parcels of land from the CCP and the new regime.[4] The "suppression of counterrevolutionaries" campaign was designed to eliminate the bureaucratic bourgeoisie—those compradores, traders, and KMT functionaries who were seen by the party as economic parasites or political foes.

After China entered the Korean War, a Resist-U.S.–Aid-Korea campaign was begun, and the threat of foreign imperialism was used to justify mobilizing the population to conduct a frenzied hunt for enemies of every kind and description. On 21 February 1951, the Beijing government promulgated a drastic decree on the "suppression of counterrevolutionaries," which legitimated, if that is the word, what was already happening in fact—a vast, undiscriminating campaign of terror and repression against all forms of political dissent unlike any other in China's recorded history. In the first half of 1951 alone, 80 percent of the Chinese population were reported to have taken part in mass accusation meetings against "counterrevolutionaries," the outcome of which was often fatal to its targets.[5]

Those executed included former Nationalist officials, businessmen accused of "disturbing" the market, former employees of Western companies, intellectuals whose loyalty to the new regime was suspect, and large numbers of rural gentry. It was not necessary to prove that the accused had actually engaged in counterrevolutionary activity; being a "latent reactionary element" was crime enough. Important victims were invariably denounced, sentenced, and shot in public, often before vast crowds of people assembled for that purpose. Lesser fry simply disappeared, their names appearing in the lengthy lists of those executed that were posted on public buildings, if at all. Newspapers were transformed into police tabloids, featuring grisly accounts of crime and punishment. The entire process seemed designed to produce maximum terror among the population, as well as to eliminate all real and potential opposition to the people's democratic dictatorship. It also left the outside world aghast.

The Communists, initially boastful of the numbers of counterrevolutionaries "liquidated" since the founding of the PRC, became more circumspect as the death toll mounted. In his report to the National People's Congress of 26 June 1957, Zhou Enlai stated that only 16.8 percent of all counterrevolutionaries had been sentenced to death, most of them between 1949 and 1952.[6] Since 800,000 cases were reported tried in the people's courts in the first half of 1951, this would mean that at least 134,400 of these had been executed. Given the ferocity of the campaign, the number of those executed (rather than merely sent to labor camps or placed under surveillance) was probably two or three times this number during this brief period alone. The U.S. State Department in 1976 estimated that there may have been a million killed in the land reform, 800,000 killed in the counterrevolutionary campaign.[7] Maurice Meisner, who is sympathetic to the need for revolutionary terror, allowed that perhaps 2 million people were executed during the first three years of the PRC.[8] Jacques Guillermaz, the distinguished French Sinologist, who served as French Military Attaché in Nanjing during the civil war and later in Beijing, estimated in his *La Chine populaire,* published in 1964, that a total of 1 to 3 million were executed.[9] He later increased this estimate to 5 million, a figure that Fairbank has cited as the upper range of "sober" estimates.[10] The highest estimate comes from Nationalist officials on Taiwan, who were not inclined to underestimate the ferocity of their victorious opponents. They alleged that 6 million urban residents and 4 million rural gentry had been killed during these years.

The People's Republic has never revealed the exact number of victims of the Terror, nor is such a revelation likely, short of the overthrow of the present regime, but it was of a magnitude as to cast a deadly pall of butchery over the new government. A million of anything is a mere cipher to the human mind, but enough tales of suffering and death reached the outside world to give these statistics a human face, reminding Americans that each of those who died was, in Richard Walker's phrase, "a thinking, loving, emoting, creative being."[11]

No story attracted more attention than that of Bishop Francis X. Ford, an American who was one of the ranking members of the Catholic Church in China. Bishop Ford had been in China since 1918, working with the Hakka minority of Guangdong province from his *see* city of Kaying (Mei Xian). After Communist guerrillas took the city in April 1949, he found the activities of his priests and parishioners gradually circumscribed by a maze of new regulations. ("Freedom of religion" was allowed, but not "freedom of assembly"; the churches were shuttered.) On 23 December 1950, the noose was tightened still further, and Bishop Ford was placed in solitary confinement. The accusations began, centering on the charge that he was an American espionage agent. Bishop Ford was given no opportunity to plead his innocence and refused to confess his "guilt." The verdict was a foregone conclusion. On 15 April 1951, nearly four months after he had been arrested, he was finally arraigned in court, where he was promptly found guilty of spying against the People's Government. Along with his diocesan secretary, Sister Joan Marie, he was sentenced to a long term at the provincial prison at Canton. Less than a year later he was dead, a victim of the beatings; the rice, cabbage, and water diet; and the endless and exhausting "thought reform" sessions brought on by his refusal to sign a confession.[12]

This case attracted wide attention in the United States, primarily because the Chinese government had chosen to vilify Bishop Ford in a nationwide propaganda campaign, by extension discrediting the entire missionary movement. Newspapers in every corner of the country denounced him as an American spy, an anti-Communist, and a counterrevolutionary. Even *Pravda* picked up the story, repeating the charges against him and claiming that he was "an important United States agent." What this crescendo of criticism was leading up to, in the opinion of Sister Joan Marie, was a show trial once the bishop confessed. But he died before he could be broken to harness.

Bishop Ford's death was kept a secret by the Chinese government for six months. When on 16 August 1952 the prison authorities belatedly informed Sister Joan Marie of his passing, it was for the purpose of having her sign a document relieving them of responsibility for his death: "Francis Xavier Ford died on February 21, 1952, of a natural illness and old age [he was sixty], despite the expert medical care given him by the People's Government." Shortly thereafter, no longer needed as an extra in a spy drama, she was released from prison and expelled from the country.

When Sister Joan Marie, gaunt and blinking, walked slowly across the bridge at Shenzhen to tell Western correspondents that Bishop Ford was dead, Americans were aghast and saddened. The *New York Times* editorialized bitterly that "we know by now what to expect of Mao Zedong's ruffians. . . . The murderers of Bishop Ford . . . have no claim upon our sympathy. They have put themselves beyond the pale."[13] Hearst columnist Bob Considine was moved to write: "The next time you feel on the verge of self-pity because of some real or imagined example of ingratitude shown you, try to remember a man from Brooklyn named Francis Xavier Ford. Ford loved the Chinese people who in the end put him to death."[14]

Many Westerners suffered similar ordeals, though few received the extraordinary public exposure that Bishop Ford did in China and in the outside world, and few died as a result of mistreatment. The new regime was from the beginning bent on driving all but a favored handful of foreigners from the country while preserving the fiction that they were departing voluntarily. Increasingly onerous restrictions on travel, communication, and business operations caused many to leave in 1949–50. Those who insisted on remaining were often placed under house arrest and, like Bishop Ford, accused of engaging in anti-Communist, counterrevolutionary, or espionage activities.[15] They were treated with increasing ruthlessness, up to and including violent abuse at the hands of government-instigated mobs, and threatened with the prospect of long prison terms. Nearly all found it expedient to quickly confess to any alleged wrongdoing in the hope (and promise) that the government would expel rather than imprison them.

Only a handful of Americans remained in China after this forced exodus. Isaac notes that, "In mid-1957 there were, as far as was definitely known, 23 Americans all told in all of China, compared to the 13,000 American residents in 1937, the last 'peacetime year.' "[16] This remnant consisted solely of the exalted and the damned. On the one hand there were the "friends of the people," individuals like Dr. George Hatem, who had served the party long and faithfully and who became a "special advisor" to the Ministry of Health, where he spoke to visiting delegations about the revolution's spectacular improvements in health care. On the other hand there were the "enemies of the people," Americans like Bishop Walsh of Shanghai who were accused of spying and were condemned to prolonged incarceration in the new government's prisons.

For every foreigner who was forced out of China there were a thousand Chinese who, in the eyes of the new regime, had been tainted by contact with them. During the "suppression of counter-revolutionaries," those who had been close to, or in the employ of, the departing "espionage agents" were especially at risk of arrest and execution. Althought their stories did not become known to a wide public outside of China, and are necessarily absent many details, the journalists, businessmen, diplomats, and missionaries who lost Chinese friends and colleagues in the Terror did not forget it.

In his 1972 book, *Journey Between Two Chinas,* the former *New York Times* Assistant Managing Editor Seymour Topping recalls the fate of J. C. Jao, a former colleague of his at the Associated Press office in Nanjing. Jao was a graduate of the University of Missouri School of Journalism, spoke excellent English, and had edited the *Qingdao Herald* before joining the AP. As a political liberal, he had initially welcomed the Communists, but was increasingly critical as they tightened their control over the population. He did not welcome the reeducation sessions that he was required to attend; he resisted confessing past ideological sins and turned down the Communists' offer of a job writing anti-American propaganda.

J. C. Jao was thus a natural target for suspicion and denunciation when the Terror began in early 1951. By that time Topping had left the country and indirectly received word of his friend's difficulties through newspaper accounts. The Shanghai *Liberation Daily* announced that J. C. Jao was one of many "counterrevolutionaries" who had been rounded up in Nanjing. He was accused of having engaged in "espionage activities" on behalf of the Associated Press, even though he no longer worked for the news agency. On 5 May the *Liberation Daily* reported that a public trial of 376 "counterrevolutionaries" had been held on 29 April in Nanjing before an audience of thousands. All were found guilty and liquidated on the spot. Among the names listed in the *Liberation Daily* of those having died on the killing fields that day was that of J. C. Jao. "Nothing was ever heard of Jao again," Topping writes.[17]

POLITICAL CAMPAIGNS

The "suppression of counterrevolutionaries" and the "land reform" were only two of the more bloody examples of political campaigns that were to become a trademark of CCP rule. While only the Hundred Flowers campaign and the Great Leap Forward attracted more than passing attention outside of China, there were many more.

Counterrevolutionaries were snared by the "Three-Antis" (*sanfan*) campaign against "corruption, waste, and bureaucratism"; the "Five-Antis" campaign against "bribes, fraud, tax evasion, theft of state property, and revealing state economic secrets"; the "Increase Production and Practice Economy" campaign; and the "Thought Reform" campaign, aimed at remolding intellectuals along acceptable Marxist-Leninist lines. And this was just during 1951–1952!

Each of these political maelstroms swept across the face of China with the suddenness and destructive force of a late summer typhoon, leaving a trail of battered victims and ruined societal structures. To be sure, not all of these campaigns were countrywide search-and-destroy missions like the "land reform." But whether they were intended to purge cadre ranks or remold public values, to adjust management practices or transform the rural economy, each produced its quota of political heretics who were publicly abused, brutalized, and frequently executed. And each produced its own trickle of refugees and accounts by journalists, further affirming the new regime's ruthlessness.

American China-watchers were as surprised by the thoroughness of these repeated socialist calls to arms as they were shocked by their violence. Ideological reeducation, a central feature of many campaigns, often involved tens of millions of Chinese in weeks or even months of meetings. The instrument used to reform their thinking was the "self-criticism," a political purification rite unique to the Maoist version of communism, in which those accused of past ideological sins or present faulty thinking confess their wrongdoing at public meetings. In the "Thought Reform" campaign, for instance, all of China's teachers were required to write detailed autobiographical confessions exposing, and disavowing, any bourgeois, feudal (that is, Confucian), or bureaucrat-capitalist attitudes they had formerly held, and swearing their allegiance to the new regime and its political theories. These "self-criticisms," once judged acceptable by the party, were then contritely read out loud before meetings called for that purpose.

As one class or group of people after another was singled out by the party for special attention, the full dimensions of what the Chinese Communist party was attempting became apparent. Chinese society was to be recast according to Marxist social theory, in which everyone was defined by membership in a class. Moreover, Chinese people were to be stripped of their Confucian ethics, for which Mao had often voiced his disdain, and were to be taught the virtue of violent social change. The "incremental objector," to use Buckley's phrase, was to be eliminated either by sweeping his mind clear of offending thoughts or, if the clutter was deemed irreparable, by shooting him in the back of the head.[18]

Americans were horrified. Not only was the imposition of a rigid system of class the antithesis of their belief in total social mobility, it violated their understanding of traditional Chinese practice. One reason for the early American infatuation with China was the perception that the lowliest farmer's son could rise by individual merit to a position of high office. By contrast, the new system of class seemed incomprehensibly unfair, and worse yet, un-Chinese.

The perception of millions of Chinese being forced to abandon their old belief system in favor of a new and alien one came to be widely held in the West. Taken as a whole, the new regime's single-minded efforts at directed social change seemed to be an effort not only to bury traditional Chinese culture, but to change the very character of the Chinese people. A *New York Times* editorial in 1955 captured the prevailing mood:

> Mainland China had been conquered by still another external group and for the time being by a set of ideas basically foreign to the Chinese concept of good living . . . the Confucian ethics that had become part of the admirable Chinese character. There is no place in the Communist world for the personal and family loyalty that were the very heart of Chinese society. There is no place for humor and generosity, for patience and kindliness, for honor and warmth of heart.[19]

Even Isaacs, who does not dwell on the repressive aspects of CCP rule, in effect gives his imprimatur to the American consensus on this point by declaring: "There is nothing ephemeral . . . about the system's intellectual robotism [and] its police terror."[20] These are strong statements for a writer who set out to chart only the shifting sands of perception, not the hard rock of reality. As we will see, however, even intellectuals who do not hesitate to rationalize the "rectification" of other classes in the name of socialist progress (to which group

Isaacs by no means belongs), are likely to be horrified when their own class is being coerced into "robotism."

In the minds of Americans, China had become a despotism capable of any atrocity. The testimony of the exiled church leader Samuel W. S. Cheng before the House Un-American Affairs Committee in 1959 that "more than 30 million Chinese have suffered persecution and death up to the beginning of the commune system" was accepted without question.[21] The *New York Times* in an editorial 2 June 1959 called public attention to "testimony before a House Committee [that] put the number of persons murdered by the Red Chinese in the past decade at about 30 million."[22]

LEANING TO ONE SIDE

Those Americans who had maintained that the new regime would chart a foreign policy course independent of Moscow were also left in the lurch. In his essay "On the People's Democratic Dictatorship," Mao squarely committed China to the socialist camp. "It was through the Russians that the Chinese found Marxism," he declared on 1 July 1949. "Internationally, we belong to the side of the anti-imperialist front headed by the Soviet Union, and so we can turn only to this side for genuine and friendly help, not to the side of the imperialist front."[23] Mao called his new policy "leaning on one side," but it soon began to resemble a Greap Leap Northward.

Mao traveled to Moscow in late 1949 for a nine-week sojourn, the upshot of which was the Sino-Soviet Treaty of Friendship, Alliance, and Mutual Assistance signed on 14 February 1950. The treaty, which Mao hailed as "eternal and indestructible," pledged Soviet support should Japan or any state cooperating with Japan attack China.[24] Squadrons of Soviet-made fighter planes were delivered that spring, and soon put an end to Nationalist air raids on military bases along the South China coast. The first Soviet advisors arrived soon after and began constructing the fifty model industrial units Stalin had promised Mao. In total, some ten to twenty thousand Soviet advisors and another fifteen hundred East European experts were to work on more than a thousand different industrial projects in China during the 1950s.[25] The Soviets agreed to extend $300 million in credits to China, but there were to be few outright gifts, either then or later.

A long duet with the Soviet "elder brothers" followed in which Russian became the principal foreign language studied in the schools, and the USSR the principal destination for Chinese students studying abroad. Centralized economic planning was adopted, with Soviet accounting and managerial methods followed to the letter. The first Five-Year Plan, launched in 1953, could have been lifted from Gosplan. The 1954 PRC Constitution was a dead ringer (in translation) for the 1936 Stalinist Constitution. The courts, the legal system, the police forces, and other institutions were Sovietized. Even Chinese architecture took on blunt Stalinoid features, as builders and building plans were imported from Moscow.

While everything Soviet was welcomed, everything Western was rejected. Russian literature, for instance, was translated into Chinese by the bale, but the only Western literature allowed in China was that which had been passed by Soviet censors and published first in Russian. While Russians were being welcomed into the country, Americans were being forcibly ejected, and those Chinese with ties to the United States, like J. C. Jao, were being reeducated, imprisoned, or executed. To Americans struggling to come to terms with a China turned upside down, the new leadership was not just "leaning to one side," as Mao euphemistically put it, but had leapt into the Soviet camp and was displaying a frenzied anti-Americanism to win Stalin's acceptance.

On 25 October 1950 as U.S. forces pursued the remnants of the North Korean army northward toward the Yalu River, beyond which lay Manchuria, they were sent reeling back by hundreds of thousands of Chinese "volunteers." These saturation tactics won ground only temporarily. The conflict soon settled into a bloody war of attrition around the thirty-eighth parallel, but the spectacle of American soldiers suffering defeats and dying at Chinese hands stunned Americans. A host of images of China and its people were effaced virtually overnight. The old China, which had patiently and philosophically endured humiliation after humiliation at the hands of foreign powers, was now itself a "foreign power," capable of military exertions beyond its borders. The soldiers of that country, long ridiculed as weak and ineffectual—"comic opera warriors," in Isaac's stinging phrase—stood revealed as formidable foes.

There was no question in the minds of Americans of what force had wrought this unexpected transformation. The Chinese Communists, who had set out to reconstruct China in their own image, were now in league with international communism, trying to spread forcibly their doctrine to other nations. When the National Security Council in 1950 classified China as bellicose and bent on subjugating Southeast Asia, it was at one with public sentiments of the time. Reports of "human wave attacks" readily confirmed the new regime's callous willingness to exchange lives for terroritory. In May 1951 General Peng Dehuai, in a desperate effort to overrun U.S. lines, lost more than a hundred thousand men in less than a week. China's enormous population of 600 million was transformed into an ocher flood, or a yellow peril, in the vocabulary of the time.

Americans were aghast by reports that prisoners of war (POWs) were being "brainwashed" to accept the party's version of the Korean War, in which the United States was the "imperialist aggressor," and to sign confessions admitting that they were "war criminals." Western notions of the proper way to treat POWs, which had been codified in the Geneva Convention, were being ignored by a dishonorable and ruthless foe. Furthermore, the sanctuary of the mind was being violated in an inhuman effort to gain propaganda advantage from prisoners. Stories of hapless Americans being broken and manipulated by Communist interrogators became a set piece of the time and seemed to come straight from the pages of George Orwell's *1984*.

It may be, as Isaacs suggests, that old images of the cruel, devious, and subtle Oriental created the appearance of a "special mystique that gave the Chinese extraordinary skill in the use of these weapons of mental and emotional torture," but this sort of mental rape did not need to feed on caricatures of inhuman cruelty or devious inscrutability in order to horrify.[26] It did quite well on its own, easily outstripping the crude and brutal torture techniques attributed to the Russians in the purge trials of the Stalin area. The term *brainwashing* was, in fact, a literal translation of a Chinese Communist party term, *xi naujin,* and referred to a set of psychological stress techniques developed by the party in the 1930s and 1940s. Rather than execute ranking members of the party or potentially useful enemies, the party preferred to harangue, harass, and cajole them into recanting their heretical thoughts and accepting the infallibility of the party. These mind-bending techniques, less rigorously applied, continued to be used in the fifties to remold the thoughts of intellectuals, "petty bourgeoisie," and others who held only mildly divergent opinions or who were too important simply to shoot. The mill was set up long before; the POWs were simply the latest shipment of grist.[27]

MUTUAL ANTAGONISM

The 1950s were years of hostility towards the PRC, hostility all the more bitter for being thoroughly requited. Mao displayed a depth of anger toward the United States or, more precisely, toward "U.S. ruling circles," unparalleled by any other important foreign leader. Typical was his "Statement Supporting the People of the Congo Against U.S. Aggression," which clamored: "People of the world, unite and defeat the U.S. aggressors and all their running dogs! People of the world, be courageous, dare to fight, defy difficulties and advance wave upon wave. Then the whole world will belong to the people. Monsters of all kinds shall be destroyed."[28]

Ill feeling between the United States and China ran so high at times that their representatives cold-shouldered each other at international diplomatic functions. At the Geneva Conference in 1954, John Foster Dulles was widely reported to have refused to shake hands with Zhou Enlai. Zhou, for his part, gave as good as he got. Tillman Durdin, by then reporting for the *New York Times* from Hong Kong, recalls meeting Zhou in Rangoon: "As I marched through the [reception] line I met Zhou, and he turned away as I offered my hand. He wouldn't shake hands. He knew me very well . . . [but] the policy had changed."[29]

Little in the steadily diminishing flow of accounts by American missionaries and businessmen, and Chinese emigres and refugees contradicted this dim view of China. Such books as Sister Mary Victoria's *Nun in Red China* (1953), Robert W. Greene's *Calvary in China* (1953), and A. M. Dunlap's *Behind the Bamboo Curtain* (1956) provided intimate, anecdotal accounts of the political and religious intolerance of the new regime.[30]

In lonely rebuttal to these sober pictures stands Julian Schuman's *Assignment China* (1956). Schuman, an American journalist who stayed on in Shanghai until 1953, when the government closed down his newspaper, the *China Weekly Review,* nevertheless declared that China had just as much freedom as the West. He attacked Christian missionaries for having links with the Office of Strategic Services (OSS) and the Central Intelligence Agency (CIA) and argued that their imprisonment and expulsion for spying was justified. He even castigated a reporter from the *Nation* for taking a slightly jaundiced view of brainwashing, insisting that such gentle reeducation was necessary to create a New China. But he was swimming against the tide of American opinion.[31]

Two highly personal accounts by young university students who escaped to Hong Kong early in Communist rule are gems of the refugee genre. Liu Shaw-tong worked as a propagandist for the party for one year before fleeing to Hong Kong in 1950. His book *Out of Red China* offers a plethora of anecdotes illustrating the mindless viciousness and absurdity of totalitarian rule. Marie Yen's *The Umbrella Garden* vividly describes the decline of Chinese academe under the influence of intellectually mediocre party cadres, who replaced the liberal arts with a curriculum that pandered to the Soviet Union and Stalin and who substituted thought reform for academic freedom.[32]

Journalists and officials of other nationalities, unlike Americans, continued to be allowed in China for short visits during these years, and their articles and books occasionally appeared in American newspapers and in English editions. Frank Morae's *Report on Mao's China* is typical of the book-length accounts, which were more commonly critical than sympathetic. Morae had been a war correspondent in China in 1944–45, and on his return there in 1952 as a member of a government delegation from India he was able to evaluate from his personal experience the changes that had occurred. On the positive side of the ledger he notes that the hyperinflation of the last years of the civil war has been brought under control and that the health care system has improved. But the most striking change he identifies is the unrelenting oppression and mind control of Communist rule, to which he devotes many pages. And, like most observers of the time, he notes the hand-in-glove relationship between the PRC and the Soviet Union.[33]

American newsmen were persona non grata in China until 1956, when the Beijing regime suddenly reversed itself and invited eighteen newsmen to tour the country. When Washington refused to sanction the delegation, three of those invited went anyway, returning to the United States to publish accounts of their visit in *Look,* the *New York Post,* and other papers. In 1957 the Washington ban on travel was broken again by members of an American "youth delegation" to Moscow, who continued on to China as guests of Beijing.[34] After the Quemoy-Matsu crisis in 1958, Beijing drew back from such contact until the end of the decade, when Edgar Snow became the first American correspondent with experience in pre-1949 China to be invited back.

A bamboo curtain, to use the terminology of the day, had rung down over China, making China-watching an arcane and tedious art. Unable to observe events firsthand, students of contemporary China disappeared into the library to pore over Communist China publications or decamped to Hong Kong to interview recent refugees. They found the collection of correct, pertinent facts about China to be arduous, and their further assembly into coherent, reliable descriptions of the general state of affairs to involve considerable speculation. Perceptions of China, even more than of Yenan during the civil war, came to be governed by a single super story.

TOTAL STATE, MASS PROGRESS

As Americans saw it, a particularly invidious form of totalitarianism had descended upon China, extinguishing the individual to the "masses," and regulating and controlling the pulse of society through "mass movements." At the same time, it was also believed that this loss of freedom was, at least in large part, offset by the great works that the now-mobilized masses had achieved. Chinese men and women, sturdy and industrious, had been inducted into a vast army, and all their enormous energies channeled into industrialization.

Work battalions were swiftly modernizing the ancient face of China—pumping oil, building bridges, raising factories—opening up the prospect of superpower status in the near future.

Virtually every foreign visitor who put his impressions to paper remarked at length on China's economic progress and prospects. Two British visitors, Lord Boyd Orr and Peter Townsend, comment that "when one considers the amount of building which has been done in the cities, the expenditure on flood control, and the cost of laying new railways and roads, the fact that China has come so far suggests that a backward poverty-striken country is being transformed—and quite rapidly at that—into an industrial nation."[35] A British journalist, George Gale, found remarkable the plethora of "factories, roads, railways, bridges—these are the most unarguable and most visible hard facts."[36] The regime published statistics showing the gains made during the First Five-Year Plan from 1952 to 1957, including a phenomenal increase in GNP of 68 percent over these years, which were widely accepted as valid. Professor Li Choh-ming of the University of California at Berkeley concluded that "as far as I could see, there is no evidence of deliberate fabrication."[37] Most American economists agreed that China enjoyed the highest growth rate of industrial production in the world in the 1950s, far ahead of Japan, West Germany, and the USSR.[38] Even those who were heavily critical of the Communist party's ideological intolerance and frequent resort to police terror accepted its claims that China was rapidly progressing toward industrialization. Richard Walker was among those who later endorsed such claims, writing that "in the first decade of Communist rule, the PRC made dramatic achievements in industrialization and modernization—steel production, for instance, reaching in excess of 12,000,000 tons."[39]

In the countryside, the party quickstepped the farmers into collectives controlled by the state and party. By 1955 the agricultural sector became integral to the planned economy. Unlike in the Soviet Union, this was accomplished without widespread resistance, since the old rural elite had already been eliminated, and without faltering in food production or lowering of food consumption. American economists were again impressed, noting that since the regime was investing heavily in industry at the expense of agriculture, it was doing well to hold its own food production against population increase.

Though unacquainted with these statistics, Americans at large had absorbed a sense of the burgeoning industrial power of the People's Republic. Most would have agreed with Gerald Clark that "specific or exact statistics in industry are in some ways irrelevant. The main point is that Chinese industry has indeed jumped ahead at a rate never envisioned by Westerners who knew the former China, and is progressing at a rate to dispel any complacency on the part of the West."[40] With the aid of a propaganda apparatus skilled at creating positive impressions, a new picture of a rapidly industrializing China became current. *Life* magazine, a publication not given to portraying revolutionary China in a positive light, in 1957 published a photo essay showing bridges being built, rails being laid, roads being constructed, and canals being dug. *Life* asserted that its picture report made it clear "that Red China has made some formidable efforts" and added, "If it reaches its set goals, Communist China, by 1962, will rank among the world's ten top industrial powers."[41] This prediction sounds ironically similar to some that Chairman Mao was making about this time. When he launched the Great Leap Forward later that year, he announced that one of its goals was to catch up with Great Britain in the production of iron and steel within three years.

The prototypical photograph of the time showed hundreds or even thousands of Chinese dressed in identical baggy blue tunics and trousers, digging at the earth with pick and hoe or carrying cement in panniers and rocks in wicker baskets, on some massive project that would take months, if not years, to complete. To Americans, the Chinese had become the blue ants, creatures who worked in swarming masses, lived in communal nests, and submerged their individuality to the collective will. Rather than scoff at the absence of modern equipment, Americans were impressed that such mammoth projects could be undertaken by men and women working with simple tools. Few disputed Mao's prediction that China would soon overtake Britain in industrial production. What could China not accomplish if its "people power" were thus harnessed and channeled?

This sense of China's burgeoning industrial might, which after the Nixon opening to China would be applauded, was at the time cause for considerable alarm. The Chinese Communist party, under the leadership of Mao Zedong, had determined to control the whole of Chinese society and had for all practical purposes succeeded. Purges had swept away the recalcitrant, and ideological remolding had domesticated the rest. The people had been impressed into work battalions called communes, and new and incalculable energies had been unleashed. The substantial economic progress achieved by totalitarian means was threatening to Americans because the PRC commanded one of the largest military forces in the world, which it did not hesitate to use, and regarded the United States as its Number One enemy and the Soviet Union as its primary ally.

THE TOTALITARIAN PARADIGM

One could accurately summarize American views of China in the fifties in one word: "totalitarian." What is remarkable about this super story is the way it came to dominate American thought about China. Unlike the U.S. war correspondents' earlier interpretation of Yenan, the CCP and the Chinese Civil War, which remained primarily an elite viewpoint, the totalitarian-China paradigm was shared by correspondent and reader, layman and scholar, and even by those who had originally supported the Chinese Communists. To paraphase Isaacs, it became clear to even sympathetic Americans that "Chinese communism" was not a significant modification of generic communism, at least in those areas which made it serve so well the purposes of bureaucratic totalitarianism.

Tai-chun Kuo and Ramon Myers, who recently undertook to assess how well Sinologists had understood the PRC in the first three decades of its existence, note that "in the 1950s, most American experts insisted on calling Communist China a totalitarian state."[42] Benjamin Schwartz told his academic readers that the vision contained in Mao's speeches was "of a totalitarian society by consent," while cautioning them that "the authority of the state, however, remains supreme, and the basic concept is still fundamentally totalitarian."[43] Richard Walker, in his book *China Under Communism*, characterized China as a "totalitarian dictatorship," emphasizing the party's reliance on the military, police, judiciary, mass organizations, and the propaganda apparatus to promulgate and enforce its policies among the population.[44] Arthur Wright, examining the differences between traditional and Communist rule, asserted that "with modern techniques and instruments of coercion at its command, the Communist regime is seeking to impose a system that surpasses in its totality anything that China has experienced in the past."[45] Walter Rostow saw Communist China as expansionist, determined to "increase the independent authority of Beijing in Asia within the limits permitted by the need to maintain the Sino-Soviet alliance."[46] John K. Fairbank concluded that the new regime had combined Communist theory and praxis with certain historical practices to create "a totalitarianism which is something quite new in China's experience."[47]

That China possessed every characteristic of a totalitarian state, as defined by Friedrich and Brzezinski in 1956, is difficult to gainsay.[48] The distinguishing features of generic communism, to use Isaacs' phrase—a Communist party led by one man, with party control over ideology, communications, the economy, the police, the judiciary, and the army—were all present and largely accounted for. One might wish to argue that Chinese totalitarianism was not purely a product of Marxism-Leninism or, with the later Fairbank, to avoid the word totalitarian altogether, but "the unprecedented degree of central control" could not be ignored.[49] That this useful descriptive typology later fell into disuse in academe had less to do with reasoned argument than with the growing sensitivity of many academics to the harsh overtones of the word *totalitarian.*

The idea that the Chinese Communist party had conducted continuous political campaigns, whose clear and calculated purpose was the ideological remolding of the population, was also well-rooted in the soil of Chinese reality. It was not merely that the party enjoyed a monopoly on the mass media through which it ceaselessly propagated its policies, or that it brutally suppressed those with dissenting views. It went further, insisting that important groups outside the party—intellectuals, businessmen, members of the middle class—actively endorse and support its policies. In 1953 a pseudonymous article in the journal *Problems of Communism* detailed how the "party presumes to dictate not only what a man may write, and how he may write it, but how and where he must spend his time in pursuit of inspiration."[50] Robert J. Lifton, in his excellent study of thought reform techniques, remarks on the importance of such milieu control: "It is probably fair to say that the Chinese Communist prison and revolutionary university produce about as thoroughly controlled a group environment as has ever existed. The milieu control exerted over the broader social environment of Communist China, while considerably less intense, is in its own way unrivaled in its combination of extensiveness and depth; it is, in fact, one of the distinguishing features of Chinese Communist practice."[51] Thought reform techniques continue in use today not only in the PRC's prisons and labor camps, but also in such political campaigns as the population control campaign and the anti–spiritual pollution campaign.

The widely perceived hostility of the Communist elite toward the United States was likewise no invention of the cold war. A fierce, deep-seated, and dogmatic hatred of "U.S. imperialism" was often apparent in Mao's speeches and writing. While it was not until the Cultural Revolution that Mao finally began to enjoy the kind of unquestioned authority that Stalin or Hitler had exercised, his views of the United States dominated in party circles from the beginning. At the Moscow Meeting of Communist and Workers' Parties on 18 November 1957, for instance, he predicted the overthrow of this "paper tiger":

> I have said that all the reputedly powerful reactionaries are merely paper tigers. The reason is that they are divorced from the people. Look! Was not Hitler a paper tiger? Was Hitler not overthrown? I also said that the tsar of Russia, the emperor of China and Japanese imperialism were all paper tigers. As we know, they were all overthrown. U.S. imperialism has not yet been overthrown and it has the atom bomb. I believe it also will be overthrown. It, too, is a paper tiger."[52]

Some have interpreted these and similar statements as mere rhetorical posturing, or argued that they reflect a tendency toward hyperbole that is intrinsic to the Chinese language. As a poet, they argue, Mao was particularly susceptible to this kind of verbal excess. Others have admitted that as a Communist revolutionary Mao would have applauded the downfall of capitalism in the United States, but they rejected as anti-Communist hysteria the idea that he was actively seeking a confrontation with U.S. troops and allies abroad in the years after Korea.

The late Soviet president Andrei Gromyko's recently published memoirs contain evidence that American fears of hostile Chinese action were not unfounded. In August 1958, then–foreign minister Gromyko secretly visited Beijing to meet with Mao Zedong, and was astonished to learn that the Chinese leader wanted the Soviets to attack U.S. troops with nuclear weapons after his forces had lured them into China. According to Gromyko, Mao's plan called for an attack on the Nationalist-held offshore islands of Quemoy and Matsu. When the Nationalists and Americans counterattacked, his armies would retreat deep into the Chinese heartland. Once U.S. forces were deep in Chinese territory, Mao said, "The Soviet Union should catch them with all its means." Gromyko wrote that he was surprised at the audacity of Mao's plan to use nuclear weapons against U.S. forces, and responded that "the scenario of war described by you cannot meet a positive response by us."[53]

But even well-founded anxieties about China could frequently be taken too far. Consider the Sino-Soviet monolith, the impression that Moscow and Beijing had joined forces in an ideological crusade to carry their Marxist gospel throughout the world. The alliance between China and the Soviet Union was real enough, based on their shared enmity toward the United States and their shared belief in the inexorable march of history. But it cast a larger shadow in the West than it warranted, because it was taken to mean not simply a limited unity of purpose, but a joining together of polities under the Communist banner. China had not merely adopted an alien ideology, it had voluntarily incorporated itself into the Soviet Union as the newest "socialist republic."

The alarm this raised in America was amplified by fear. Isaac remarks that "in the same season of 1949 that China fell to the Communists, Russia exploded its first atom bomb and had become something new in the American cosmos: A foe to be feared."[54] Many Americans consequently exaggerated the degree of solidarity between the USSR and China, perceived in China's early adulation of things Russian its irreversible Sovietization, and saw in China's intervention in Korea its willingness to provide foot soldiers for Moscow's wars. Anxious Americans feared that the Communist movement had a manifest destiny of its own.

The principal flaw in the American super story of the fifties was the perception that the Communist party's control and regimentation was enabling it to transform China into an economic superpower overnight. In the early years, the People's Republic of China had indeed tamed inflation, repaired the destruction wrought by the war, and returned production to prewar levels. But growth in the mid-fifties was slower than the 9 percent per annum claimed, and during the turmoil of the Great Leap Forward it virtually ceased. Writing in 1968, T. C. Liu and K. C. Yeh estimated that by 1952 the Chinese gross national product had recovered to 1933 levels and that for the next five years the GNP grew at a rate of approximately 6 percent a year, hardly a record-shattering clip for a country with a per capita income at that time of about one hundred dollars a year. They characterized the years from 1958 to 1965 as a period of "further industrialization without growth."[55] After 1979 Chinese economists readily admitted that despite continued investment by the regime in industry, the economy as a whole had become increasingly unproductive after 1957.[56]

Those who were deeply worried about a Communist China on the march were also led to warn their countrymen of the danger, sounding the tocsin all the louder for good effect. Michael Croft, who visited China as a member of a youth delegation, cautioned that "it is not only foolish but may prove fatal to shut our eyes to what is happening [in China] simply because it seems so very far away. . . . Distance has not prevented China from emerging, within a few years, into a world power of the first magnitude and ultimately, I believe, it will not prevent China, still firmly allied to the Soviet Union, from gaining effective control over most of Asia, with catastrophic repercussions upon the western way of life."[57] Economic progress enhanced the fearfulness of China as an opponent; fear, in turn, added to perceptions of its burgeoning economic power.

One consequence of the mistaken belief that the New China was advancing industrially at a blistering pace was a gradual muting of criticism over its lack of civil and political rights. Most political observers saw the two as inversely related, convinced that it was precisely the denial of individual liberty and the imposition of intense intellectual conformity that made possible China's smoothly running collective economy. What did it matter if the Chinese were denied freedom of speech if they were, for the first time in history, gaining in the race for subsistence? Would they not willingly (if given the choice) trade in their election ballots for a chance to raise their standard of living to that of the Western world? It was upon this argument that a new, more favorable view of China would be constructed in the sixties.

5

From Hostility to Second Admiration

❧❧❧

Man's love of truth is such that when he loves something which is not the truth, he pretends to himself that what he loves is the truth, and because he hates to be proved wrong, he will not allow himself to be convinced that he is deceiving himself.

—St. Augustine
Confessions

From the beginning several U.S. scholars and journalists privately questioned the usefulness of the totalitarian paradigm for understanding Communist China. It was difficult for those who had been in China before 1949 to accept that the PRC was not romantic Yenan writ large and that the charismatic Zhou Enlai and his colleagues were presiding over a Red Terror. Students of Chinese history, no less than admirers of the one-time "agrarian democrats" of Yenan, found the thought of the vast panoply of Chinese civilization collapsing into a totalitarian state utterly distasteful and a few rejected the possibility out of hand. Barred from China themselves, both groups of China-watchers sought counterevidence, or at least encouragement, in the reports of visitors.

Like the Soviet Union before it, once the Communist government was firmly established in power it vigorously set about improving its international prestige through the use of what Richard L. Walker has called "cultural diplomacy."[1] Thousands of carefully selected foreigners representing dozens of countries in Europe, Asia, and Latin America were issued invitations to "come and see" the New China and its achievements during the 1950s. The political inclinations of the invitees ranged from the hard left, who went to marvel, to the merely liberal, who went with an "open mind," but they were all articulate and influential members of their societies. Americans were excluded.

As soon as these visitors, organized into special delegations, crossed the border between Hong Kong and Shenzhen—the customary entry point into China—they stepped onto an invisible conveyor belt. For the next week or two they were carried effortlessly from city to city past modern factories, impressive public works, and "typical" communes. Side trips to such attractions as the West Lake at Hangzhou, or Nanjing, provided exotic relief, while Protestant or Catholic church services were available in major cities for the devout or merely curious. But leisure time was scarce; the belt moved at dizzying speed. The high point of the tour came when they reached Beijing, where they were ushered into the presence of Mao Zedong, Zhou Enlai, and other top leaders for tea and chit-chat with these revolutionary legends.

Everywhere they went they were treated with the exquisite hospitality reserved for honored guests under the Li, the Confucian code of correct manners. They were fêted by senior party officials at sumptuous banquets in city after city. "What greater joy," these officials would toast them, quoting Confucius without a trace of irony in their voices, "than to welcome guests who come from afar." Visiting factories, the guests would be escorted by the factory director, who at the end would walk them to the entrance and bow them farewell with all ceremony.[2] It is hard to exaggerate the effect such charming solicitousness had on foreigners unfamiliar with such protocol. Who could forget the sight of China's premier personally selecting a choice morsel of some Chinese delicacy and putting it in your rice bowl at a banquet in your honor?[3]

Basking in this sunny and courteous treatment, foreign guests were almost insensibly acclimatized to Communist China without ever learning much about it. Few paused to wonder how the practices of the former Confucian elite had survived the regime's well-known proletarian ardor. Fewer still asked themselves how they came to deserve such feudal deference. Chinese hospitality was so charming, Chinese amenities so gratifying, and Chinese politeness so frictionless that most accepted their treatment without question. And if after leaving China they began to reflect on the underlying reason for their hosts' solicitousness, their pleasantly memorable visit made it almost impossible for them to be publicly critical of the regime on this or any other count. One said positive things or nothing at all.

China created its pleasant illusions not with smoke and mirrors but with careful choreography and compulsive attention to background detail. "When your Prime Minister Clement Attlee visited Guangzhou in 1954, not only were the fronts of all the buildings he would pass freshly painted for the occasion, but people who worked or lived along the route were rehearsed in their roles for three months before he came," one of the extras told the British journalist Dennis Bloodworth afterwards. "Even an old chap who sold cigarettes from a pitch outside our office—one stick at a time—was given ten lessons in what to say if by chance the foreigners stopped and asked him something. It was standard procedure."[4]

Robert Loh, who performed in this meticulously directed theater for seven years, gave the world an unusual look backstage after fleeing to Hong Kong in 1957. As a personal assistant to the Chen brothers, once the biggest of Shanghai industrialists, he had helped them to entertain foreign visitors on more than fourscore occasions. Convincing skeptical Western businessmen that Chinese capitalists had welcomed the expropriation of their enterprises had been demanding work, requiring much careful preparation:

When the guests [French industrialists] were admitted to the sitting room, they could not hide their amazement at the luxurious standard of living these ex-capitalists were enjoying under Chinese Communist rule. Through a French window, they could see a large garden full of flowers. A neatly dressed governess was wheeling a child across the lawn, with two dogs frisking about them. In the adjoining room, the eldest daughter was practicing the piano. Everything seemed so peaceful and natural that no one could possibly guess that each of these details had been carefully planned and rehearsed. No wonder one of the French ladies remarked, "I have never seen a more contented family."[5]

When Mr. Loh's boss was asked, as he invariably was, how it was possible for him to willingly abandon all his property to the state and endorse Communism:

> [He] assumed a serious expression, paused for a moment, as though for thought, and answered slowly, "When the Communists first occupied Shanghai, we were very apprehensive, if not for our lives, at least for our property. . . . we have come to realize that the Chinese Communists never deceive people. . . . My business, which was drifting before, is now growing and developing. As to my personal mode of living, it has remained the same since my business became joint with the state. . . . The younger generation, imbued with the ideals of socialism, realizes that gain without effort is shameful. So even if I were able to bequeath my property to [my children], they might refuse to accept it. Under the circumstances, there is no reason why I should not support the Communist Party and accept socialist transformation.[6]

This oration, delivered in a fashion worthy of Sir Laurence Olivier, usually had his guests nodding in agreement. In the case of the French industrialists, Loh reports that they were completely won over: "[They] shook Mr. Chen's hand, saying: 'If the French Communists adopt the policy of the Chinese Communists, we shall have nothing to say against it.' This phrase was printed in all the newspapers on the following day. Even Mao Zedong used it in one of his speeches many months later."[7]

The cost of staging these elaborate performances, whose casts consisted of the populations of whole factories and communes, for an endless series of foreign delegations must have been staggering. And the numbers of visitors to be entertained kept increasing throughout the fifties, going from dozens to hundreds to a thousand or more in 1959 and 1960, when the achievements of the Great Leap Forward were being touted. Yet the favorable notices that resulted must have made such extravaganzas, in Beijing's view, well worth the expense. "China is in great vogue," wrote a Brazilian critic at the time. "It is fashionable to travel to China and see the places that the Chinese government has prepared for visitors. . . . Parliamentarians, writers, journalists, rush to get there and come back roaring with enthusiasm, with exaggerated eulogies for the . . . regime and its extraordinary achievements in progress and wealth."[8]

Latin Americans were not alone in their remarkable susceptibility to the regime's pretensions. Well-educated visitors from a dozen countries unhesitatingly generalized from the little they had heard and seen that all of China, under the guidance of wise and caring leaders, had achieved social justice, equality, and rapid modernization. William Ratliff's description of Latin American visitors can fairly be applied to all: "The majority . . . who went to China hoped to find an underdeveloped country overcoming enormous obstacles in its drive for social and economic progress, and, since they saw only what the Chinese had prepared for them, this is just what they found."[9]

Even greater than the joy of welcoming guests from afar, from Beijing's point of view, was the joy of sending them back to their native lands to serve as willing missionaries for the New China. As anticipated, they were a prolific group, who after their exit from China hastened to vent their newfound expertise in interviews, speeches, articles, and books. By 1960 a dozen Indian visitors had written books about the People's Republic following a guided tour in that country; all but two were panegyrics.[10] In Latin America, whose intellectuals found China's anti-Americanism particularly appealing, numerous volumes appeared but "none of them is critical in tone, nor even merely a dispassionate account."[11] The English-speaking world, too, saw a rash of such publications, many of them highly partisan.[12] An army of paid public relations consultants could have been no more effective at improving China's international image than these enthusiastic volunteers.

Beijing was sufficiently confident of its stagecraft that the occasional muffed line was shrugged off. As a Chinese official remarked to a disenchanted Chilean student who, after fifteen months in China during 1960 and 1961, was about to return home: "You have perhaps found bad things here, but you can say what you wish. No one will believe you because many foreign delegations come here who say the contrary."[13] He was right. The reports of the few visitors who refused to take the official show-and-tell for truth were dismissed as biased by the many who had. Outside the United States, their views swept the field.

Most of these visitors flatly denied that the People's Republic of China was governed by a totalitarian regime that forbade its citizens the free practice of their religion, subjected them to humiliating re-education sessions, and executed those branded as counterrevolutionaries. Simone de Beauvoir returned from her guided tour in the mid-fifties to assert that "life in China today is exceptionally pleasant." This she attributed to the enlightened rule of renaissance men: "Plenty of fond dreams are authorized by the idea of a country where the government pays the people's way through school, where generals and statesmen are scholars and poets."[14] Hewlett Johnson, the dean of Canterbury, came away from extended conversations with officials of the "Chinese Christian Churches" convinced that the expelled missionaries who spoke of widespread religious persecution of Chinese Christians were wrong. "[N]o persecution of missionaries or Christians has been countenanced by the Government," he asserted. Reeducation sessions, with their mandatory public self-criticisms, instead called to mind "primitive Christian professions of a humble and contrite heart, and also the story of the communal forgiveness of the early Christian communities . . . [S]uch an outlook, permeating to the many millions as yet untouched, gives promise of unimaginable moral strength."[15] Basil Davidson found nothing objectionable in the reeducation (he used the term *remoulding*) of intellectuals, because it was carried out humanely for a high moral purpose: "[R]emoulding does have the effect of wiping out memories of the past, of healing wounds in Chinese society, of leaving men and women with a sense of freedom to develop new attitudes towards each others' and their work." In any case, the Chinese state was "authoritarian only towards a minority—a minority who are not workers or peasants. This will come unpleasantly to those who like to fool themselves that China is achieving her success by dictatorial methods: the truth is that China's successes are being achieved—and can only be achieved—by the voluntary and even enthusiastic effort of most of the people of China."[16]

Many visitors, extrapolating from Chinese contacts who all spoke with one voice, came to share the view that the Chinese Communist party had converted the Chinese masses into a moral community whose enthusiasm for collective undertakings was unbounded. James Bertram, a New Zealander whose experience in the countryside was limited to a visit to a state-run dairy farm, nevertheless pronounced collective agriculture a smashing success. "The first impression remains the lasting one," he wrote in 1957, "that of a whole population cheerfully associating in group activity, and finding it better than the old back-breaking toil in solitude. . . . the slogan of 'Land to the Tiller!' has been made a reality; and . . . collectivization does not seem to threaten it."[17] Ignorance and inclination combined in Bertram's imagination to create a peasantry eager to be free of the burdensome toil of running their own family farms so that they could join with thousands of their neighbors and farm the land in common under the direction of cadres appointed by the state.

The high tide of China's cultural diplomacy in the fifties coincided with the Great Leap Forward and produced favorable notices for years afterwards. Scott Nearing, visiting China in late 1957 at the beginning of the Leap, "found a China completely transformed since my first trip there in 1927. The Communists had eliminated the scourges that were rife thirty years earlier. . . . Industrialization was being enthusiastically promoted. . . . Cooperatives in agriculture, in trade, and in handicrafts had become a prominent feature of Chinese economy. . . . A flood of energy, idealism and high striving marked the mood of China."[18] Renée Dumont, a French professor of agriculture, returned from China convinced that the mass labor projects he had witnessed could not have been undertaken "without the *active* and *voluntary participation* of the *majority*," and were a result of the party "marrying its authority to the peasant's consent." The British author Sir Herbert Read, who visited China in 1959, thought that the people's communes "may . . . be of great significance to other parts of the world. . . . It does not matter what the system is called: it is a living reality and the Chinese Communist Party itself claims that it is an entirely new form of social organization . . . *what counts more than statistics is the happiness and contentment of the peasants.*" Professor Charles Bettleheim of the Sorbonne declared that economic progress made during the Great Leap Forward "implies great clearness of thought, a lucid vision of all the possibilities of development . . . shared by the masses." He believed he was witnessing "a real technical revolution coming from the masses themselves."[19]

Sir Cyril Hinshelwood, president of the Royal Society of Great Britain, excused the "inevitable restrictions" of a "communist organization" because "the Chinese people never had much personal liberty and *it is quite likely that many of them are now freer in some ways than they have ever been.* The eminent British Sinologist Dr. Joseph Needham wrote in 1958 that criticism of the communes was ethnocentric: "If they [the critics] had any experience in the slavery of the Chinese woman throughout the ages to the charcoal or brushwood stove and the primitive water supply, they would understand that the cooperative farm, . . . restaurant (*sic*) and the public bath today seem more like heaven on earth to millions." He lauded the "emancipation of women to follow careers . . . on the farm, railway or factory." He compared the commune mess halls to the cafeterias at Cambridge and other universities, claiming that their existence was "a matter of pride in China today, not of compulsion or regimentation." The British correspondent Felix Greene, from whose book these visitor's reports come, commends them to the reader as factual, fairminded, and balanced.[20]

THE LIBERAL COUNTEROFFENSIVE

Few of these books were published in the United States, and those that were sold poorly. The public at large was not favorably disposed toward a China that had intervened in the Korean War, was allied to the Soviet Union, and seemed to be espousing a communism even more radical than Moscow's. Nevertheless, despite their limited circulation, these firsthand accounts had a certain impact in intellectual circles. Academics and others with special interests in China, frustrated by their lack of access to that country, combed these books for clues to current conditions. Those China-watchers who were unconvinced that the totalitarian paradigm captured either the substance or the essence of Chinese actuality found in them much support for their own views.

In their paradigm, which we will call the "modernizing communist regime," the People's Republic of China was a successfully modernizing state whose communism (with a small *c*) was tempered by China's past and whose advances had not been costly in human terms. So out-of-step was this perspective in the fifties that its partisans initially advanced it with great caution. Fairbank remarks that be-

101

cause of the "overriding importance of political orthodoxy . . . [i]t became second nature to indicate at the beginning of an article, by some word or phrase, that one was safely anti-Communist."[21] The strongly anti-Communist tenor of the time accounted only in part for the China-watchers' reluctance to state openly that communism had been good for China. As a group, they had been scorned in the recent past by the American public, accused of misdiagnosing the civil war, misreading the intentions of the Chinese Communist party, and even contributing to the Communists' rise to power.[22] A bold dissent from the reigning orthodoxy might lead to their being accused of apologizing for the Chinese Communists.

Not that the New China's partisans passively accepted the existing monopoly on perceptions of the new regime. While the promotion of a positive image of Chinese communism was problematic, the reigning paradigm (and its adherents) could be attacked as simplistic, erroneous, and confused. Richard L. Walker's *China Under Communism*, which characterized China during the first five years of Communist rule as a "totalitarian dictatorship," was the target of several particularly venomous reviews.[23] The China historian Mary C. Wright was one of those who took offense at Walker's description of the way in which the Communist party in China eliminated or coopted all political opposition, subjected all economic activity to state planning, and controlled the media to promote its ideology and policies. Rather than directly attacking the "Communist China as Totalitarian Regime" paradigm or advancing her own, Wright chose instead to berate Walker personally for writing a "chaotic and confusing" book.[24]

In more popular forums, these China-watchers sought to explain to the American people that such unhappy features of Beijing's governance as the persecution of intellectuals, the purges of "class enemies," and the denial of religious freedom were historical in origin. It was not ideology and organization that had created a police state, they argued, but China's history and culture. Though no sensible student of China would dispute what John Lukacs calls the historical relevance of national character, the view they advanced was remarkably selective in attributing negative features of Communist rule to China's past, rather than to standard Marxist machinations, or to Mao's unique and evil genius.

Professor Fairbank was a leading exponent of such continuities. Writing in the *Atlantic Monthly* in 1957, he asserted that "the Chinese culture area is a political universe in which a centralized Chinese despotism stands supreme. . . . we now face an apparently high degree of compatibility between Soviet totalitarianism and old-style Chinese despotism." The regime's controls over "prices, persons and minds, mobilizing of patriotic youth, collectivizing the rural economy and pushing of industrialization" were "remarkable successes" and "great achievements," but not really surprising when illuminated by Fairbank's historical lantern.[25]

The idea of China as an unalloyed despotism, governed by a single, all-powerful emperor through an ideological elite that brooked no competition, was a hoary one. Chinese emperors had ever been intolerant of political dissent. By insisting on this historical connection as the primary explanation of the new regime's indifference to human rights and political liberty, sympathetic China-watchers could finesse, or even avoid entirely, embarrassing questions about the impact of Marxist ideology and Leninist political organization. If the new rulers of China gave short shrift to the idea of democracy they had once seemed to promote, well, neither had Confucius been an advocate of popular rule. If the Beijing regime was centralized, bureaucratic, or even despotic, well, that description would have fit a dozen dynasties. These Sinologists were in effect asserting that China's history is its destiny and that its political culture *qua* culture is unique. The utility of this position was that it enabled criticism of Communist China to be dismissed as either historical ignorance or cultural sacrilege, uninformed or ethnocentric quibbling deriving from a narrowly Western perspective.

Both communism and Confucianism purport to derive their legitimacy by elaborate ideological rationalizations—myths, if you will. The central political myth of Confucianism was that the emperor and his mandarins ruled the Middle Kingdom through moral example, and that as long as they maintained Confucian standards of public virtue, they would enjoy a "Mandate of Heaven." The primary evidence of the continued existence of heavenly favor, of course, was the survival of the dynasty. The central myth of communism is that the leaders of the party ("the vanguard of the proletariat") are temporarily exercising dictatorial power on behalf of "the masses" for only as long as it takes for the state to "wither away." The "masses," of course, must be persuaded to accept this version of affairs.

Obviously both of these myths disguised the reality of a despotic state that derived its power not from the just consent of the governed, but from force or the threat of force. There is one striking difference, however. It is one thing to insist that those who govern exhibit a certain moral character in the course of performing their public duties. It is quite another to require the governed to submit to educational remolding to eliminate any ideas or attitudes threatening to the regime. All other things being equal, leadership by example inspires trust in government, while rule by rigid precept produces fear.

The mystical invocation of Culture and History to explain Chinese Communist party policies and practices is all the more odd in view of Mao's conscious and violent rejection of China's past. Mao was convinced that Confucian social and cultural mores—the traditional class system, the family system, the ideological system—had to be extirpated before his ideal egalitarian society could flourish. These "feudal tails" were viciously attacked from the beginning, not merely driven underground to reappear in Marxist garb.[26] Self-avowed Marxist scholars can be refreshingly candid on such matters. Professor Maurice Meisner, a leading Marxist historian of China, asserts that "[T]here is little evidence to support the widespread assumption that modern Chinese revolutionary change can be understood in terms of the survival of traditional patterns of thought and behavior . . . the aim was not to revitalize old Chinese traditions but to find ways to bury them."[27]

Those similarities between the old Confucian-based political order and the new Marxist-based one that have been identified often have an abstract, formal, or even trivial character. Take, for instance, Professor Ping-ti Ho's finding that "while the Maoist ideology and the unprecedented power of organization are distinctly new wine, this new wine is contained in a two-thousand-year-old bottle of authoritarianism."[28] Given that governments based on the principle of individual freedom have been rare in human history until quite recently, the reappearance of authoritarian rule after 1949 scarcely constitutes convincing evidence of continuity. Some form of dictatorship was the most likely outcome.[29] Far more striking than any connections between China past and present, and more deserving of remark and analysis, was the organizational, ideological, and policy isomorphism between the PRC and the USSR.

Professor Fairbank and others seldom addressed the topic of communism in its generic sense, since they disapproved of the notion that it had a fixed and transnational character. Indeed, they almost never used the term. When they did it was often placed in parentheses. For them "communism" was a pliable ideology that, when transplanted across national and cultural boundaries, easily assumed the character of its new practitioners. A China under the rule of the Chinese Communist party was still China; to call it Communist China was needlessly pejorative. Fairbank, Richard Thornton concludes, "saw Communism in China as a wholly national movement with exclusive indigenous roots."[30] There were problems with this point of view, of course, not least that it required overlooking a substantial set of homologies between China and the Soviet Union. But the alternative was even more distasteful. How could they possibly agree with anti-Communists, whom they despised, that there were in truth similarities among the several Communist regimes? How could they bear contributing to the anti-Communist attitude of the American public that they were accustomed to dismissing as "hysterical" and "paranoid?"

The clearest statement of how these political convictions determined scholarly tactics comes from Fairbank himself: "I was committed to viewing 'communism' as bad in America but good in China," Fairbank writes, "which I was convinced was true. This led me to claim China and America were different 'cultures' or 'social orders'—also true. It followed that area specialists like me had esoteric knowledge of these cultural-social differences between China and America. The question was whether we could impart it to our fellow citizens and make them all area specialists (in the sense of understanding cultural-social differences). It was a tall order but the only way to keep American policy on the right track."[31] Fairbank and others like him understood that warm relations with the Chinese Communists would be possible only after Americans had been educated to understand how "good" communism had been for China. It would be a decade before that prospect began to be realized, but in the meantime the bonds of acceptable discourse had been loosened enough by the Sino-Soviet Split to permit Fairbank and others to abandon their defensive redoubts of "culture" and "history" and attempt to seize the offensive.

THE SINO-SOVIET SPLIT

Unbeknownst to the West, tensions between China and the Soviet Union had been on the rise throughout the fifties. Mao, who had only grudgingly recognized Stalin as the senior partner in their relationship, refused to concede this status to Stalin's blustering successor. Khrushchev's scathing denunciation of Stalin's crimes in 1956 surprised and dismayed the Chinese leadership, which complained about Moscow's "failure to consult with fraternal parties in advance," and privately regarded this attack on one of communism's greatest leaders as rank apostasy. Mao, in particular, was livid, perhaps because of the unhappy implications of de-Stalinization for his own flourishing domestic personality cult.

At the Tenth Plenum of the Central Committee in 1962, Mao recalled his escalating troubles with Soviet leaders: "In 1958 Khrushchev wanted to set up a Soviet-Chinese combined fleet in order to seal us off [from attacking the islands held by Taiwan]. In 1959, at the time of the border dispute with India, he supported Nehru. At the dinner on our National Day he attacked us. . . . Today . . . we are called 'adventurists, nationalists, dogmatists.' "[32]

Khrushchev's complaints were more public. On 1 December 1958 he told Senator Hubert Humphrey that the Chinese communes would never succeed, a statement that a short time later found its way into the pages of *Life* magazine.[33] In June 1959, worried that Mao might drag the USSR into a nuclear conflict with the United States, Khrushchev unilaterally abrogated the 1957 agreement on military technology—a pact that was to have provided China with an atomic bomb. On 18 July 1959 he publicly denounced the communes, blaming their establishment on certain unnamed people who "do not properly understand what communism is or how it is to be built." In 1960 he suspended all technical assistance to China, ordering

Soviet engineers and technicians in China to roll up their blueprints and return home.[34]

The West watched in amazement as the one-time "fraternal parties" began upping the rhetorical ante like losing poker players desperate to recoup their losses. In Moscow on 23 October 1961, by ceremoniously walking out at the head of his delegation, Zhou Enlai protested the decision of the Twenty-second Communist Party of the Soviet Union (CPSU) party Congress to criticize Albania and remove Stalin's body from the Lenin Mausoleum. In 1963 Mao accused Khrushchev by name of committing the Marxist heresy of "revisionism," singling out for particular opprobrium the notion that communism could "peacefully coexist" with capitalist imperialism. Moscow, in hardly less heated terms, accused the Chinese leadership—by which they clearly meant Mao—of "adventurism, dogmatism, and factionalism." A long and public exchange of extremely vitriolic letters between Beijing and Moscow ensued.[35]

The piecemeal demolition of the "lasting and indestructible eternal friendship" between the PRC and the USSR came as a great surprise to Americans, and their mental map of the world began to blur and shift. They had previously visualized China as a Slavic Manchukuo, in Dulles' phrase, a bulbous appendage of the Moscow-directed world Communist movement hanging down into the heart of East Asia. Now this map dissolved into a radically new configuration, one in which China was seen as a continental-sized country in its own right. In place of "monolithic international Communism" emerged two bitterly feuding states.

Neither country had abandoned communism—Mao especially seemed more rabidly anti-American than ever—but the world nevertheless assumed a new, less threatening shape for many Americans. In the general relaxation of tensions that followed, the obvious policy differences between the Communist giants, as they were then called, weakened the argument for applying generic labels of *Communist* or *totalitarian* to such states. Both terms were criticized as insufficiently scientific, even prejudicial. Nor could the Great Leap Forward be understood, by Khrushchev or anyone else, as a Stalinist five-year plan.

It was during the Great Leap Forward that China-watchers began to grasp that Mao Zedong might better be called a radical utopian than an orthodox Marxist in the Stalinist mode. In place of a rigid system of central planning, he had conjured up a vision of an anencephalic economy composed of 80,000 identical cells. Each commune was to remake itself into a self-sufficient and interchangeable unit producing its own food, fertilizer, steel, machines, and small arms. Human beings, too, were to be made self-sufficient and interchangeable. Mao was convinced that distinctions between intellectual and peasant, official and worker, and even man and woman could be effaced by means of manual labor and ideological reeducation. The result would be an androgynous Socialist Superman who could "use a pen to write articles, a hoe to weed, a gun to fight, and a platform to make political propaganda."[36]

All that would be required to effect such changes, as Mao suggested in his famous parable "The Foolish Old Man Who Removed the Moutain," was a supreme effort of human will. This was not historical materialism, in which ideas were merely pale reflections of economic desiderata, but idealism on a grand scale, an anticipated triumph of mind over matter. For Mao, the sword of ideas could not only be removed from the stone of substructural economic reality; it could shatter it.

A new view of the People's Republic, which emphasized the vision and policies of Mao Zedong and his colleagues and their effect on society, began to be advanced openly. The task of evaluating American scholarship in terms of evolving American perceptions of China is daunting, and an exhaustive and systematic review of this material is a task that must be deferred to an interested scholarship. A massive number of academic articles and books on China appeared each year from the late fifties onward, as recently established East Asian studies' programs at Harvard University and elsewhere began minting new scholars by the dozen. In the brief survey that follows here, I refer only to works on contemporary China that advance and illustrate the new paradigm which, following Kuo and Myers, we may call the "modernizing communist regime."[37]

The Great Leap Forward and Khrushchev's criticisms led Professor Benjamin Schwartz to remark in 1960 that Stalinist policies had not been fully adopted in China because the "subjective outlook of Mao Tse-tung and his entourage are equally important. . . . one of the peculiar features of Chinese communism is the whole area of phenomena known as 'thought reform' and 'remoulding.' "[38] Similarly, Professor Joseph R. Levenson wrote that "Mao would transform the peasants (and everybody else) through voluntarism . . . politics takes command, superstructure takes priority, over the substructural means of production—and of destruction."[39] Professor Victor Li saw the Soviet-style legal system of the early and mid-1950s increasingly give way to Maoist-style efforts to reform behavior by instilling new values and norms.[40]

China-watchers agreed that the shift from the five-year plans of the early 1950s to Maoist mobilization campaigns like the Great Leap Forward had caused huge fluctuations in economic activity. But as Kuo and Myers point out, "Most experts did not associate these violent swings in economic policy and activity with any severe setbacks for the people's welfare or with a decline in goods, services, and physical capital. . . . leading economists considered the first two decades to be periods of moderate growth."[41] Typical in their view was Alexander Eckstein's assertion that the PRC economy as a whole consistently experienced annual rates of GNP growth per capita of 2 to 3 percent and that even "the rate of farm production growth in China may be considered as eminently respectable although, placed against the formidable pressure of population and the rather rapid rate of population growth, it does not seem adequately to have met the requirements of the country's industrialization."[42]

China was industrializing in a way that avoided the alienation, anomie, class exploitation, and other serious dysfunctions that had once afflicted the West. Kurt Mendelsohn, a British physicist, maintained in 1961 that "for the workers in the West . . . industrialization always savors of enslavement and exploitation. The industrial revolution has left a bitter taste. Things are different for the Chinese. There, the Communists are not, as with us, a force which tries to destroy a well-established pattern of society. On the contrary, they have brought order and peace. . . . Technology is a great and joyful experience, an adventure into which they have thrown themselves with enormous enthusiasm."[43]

If there was occasional political turmoil and instability, this was only because the leadership had not yet fully instilled proletarian values and institutions in the population to replace now-defunct traditional ones. Professor Michel Oksenberg, who was to become President Carter's China advisor, speculated that "rapidly expanding transportation systems often destroy existing institutions (marketing systems, kinship loyalties, etc.) more rapidly than new institutions can develop that can perform equivalent functions. Thus . . . an increased probability of the disintegration of society paradoxically may be one of the short-run effects of improved communications." If Oksenberg's speculation seems to slight the role that Mao and his colleagues played in deliberately destroying the free market and extended family ties, then his necessity defense of the Maoist personality cult is truly novel: "While the new institutions are taking root [he conjectures], resort to the unifying symbol of the ruler—in China's case, Mao—may be an appropriate response."[44]

Advocates of this new paradigm ignored, rather than refuted, the totalitarian state paradigm they sought to replace. Their emphasis was on a visionary leader's attempt to transform society, not society's control by a party apparatus and police forces. Fluctuations in grain production and industrial output were admitted (in contrast with the steady, incremental advance implicity assumed by the totalitarian model), but the idea that the Chinese people had been adversely affected was dismissed. China's obvious instability was blamed on the absence of universally accepted values and institutions. The possibility that this chaotic state of affairs had resulted in part from systematic attempts to demolish mediating institutions that would inhibit party control—the totalitarian state hypothesis—was left unexamined. There was no place in their view of China for purges, penal colonies, and political prisoners. Though few of the proponents of the modernizing communist regime paradigm would have been comfortable stating their central thesis so baldly, they believed with Fairbank that Mao's home-spun "communism" (with communism in quotation marks) had been good for China.

FEAST OR FAMINE?

American journalists were able to contribute little to the understanding of China under communism, since the PRC remained generally off-limits for Americans throughout the 1950s and 1960s. An exception was made for Edgar Snow, who in 1960 became the first American correspondent with prior experience in China invited to return. Barred from China themselves, China-watchers awaited the verdict of someone who had followed the Chinese Communist movement from its early days in romantic Yenan, and whose friendship with the charismatic Zhou Enlai and the colossal Mao Zedong dated from that time.

Snow was an old-line socialist and longtime admirer of the Chinese revolution. In his pre-1949 works, Snow tried to adhere to the standards of objective reporting; his errors were the unconscious product of his ideological enthusiasm. The same cannot be said of the books and articles that he wrote after the founding of the PRC. His oft-stated determination that Americans should view the changes in China in the most positive light possible allowed major errors and omissions to creep into his efforts. If he had sympathized with the revolutionaries out of power, he apologized for them once they were in power. The stalwart opponent of Chiang Kai-shek's one-man rule found in Mao's dictatorial tendencies nothing more insidious than an expression of China's tradition of autocracy. The onetime critic of Nationalist corruption remained oblivious to the corrupt new elite that had been created. Even the armed occupation of Tibet in 1959 by Chinese troops elicited from this harsh critic of Western imperialism only the cruel comment that Tibetans must "adapt or perish."

Both the length and timing of Snow's 1960 visit bear reflection. The Great Leap Forward had just shuddered to a halt. Promising "three years of suffering leading to a thousand years of happiness," it had led instead to what were being euphemistically called "the three difficult years." Emaciated hordes of starving refugees came tottering across the Hong Kong border in 1960–62 and told of villages stricken with hunger. Yet at the height of this disaster, Snow was allowed to poke about the country for five months (and could have stayed longer). Was the China-watcher whom Zhou Enlai had called in 1937 "the greatest of foreign authors and our best friend abroad" invited in the hope that his reports would counteract the bad publicity that followed the failure of the Leap? Once again Snow did not disappoint his sponsors.[45]

The book that resulted, *The Other Side of the River: Red China Today* lauded the Communist party for creating a new, modern

China. Snow reported that the Chinese willingly threw themselves into campaigns to build roads, dams, and bridges during the Great Leap Forward, but fails to mention that many were reluctant volunteers at best, dragooned on pain of labor reeducation into working on projects that often turned out badly. He cites mass participation in choosing local governments as evidence that oxymoronic "democratic dictatorship" really worked, but neglects to tell his readers that voting for the party-approved slate of candidates was mandatory.

Snow's defense of the less pleasant aspects of life in the People's Republic lent an apologetic air to his narrative. The Cult of Mao was simply a historical inheritance: "Nations which for centuries have been ruled by authoritarianism may cast aside one skin and pick up another but they do not change chromosomes, genes, and bodies in a generation or two."[46] Chinese surveillance of foreign residents "was smooth, unobtrusive, and probably efficient"; but America employed similar techniques: "I never got a letter from China that had not been obviously opened and delayed."[47] (Note the disproportion here, since mail from China, especially mail addressed to Edgar Snow, was in a special category as far as the U.S. government was concerned. Beijing, on the other hand, opened every piece of foreign correspondence received by its citizens, trusted party members and counterrevolutionaries alike, well into the eighties, and is probably doing so now.) Snow admits that with the exception of what they learned from the movies, Chinese leaders had little knowledge of the United States, but he quickly adds that Zhou Enlai spoke English. "Has the United States ever appointed a Chinese-speaking Secretary of State?" he trumped.[48] Snow had peculiar ideas about diplomatic intercourse; if Chinese, instead of English, were the language in which the diplomatic affairs of a hundred nations were conducted, Henry Kissinger would surely have learned to say more in Chinese than the *Ni Hao?* ("How are you?") he used to greet Zhou.

Adhering to the paradigmatic view that economic fluctuations had occurred during and after the Great Leap Forward but had caused no serious problems for the people, Snow flatly denied that there was a famine: "One of the few things I can say with certainty is that mass starvation such as China knew almost annually under former regimes no longer occurs. . . . I diligently searched, without success, for starving people or beggars to photograph." Although he conceded that some people were suffering from "severe malnutrition," he thought that it had probably not led to any significant number of deaths.[49] Coming from someone who had traveled around the country for months during a time when millions of people were withering and dying in China's worst famine of the twentieth century, such statements now read like an almost willful denial of reality. They call to mind the *New York Times* correspondent Walter Duranty's now infamous denials of famine in the Soviet Ukraine and North Caucasus in 1932–33, years in which Robert Conquest later estimated that 6 million had died.[50]

Did Snow know about the famine and deliberately deceive his readers to protect his access to China, as Duranty did in the Soviet Union? Or were the Communist leaders able to deceive him with their denials of food shortages? Or did he perhaps overlook the truth in his haste to validate his past optimism about Chinese communism and to correct misimpressions about a regime that he considered unfairly maligned in the Western press? It is impossible to choose among these alternatives. It is known that Snow spent two days in the company of Zhou Enlai, who provided him with statistics on grain production that later turned out to be false. The premier's attentiveness may well have been part of a concerted campaign.

Of that time, China historian Edward Friedman has written that "foreigners were fed a diet of lies to spread outside the country, to the effect that there was no famine in China."[51] A Chinese-speaking British doctor, J. S. Horn, a medical advisor of the Beijing regime, challenged reporting in the *New York Times* about a famine: "As a doctor, I should be quick to notice signs of malnutrition and a daily intake of 600 calories [the reported caloric intake] would rapidly produce severe symptoms. Yet the general health of the people appears to be good." Another foreigner resident in Shanghai wrote to a friend abroad that "to say that China is experiencing a famine is grossly untrue."[52] The British journalist Felix Greene returned from a visit to China to announce, in tones reminiscent of Snow, that "the indisputable fact is that the famines that in one area or another constantly ravaged the farmlands of China, and the fear of starvation, which for so long had haunted the lives of the Chinese peasants, are today things of the past. . . . improvements in [China's] food conditions, as I and others found them, has probably been one of its greatest achievements. . . . In 1960 . . . I saw no signs of serious malnutrition."[53] Anna Louise Strong, who was the most faithful of foreign camp followers of the regime, knew better but kept her complaints to herself. "I am not allowed to admit that anyone in these three years ever starved to death," she noted in her diary.[54]

The "firsthand" verdict of Snow and others on the famine was widely accepted, even by many American China-watchers, who denied or at least downplayed one of the greatest human tragedies of our century. Snow's views received a respectful hearing at Harvard and elsewhere after his return to the United States. Fairbank's introductory history of modern China, *The United States and China*, devotes just one sentence to the subject: "Malnutrition was widespread and some starvation occurred."[55] Harrison Salisbury of the *New York Times* in his 1973 China travelogue (dedicated to Edgar Snow) passes over this catastrophic event without mention.[56] Others went even further, claiming that because of China's efficient food distribution system, famine was impossible.[57] Professor C. P. Fitzgerald, a historian of China, claimed that during these difficult years "the Commune system . . . saved the lives of millions, simply because resources were centrally controlled, and rationing made possible."[58] Ditto Professor Maurice Meisner: "Massive famine was avoided (but only barely) through the institution of a highly efficient system of rationing and by huge wheat purchases from Australia and Canada."[59] Dr. José de Castro, former president of the Food and Agriculture Organization of the United Nations, in the fall of 1959 wrote, "New China's victory over the eternal plague of hunger is as startling an event as the conquest of interplanetary space."[60]

Can these and other China-watchers fairly be faulted for not knowing about, or at least not writing about, a disaster that Beijing worked so hard to keep under wraps? Despite the misinformation that Beijing was busy disseminating, much reliable information was available at the time. Hong Kong-based correspondents as a group were certainly not deceived by Beijing's efforts, and as food shortages spiraled into famine in 1961, reports proliferated in the nation's newspapers and newsmagazines:

Red China is in heavy trouble this time. 'Natural calamities,' crop failures, famine are only part of it. (*U.S. News and World Report,* 20 February 1961)

Taxed to the limit of their endurance by the tightest rationing of food in the modern history of China and near-famine conditions in some areas, the Chinese are reported to be reacting to the situation by rejecting Government regulations and even organizing anti-Government movements. (*New York Times,* 15 April 1961)

Things are going from bad to worse inside Communist China. . . . It's a land of hunger. (*U.S. News and World Report,* 2 October 1961)

The story of starvation inside China . . . is far grimmer than the outside world has been told. (Drew Pearson, *San Francisco Chronicle,* 5 November 1961)

The sour-tasting new soy sauce is said to be made of human hair. (*Time,* 1 December 1961)

Such reports continued in the spring of 1962, as China relaxed its border patrols and the flow of refugees into Hong Kong reached high tide, bringing with them tales of hunger and privation:

Communist China is a land of massive malnutrition and hunger. Three successive years of poor harvest have reduced the food available to most Chinese to little above the barest subsistence level. (*New York Times,* 22 April 1962)

Refugees rounded up by Hong Kong patrols today claimed that hundreds of Chinese have died of starvation while trying to reach the border. One said it was impossible to get enough to eat to keep alive in his village. (Associated Press, Hong Kong, 15 May 1962)

The migrants in fact were fleeing grim conditions of hunger. . . . It is now no longer considered absurd for observers of the China scene to talk of the possibility of a break-up of the Communist regime or revolt against it. (Tillman Durdin, *New York Times,* 27 May 1962)

Ordinary Americans accepted the existence of a famine in Communist China as a tragic but incontrovertible fact. "There is now a severe food famine in Communist China," a 1961 Gallup Poll question on the subject began. "Do you think the United States should or should not offer to send some of its surplus foods to this country?"[61]

Many contemporary press accounts questioned the regime's contention that 1960 had seen the severest and most widespread natural calamities of a century, placing the blame for the food shortages instead squarely on the shoulders of the Chinese leadership. "The Famine Makers—A Report on Why Red China is Starving" ran the accusatory headline of a *U.S. News and World Report* (9 July 1962) story, which laid the blame on "Communist Bungling." Similar accusations were flying in China. In January 1962, in a speech highly critical of the calamitous Great Leap Forward, the PRC chairman Liu Shaoqi was reported to have said that "our economy is on the brink of collapse. . . . our losses in manpower, fertile soil, and natural resources have been so heavy that it will take seven to eight years to put matters straight. . . . the masses [have] starved for two years."[62] This was, to be sure, a veiled attack on Mao, and Liu may have overstated the country's difficulties to compromise his rival. Even so, one would not have expected such an admission by China's Number Two leader to be simply ignored by China-watchers after it became public. But it was.

The same fate awaited the equally sober and far more accessible conclusions of Laszlo Ladany, a respected China scholar. Writing in the 10 August 1962 issue of *China News Analysis,* he asserted that the years from 1960 to 1962 in China had seen a "real, black famine." His "realistic estimate" of the number of lives lost to starvation and deficiency diseases during this period was 50 million. This estimate disappeared as if dropped into a real, black hole. Also ignored were army documents captured in 1961 that revealed the virtual annihilation of entire villages in Henan Province. The provincial officials in charge continued insisting even after the famine had struck that the Great Leap Forward was a triumph, proving their success by making regular shipments of grain to the cities. The commune system, lauded by Fitzgerald for saving lives by "rationing," made it possible for officials to extract the last bushel of grain from the peasants and greatly exacerbated the magnitude of the disaster. When relief grain finally arrived, the survivors were too weak to queue for the food.[63]

By the seventies, the magnitude of the disaster was clear. In 1973 the meticulous German scholar Juergen Domes estimated that at least 10 million, and possibly a multiple of that figure had perished.[64] In 1976, Ivan and Miriam London published "The Three Red Flags of Death," an account of the famine based upon in-depth interviews with refugees conducted in Hong Kong in the mid-sixties.[65] By 1981, with the de-Maoization campaign in full swing, even an official Chinese journal, *Economic Management,* admitted to 10 million "excess" deaths during this period. The most reliable figure comes from the demographer John S. Aird, whose analysis of the 1981 census data led him to conclude that the net population loss during the famine years 1959–1961 was perhaps as much as 25 million people.[66] What Fairbank called "some starvation" may well rank as the worst famine of the twentieth century.

Those China-watchers who denied the reality of the famine ultimately owe their incomprehension not to the reports of Edgar Snow and others, but to the iron constraints of their own paradigm. Snow simply told them what they expected to be told: the widespread natural disasters in 1960 had resulted in food shortages, but famine had been averted by the efficient distribution of food. In modernizing communist China, death by starvation was a thing of the past.

The totalitarian paradigm better served its declining number of scholarly adherents. To be sure, it neither predicted the famine nor provided a complete context for understanding its occurrence. But it did equip its adherents with a blueprint of the totalitarian command and control apparatus that Mao had at his fingertips, and it did alert them to the possibility that he and other leaders could act callously and brutally toward those who did not respond enthusiastically to their dictates. Such insights took them a long way toward understanding the reports of famine that surfaced in refugee accounts and the popular press at the time.

The totalitarian paradigm continued to dominate in the popular mind as well. Because of China's espousal of a communism more radical than Moscow's and because of Beijing's aid to North Vietnam, most Americans regarded Communist China, if not the Chinese, with enmity. Public opinion, usually conceived of as weightless and transient, remained strikingly set against "Communist China" throughout the fifties and early sixties. It was consistently seen as a rogue nation, ill-suited to the polite discourse and diplomatic niceties of international relations. Large majorities of Americans continued to oppose its admission to the United Nations until this was an accomplished fact in 1971.[67] Indeed, so savage and aggressive was its reputation that by the mid-sixties it was "Communist China," and not

"Russia," that Americans identified—by two-to-one margins—as "the greater threat to world peace."[68] In early 1965 Gallup actually hypothesized a war between the United States and Communist China, and asked respondents which side Russia would more likely be on.[69] Communist China was the country that Americans liked least, ranked in 1968 at the bottom of a list of twenty-eight nations that included the Soviet Union, Cuba, and North Vietnam.[70] It was during this period that the "Communist Chinese people," suffering from the general disrepute of their country and its leaders, were described by Americans as "ignorant," "warlike," "sly," and "treacherous."[71]

With few exceptions, academic China-watchers who disputed these attitudes had neither the inclination nor the skills to write for a larger audience. Their views, published in scholarly journals of limited circulation like the *China Quarterly* or in books with limited press runs, or expressed before captive audiences of college freshmen, had little immediate impact outside their own community. Yet in just a few years, this situation would change dramatically. A younger generation of China-watchers, radicalized by the Vietnam War, would seize the moment to advance their even more favorable view of the "revolutionary socialist" regime that governed China.

6

The Second Age of Infatuation

꧁꧂

Not finding anything about them which seemed to conform to their ideals, they [the Physiocrats] went to search for it in the heart of Asia. It is no exaggeration to say that everyone of them in some part of his writings passes an emphatic eulogy on China. . . . That imbecile and barbarous government . . . appeared to them the most perfect model for all of the nations of the world to copy.

—Alexis de Tocqueville
Quoted in Lewis M. Coser, *Men of Ideas.*

It was perhaps only natural that as the Vietnam War dimmed America's faith in her own character and virtue, Communist China would begin to arouse brighter and kindlier emotions. China had, after all, come to be seen as the totalitarian antithesis of the democratic United States, a position that now seesawed into China's favor. Antiwar activists who condemned their country's involvement in Vietnam applauded China's assistance to its fraternal North Vietnamese ally. Those who went on to reject America's individualistic ethic and free market economy—as many did—found China an inspiring model of communal endeavor, and in the Cultural Revolution a noble experiment to purify an already selfless people. Illuminated by the black light of their own alienation, the People's Republic shone lustrous in the distance.

Among the first political pilgrims, to use Paul Hollander's phrase, to travel the road between Hanoi and Beijing were Staughton Lynd and Tom Hayden. They were allowed to embark upon this journey after they demonstrated their opposition to U.S. imperialism and their friendship for Chinese socialism in the most convincing way possible: They had applied in person at the PRC Embassy in Hanoi in late 1965 for a travel visa.

If Snow was an old-line socialist and longtime admirer of the Chinese revolution, then Lynd and Hayden were the forerunners of a new generation of American visitors radicalized by their opposition to the Vietnam War. Estranged by what they perceived as the imperialistic, immoral behavior of their country, they cast about for a just society, free of capitalistic greed and imperialistic ambitions, and discovered China. Pariahs in their own country, where their views were still anathema, they wrote movingly of having discovered a country whose elite shared (or so they thought) their views: "[W]e felt empathy for those more fully 'other' members of the other side, spokesmen for the Communist world in Prague and Moscow, Beijing and Hanoi. After all, we call ourselves in some sense revolutionaries. So do they. After all, we identify with the poor and oppressed. So do they."[1]

Coming from an America in discord (to which they had contributed), Lynd and Hayden reveled in the New China's community of purpose: "Walking before breakfast . . . we passed a group of women energetically singing before starting a day's work. Everywhere is the pulse of purposeful activity."[2] This new socialist brotherhood and sisterhood, achieved by the total elimination of class distinctions, had enabled startling advances to be made: "Everywhere in Beijing the old society is being replaced by the new. . . . The point is that progress is everywhere. Millions of Chinese are involved in its creation. In Peking we saw thousands of people digging a canal while music blared from outdoor loudspeakers."[3] To the uninitiated, it may seem but simple common sense to prevent drought by building irrigation canals, but to Lynd and Hayden it was a triumph of Mao's Thought, the relevant chapter and verse of which they recite: "A bad thing cannot automatically change into a good thing. Such a transformation demands a certain condition. What is it? It is the firm resolve to fight against natural calamities. Without that resolve bad things cannot be turned into good things. To turn bad things into good things we cadres and commune members must have the revolutionary drive shown by the 'Foolish Old Man Who Moved Mountains .' "[4]

On all things they accepted the assurances of their hosts over the evidence of their senses. Slightly taken aback when all Chinese they questioned attributed the country's progress to the turgid "Thought of Mao Zedong," they nevertheless concluded from discussions with their guides that this was not hero worship or the "cult of the individual" but simply "the Chinese way to analyze development."[5] They began to fret when each time they visited a restaurant they found themselves "escorted to a separate room, where we could talk easily while eating." But they were relieved to find that this was unrelated to the ugly capitalist vice of inequality: "[W]e were told the restaurants are open to all, food is the same for everyone, and prices are low."[6] Had they rubbed elbows with the noisy proletariat outside, they would have found that such rooms were actually restaurants within restaurants, where VIPs like themselves could dine on specially prepared dishes in solitary splendor.

By praising the character and values of China, it should be clear, these radical academics (Lynd was a tenured professor, Hayden a graduate student) were condemning their own society, which they saw as morally inferior, if not bankrupt altogether. Socialist societies like China, which embraced collective economic strategies and presented themselves as cohesive societies, represented a higher moral order. This attitude, initially limited to a handful of extremists at elite universities in the mid-sixties, had by the end of the decade come to be the dominant view among the liberal elite.

Once again China was to be a model for the West. Just as the domestic debacle of the depression provoked a surge of interest in socialism and communism among the liberal intelligentsia in the thirties, so did America's involvement in a seemingly unwinnable foreign war thirty years later lead to a renewed fascination with these ideologies and their vision of a new society. Once again, it became perfectly respectable to assert, as Robert Heilbroner did in 1969, that socialism promises "a wholly new kind of society, free of invidious striving and built on motives of cooperation and confraternity."[7]

Heilbroner and others were especially entranced with the novel form of socialism that was evolving, free of the taint of Stalinism, in the People's Republic. They were attracted by the utter confidence that the Chinese people seemed to repose in their leader and his vision of a selfless, communitarian society. And they accepted without question the most outrageous claims of the Maoist state that tremendous advances in the human spirit had been made in the Cultural Revolution. It was The Idea of a totally new form of society that appealed to them, not the details of its organization.

THE REVOLT OF THE RED GUARDS

Just when China began to attract the widespread interest of the outside world, it became almost impossible to obtain reliable information about events there. In the summer of 1966 the entire country was convulsed by Chairman Mao's last and greatest political campaign, the Great Proletarian Cultural Revolution. Mao's avowed purpose was not only to overthrow "those within the Party who are in authority and taking the capitalist road," but also "to demolish all the old ideology and culture . . . and create and cultivate among the masses an entirely new proletarian ideology and culture, and entirely new proletarian customs and habits." Mao had declared war on his world.[8]

The engine of this transformation was to be China's youth. In response to Mao's call for an army of Red Guards to lay siege to the citadels of feudalism and capitalism, the young enlisted by the millions. The new recruits were issued Little Red Books as their training manuals and received their marching orders from Mao's wife and mouthpiece, Jiang Qing: "Beat down the capitalist-roaders in power! Beat down the reactionary bourgeois authorities! Sweep away all wicked demons and evil spirits! Do away with the Four Old Things: old thought, old culture, old customs, old habits. The Thought of Mao Zedong must rule and transform the spirit, until the power of the spirit transforms matter!"

Such rhetoric had an electric and disinhibiting effect on these youthful enlistees, whose adulation for their oracular leader quickly transcended all bounds. The "Great Helmsman" was "the sun of our heart, the root of our life, the source of our strength." His Thought was "a compass and spiritual food . . . a massive cudgel swung by a golden monkey . . . a brilliant beam of light exposing monsters and goblins . . . the source of all wisdom."[9]

Young zealots in khaki uniforms with red armbands took over the cities, conducting neighborhood-by-neighborhood, house-by-house searches for anything "bourgeois"—that is, anything that could be connected with the past or with the West. Western suits and traditional Chinese gowns, crosses and graven images of the gods, Dickens's novels and kung fu tales, cheap Western kitsch and priceless porcelain—all were smashed, burned, or seized. People suspected of having "bourgeois thoughts" fared no better. A talented pianist had his fingers fractured because he played Chopin. The author of the famous novel *Rickshaw Boy,* Lao She, was beaten so brutally that he committed suicide to end his suffering. A Buddhist nun was stripped naked and physically abused. The number of victims of this Chinese Inquisition quickly mounted into the millions. In Beijing these homicidal ruffians served Mao as a kind of Black Hand, an arrangement that allowed him to have his enemies in the party, government, and army arrested, reviled—and even killed as traitors, renegades, and capitalist roaders—while he kept decorously above the fray. Once the Red Guard groups had disposed of counterrevolutionaries throughout the land, they turned on each other. Small clashes between rival bands armed with sticks and swords quickly escalated into major set-piece battles between regimental-sized units equipped, in some cases, with mortars, artillery, and tanks.

The outside world, while receiving a surfeit of Maoist rhetoric— the *Little Red Book* was published in a dozen languages—was largely spared the sight of Maoism in action. The Foreign Ministry refused the visa applications of would-be visitors, expelled or imprisoned those foreigners already in the country, and closed down the country's embassies abroad. Even the PRC embassy in Hanoi, which remained open, stopped issuing travel visas. These restrictions eased only late in 1969, after the army had intervened to restore societal order. The mindless violence of the intervening years thrust itself on the West's attention only at rare intervals—for example, when rampaging Red Guards burned down the British chancery in Beijing in the summer of 1967, or when dozens of mangled and bloated corpses from factional strife in the city of Wuzhou washed up on the beaches of Hong

Kong in July 1968. When they appeared at all, reports of savage battles in the provinces between rival Maoist armies were relegated to the back pages of the newspapers. Tillman Durdin's account of "fighting in Guangxi over a period of months rivaling that of hostilities in the Vietnam war" was buried on page 11 of the *New York Times*.[10]

THE REVOLT OF THE ACADEMICS

By 1966, the enormous investment in China studies by foundations and the federal government had already, in the opinion of Professor Fairbank and others, generated handsome dividends. "[D]espite its inaccessibility to Western observers," the *New York Times* wrote in summary of their views, "the application of sociology, psychology and economics to what facts are known has already dispelled much of the mystery surrounding the mainland society, and has even shed some light on the motivations of its people. . . . [N]ot only does the United States lead the world in China studies but . . . impressive progress has been achieved." Fairbank himself believed that the major remaining hurdle for foreign scholars was the unavailability of scientific statistics, which made it difficult to analyze economic growth and social change. He characteristically attributed the government's reluctance to publish detailed and accurate information to the absence of a statistical tradition. "Until recent times, according to the scholar [Fairbank], the Chinese did not possess a statistical service."[11] That totalitarians have a natural penchant for secrecy seems not to have occurred to him.

On the eve of the Cultural Revolution, then, leading Sinologists had sanguinely announced that they were well on the way toward demystifying China—and could complete the job if only they had a few more numbers. It would be unfair to fault them for their collective failure to predict the political cataclysm that followed, since it was without precedent in Chinese history. And it must be recorded that the State Statistical Bureau was abolished in the early days of the Cultural Revolution, a victim of radical Maoists who wanted to conceal the country's mounting production losses from their own people and from the world. Cipherless, academic China-watchers could only attempt to narrate the Cultural Revolution's serpentine course from afar.

Scholarship quickly became mired in politics. No group of American academics recoiled more fiercely from the Vietnam War, participated more vigorously in campus protests, or applauded more enthusiastically the socialist experiment underway a few hundred miles to the north, than the China scholars. In part this activism reflected the natural tendency of experts to exaggerate the importance of their specialty. To Great Han chauvinists (of whom there were many) it was self-evident that Vietnam was in China's—not the United States'—sphere of influence. It was equally obvious to some that the momentous upheaval in China would change the face of Asia, if not the world. Like the French philosophes and physiocrats, alienated from the *ancien régime* and desperately seeking a substitute, numerous younger students and scholars seized upon a China that they could see only dimly as a model for other countries, even for the United States.

Those who shared this perspective in 1968 organized themselves into a Committee of Concerned Asian Scholars (CCAS). Their "concerns" were manifold: They called for the abrogation of the U.S.-Japan security treaty "which has turn[ed] Japan into a bulwark of American empire in Asia"; "an immediate end to the bombing of Vietnam, an end to the genocidal war in that country, and a withdrawal of U.S. troops to begin immediately"; and "a new policy toward China . . . withdrawal of American forces from Taiwan, and termination of all military aid to the dictatorship of the KMT government."[12]

They did not hide their contempt for scholars less committed to these propositions than themselves: "We first came together in opposition to the brutal aggression of the United States in Vietnam and to the complicity or silence of our profession with regard to that policy. Those in the field of Asian Studies bear responsibility for the consequences of their research and the political posture of their profession." Past scholarship on Asia was hopelessly compromised: "We recognize that the present structure of the profession has often perverted scholarship. . . . prevailing trends in scholarship on Asia . . . too often spring from a parochial cultural perspective and serve selfish interests and expansionism." Now it was time for a corrective: "The CCAS seeks to develop a humane and knowledge-able understanding of Asian societies and their efforts to maintain cultural integrity and to confront such problems as poverty, oppres-sion, and imperialism. . . . Our organization is designed to function as a catalyst . . . and a community for the development of anti-imperialist research."[13] Their newsletter, the *Bulletin of Concerned Asian Scholars,* established in May 1968 as a vehicle to organize campus protest against American involvement in Vietnam, gradually evolved into a scholarly periodical devoted to publishing "anti-imperialist research" on contemporary Asian societies.

Concerned Asian students and scholars rejected out of hand what James Peck called "the professional ideology of America's China watchers"—the notion that America should be the nonimperial guar-antor of the independence of Asian nations against communism, buying time while they gradually and nonviolently assimilated into the modern world of science, technology, and rational organization. "Instead of an evolving world order of independent self-determining states under the benevolent protection of America," Peck wrote, "the revolutionary Marxist sees capitalism as necessarily generating con-ditions that develop one part of the world system at the expense of another. Thus bourgeois nations face proletarian ones and revolu-tionary socialism is rooted in the semi-peasant, semi-proletarian masses of the Third World rather than in the developed metropolitan capitalist societies."[14] Why should Third World nations not violently reject participation in an economic system weighted in favor of the West which, in the words of one "revolutionary Marxist" cited by Peck, "doomed them to stagnation and regression?"[15]

It was no wonder that those who had held such views should come to admire Mao's China. Mao had refused to play the losing hand of international development poker that China had been dealt by the capitalistic West. Instead, arrogantly asserting his country's inde-pendence, he cashed in its chips—and everyone else's within reach—and risked the lot in a game of economic solitaire. It was very much a bootstrap operation, with no help from anyone except the Soviets, and even this was shortlived. Mao and the masses had parlayed this stake into a prosperous, egalitarian China, in the process inventing a socialist alternative to capitalism. If the Maoist path to development had worked in China as advertised, it might well be the answer for other "semi-peasant, semi-proletarian" Third World countries eager to opt out of the capitalist world system. Something of the excitement generated by this discovery is conveyed in the following quotation, from the *Bulletin of Concerned Asian Scholars:* "During the past sixty years, one of the world's great cultures has been transformed by a profound revolution which touches virtually every aspect of life in that society. As China continues the struggle to fully control her own destiny and to put her revolutionary ideals into practice, the rest of the world looks on with no little fascination tinged with a certain amount of envy, residual misunderstanding, skepticism and admiration."[16]

The new mirror of China that issued from pages of the *Bulletin* and other scholarly journals was the most polished yet.[17] Rejecting such dry and precise terms as *totalitarian, Marxist-Leninist,* or even plain old *communist,* the concerned Asian students and scholars settled upon the stirring and capacious descriptor *revolutionary socialism* to christen their interpretation of events in China. They believed that the Thought of Chairman Mao had raised the consciousness of Chinese man and that under his tutelage the revolutionary masses had significantly improved their material well-being *and* had substantially advanced toward a more egalitarian society—especially since the Cultural Revolution, which had been launched for that very purpose. Best of all, unlike the capitalist mode of development, these successes had come at virtually no cost to society.[18]

The Stanford economics Professor John G. Gurley, a leading advocate of the new paradigm, pronounced, in several articles and books, revolutionary socialism as practiced in China to be the economic equal—and moral better—of the free market:

Perhaps the most striking difference between the capitalist and Maoist views concerns goals. Maoists believe that while a principal aim of nations should be to raise the level of material welfare of the population, this should be done only within the context of the development of human beings, encouraging them to realize fully their manifold creative powers. And it should be done only on an egalitarian basis—that is, on the basis that development is not worth much unless everyone rises together: no one is to be left behind, either economically or culturally. Indeed, Maoists believe that rapid economic development is not likely to occur *unless* everyone rises together. Development as a trickle-down process is therefore rejected by Maoists, and so they reject any strong emphasis on profit motives and efficiency criteria that lead to lopsided growth [italics in the original].[19]

The reason that most other economists had missed the advantages of revolutionary socialism, according to Professor Gurley, was that they "suffer[ed] from an ailment common to most of economics—a narrow empiricism," which he dismissed as "a lot of . . . fussy statistical work."[20] His co-paradigmaticists took statistical descriptions of China's economy with equal insouciance, especially when they did not reflect well on the country. "Especially in the short run," wrote Professor Carl Riskin, "growth rates, even if completely accurate . . . mean very little. . . . The real question regarding China's growth potential is whether Chinese communism . . . can evolve a social system under which the population will willingly make heavy sacrifices over an extended period of time . . . [W]hatever the vagaries of the growth rate mongers, in the things that count for the future the Chinese have already compiled an impressive record."[21]

The one conviction shared by all concerned Asian scholars was that the Maoist theory of development had been adopted by the masses as their own, and as such constituted a truly proletarian ideology. "[T]he overwhelming impression of China is vitality—the enthusiasm, the humor, and the tremendous commitment of her people to this new China."[22] What matter if the aftermath of the Great Leap Forward had seen disastrous declines in food production, "there is no evidence that workers were not motivated to upgrade skills during the Great Leap (introduction of industrial technology to peasants during the 'backyard iron and steel movement' is one of the few generally conceded virtues of the movement)."[23] What matter if production spun out of control as rational planning was abandoned, "the policies of the Leap found crucial sources of support within Chinese industry, both from amongst the leading cadres at the enterprise level as well as some economic planners . . . who . . . were united on their general unhappiness with the Soviet one-man management system."[24] What matter if some women complained of their forced induction into the work force during this campaign, most agreed this was a necessary step toward "woman's emancipation" in China and a means of reinforcing their commitment to work.[25] In general, the concerned scholars regarded mass campaigns "not as the visions of a minority bent on forcing people into a revolutionary mold," but as public-spirited and widely supported efforts to "rally people around real and vitally important issues of universal political concern."[26]

Unlike their predecessors, for whom the possibility of famine after the Great Leap Forward was real enough to warrant refutation, this new generation of China scholars blithely maintained with Professor Benedict Stavis that "China is almost unique in Asia as a land free of widespread hunger, malnutrition, and famine. Virtually every group of visitors, whether reporters, medical specialists, or agricultural scientists, has been stunned by the nutrition and health of the Chinese population. . . . China is especially successful in distributing food fairly over time, space, and social standing. . . . [T]he state can meet emergency needs and prevent famine."[27] When William F. Buckley suggested to Professor Ross Terrill that there had been a famine in China in the early sixties, Terrill's response was snappish. "That was not a famine," he declared. "If you think that's a famine, you don't know what famines were like in Chinese history."[28] Professor Gurley thought China had outperformed even the United States in the fair distribution of food: "The Chinese—all of them—now have what is in effect an insurance policy against pestilence, famine, and other disasters. In this respect, China has outperformed every underdeveloped country in the world; and, even with respect to the richest one, it would not be farfetched to claim that there has been less malnutrition due to maldistribution of food in China over the past twenty years than there has been in the United States."[29]

In their most expansive moods, the concerned scholars imagined that Chairman Mao and the Chinese Communist party had invented a solution to the problems of mankind. "How can people break the shackles of oppression, poverty, and fear, how can they translate their hopes and dreams into dynamic action to expand human freedom and possibility? How can men stand up?" asked Professor Mark Selden, one of the founding fathers of the Committee of Concerned Asian Scholars. His answer: "The Chinese revolution offers inspiration not only to those who would expel colonial oppressors. Nor is its message limited to new nations striving to overcome poverty, economic stagnation, and domination by the industrialized metropolitan powers. It addresses men and women everywhere who seek to create a society free from stifling oppression, arbitrary state power, and enslaving technology."[30] Perhaps only Selden's final claim has merit. Mao's repeated purges of intellectuals, culminating in the Cultural Revolution's assault on higher education, are recognized today as having cost China a generation or more of technological and scientific development, a lesson for societies everywhere that fear "enslaving technology."

THE CULTURAL REVOLUTION EXPLAINED

Those working within the revolutionary socialist paradigm had made a commitment, in the words of Professor Gurley, "to deal with China on its own terms, within the framework of its own goals, and its own methods for attaining those goals."[31] So it is not surprising that their explanation of the initial phase of the Cultural Revolution (1966–69) closely paralleled Beijing's own (at least the explanation that dominated in China until the fall of the Gang of Four). In their view, Chairman Mao had launched the Cultural Revolution to "rekindle the sputtering flame of China's revolution and to immunize the Chinese people against the pernicious virus of Khrushchev's apostate 'revisionism.' "[32] The youthful mayhem that ensued, though encouraged by Mao in order to create "a generation of revolutionary successors" tempered in the fire of revolution, was at the same time a largely spontaneous mass movement. Professor Edward Friedman maintained that urban-rural and class tensions in China were running so high by the mid-1960s that virtually anything could have triggered a societywide detonation.[33] During their struggle against ideological impurity, the Red Guards discovered to their horror that 'revisionists' were occupying high posts within the party—foremost among them Liu Shaoqi and Deng Xiaoping—and indeed within their own ranks. A just and holy war ensued. There was some loss of life, but the violence was greatly exaggerated in the Western media and by those who persisted in seeing China as a totalitarian regime.[34]

130

It was in their evaluation of the accomplishments of the Cultural Revolution that the concerned Asian scholars really hit their stride, claiming to see everywhere the signs of a wondrous progress toward a society at once wealthier and more egalitarian. "Perhaps in no area of the economy have China's achievements been so strikingly successful as in their handling of agricultural collectivization and, with special emphasis since the Cultural Revolution, in raising the standard of living in the countryside to bring economic and social conditions in the rural areas closer to those of the towns."[35] The stunning transformation of the cities left them groping for words: "It is difficult to convey our growing amazement as we explored Shanghai. China has overcome almost all the tragic problems of Asia's cities," which included slums, inadequate sewer and urban transportation systems, and insufficient electrical power.[36]

The claims made by these earnest pilgrims on behalf of their New Jerusalem were, without exception, false. Agricultural collectivization was a costly failure, urban-rural disparities were increasing throughout the sixties and seventies, Shanghai's infrastructure was decaying at an alarming rate—the list goes on and on.[37] These errors did not always involve duplicity, either of the Chinese or their foreign admirers. For example, Professor Ross Terrill, an Australian expert on China, was informed by Chinese officials that a high school education had become nearly universal, with 80 to 90 percent of young people now graduating in most provinces. Struck by this "splendid achievement," he cited it in books, articles, and television talk shows as a prime example of the good this social movement had brought.[38] What Terrill didn't mention, undoubtedly because he didn't know, was that during the Cultural Revolution communes throughout China had been ordered to establish their own senior high schools. Local officials, anxious to comply with this directive yet without the resources to do so, had resorted to a little verbal sleight of hand. They had renamed the ninth grade classes of local junior high schools "senior high schools." Rural schoolchildren received no more education than before, but now they finished junior high school after a truncated two-year course of study, and "graduated" from "senior high school" a year later. Terrill had taken his informants at their word and had been deceived about education in China; his readers had taken Terrill for a China expert and had been deceived in turn.

Yet no lie, in the strict sense of the word, had ever been told to or by him. The chain of duplicity was linked together not by lies but by credulity.

Even after the first waves of disillusioning revelation had struck American shores, Professor Gurley in 1976 was still able to write the following accolade to revolutionary socialism: "The truth is that China over the past two decades has made very remarkable economic advances . . . on almost all fronts. The basic, overriding economic fact about China is that for twenty years it has fed, clothed, and housed everyone, has kept them healthy, and has educated most. Millions have not starved; sidewalks and streets have not been covered with multitudes of sleeping, begging, hungry, and illiterate human beings; millions are not disease-ridden. To find such deplorable conditions, one does not look to China these days but, rather, to India, Pakistan, and almost anywhere else in the underdeveloped world. These facts are so basic, so fundamentally important, that they completely dominate China's economic picture, even if one grants all of the erratic and irrational policies alleged by its numerous critics."[39]

Toward the violence, limited but real, that in their eyes had made this magnificent transformation possible, concerned scholars were of one mind. They thought China an exception to Heilbroner's formulation that "the real resistance to [socialist] development comes not from the old regimes, which can be quickly overcome, but from the masses of the population, who must be wrenched from their established ways, pushed, prodded, cajoled, or threatened into heroic efforts, and then systematically denied an increase in well-being, so that capital can be amassed for future growth. This painful reorientation of a whole culture, judging by past experience, will be difficult or impossible to attain without measures of severity."[40] On the contrary, revolutionary China scholars believed that the consciousness of the Chinese had been so uplifted by the Thought of Chairman Mao that official commands and state coercion had been unnecessary; the revolutionary masses themselves had reinvented China. The violence unleashed in often terrorist fashion by the Red Guards was not only proper but requisite—the righteous fight of a people to free themselves from their feudal and bourgeois past. Concerned scholars no more sympathized with those who suffered and died at the hands of the Red Guards than European Christians in the Middle Ages had agonized over Moslem casualties in the Crusades. Only the violence exerted by the capitalist democracies, both on Third World peoples abroad—particularly acts of war by the United States in Vietnam—and on oppressed classes at home, seemed to them repugnant and utterly unjustifiable.

James Peck contrasted this attitude, which he characterized as that of the "revolutionary Marxist," with that of "the China scholar . . . [who] defines violence narrowly as a quality of individuals or groups who challenge existing arrangements. The revolutionary Marxist, on the other hand, concentrates on institutional violence, the human costs of stability, and the violent powers of the ruling elites. And while the former stress the immediately obvious kinds of social violence, the latter insist that order, like violence, is politically defined and that the conceptions of orderly and nonviolent change only reflect the interests of those powerful enough to enforce their definitions upon the population."[41] The Red Guards put the same point much more succinctly in one of their slogans: "It is Right to Rebel!" Correctly fearing that their bourgeois colleagues might not understand the subtlety of their reasoning, however, concerned scholars downplayed—when they mentioned it at all—the mass violence that had wracked China.

The concerned scholars were convinced that the ideals of truth, objectivity, and hard intellectual analysis espoused by earlier cohorts of China-watchers were poses designed to obscure their underlying hostility to revolutionary movements. They gave the totalitarian paradigm short shrift, attacking it as a knee-jerk response to the cold war. But they reserved their special rancor for the "modernizing communist China" advocates, and engaged in long and polemical attacks on them in the pages of the *Bulletin:*[42] Fairbank was accused of the "internalization of the rightist world view, that is the continuing legacy of McCarthyism. . . . Anticommunist liberals . . . ended up serving as intellectual bellboys . . . provid[ing] the sophistication and complexity for the rigid and confining outlooks of the Cold War."[43] Professor Ezra Vogel's *Canton Under Communism* was disparaged as "typical of American liberal scholarship . . . embod[ying] many of the assumptions and values of the school: the commitment to modernization as inevitable, good, and rational; the related belief in rational administration; the love of order and regularity; the tendency to comprehend revolution largely in terms of techniques of manipulation and control; and its corollary, the tendency to ignore, devalue, or treat primarily as a component of administration the force of revolutionary spirit, class struggle, and commitment."[44]

However badly it failed to explain the Chinese reality, the revolutionary socialist paradigm easily passed the principal test of an aspiring orthodoxy: It succeeded in coopting its victims and opponents. Even as Professor Fairbank and other older China-watchers were gently disputing some of its more radical conclusions (Fairbank's response to Peck was remarkably mild, all things considered), they were drawn along in its wake and eventually accepted many of its assumptions and conclusions. By 1972, Fairbank was sounding like the most infatuated of political pilgrims: "The people seem healthy, well fed and articulate about their role as citizens of Chairman Mao's New China . . . the change in the countryside is miraculous. . . . The Maoist revolution is on the whole the best thing that happened to the Chinese people in centuries. At least, most Chinese seem now to believe so, and it will be hard to prove it otherwise. . . . Maoism, including Marxism-Leninism, has got results . . ."[45] John S. Service, once a leading State Department authority on China, returned from a visit to that country to declare that "life is obviously better for the great majority. There is no longer starvation and bitter poverty. . . . Perhaps the single word that best describes [the prevailing attitude] is egalitarian. It is exemplified, of course, by everyone being a 'comrade.' " Struck by the realization that he had not heard any swearing or cursing during his month in China, he hypothesized that "this new civility may owe something to the example of a state and party that seem to prefer governing by persuasion and propaganda rather than by command and force. One wonders, though, if it does not also have some foundation in the much more comfortable, stable life enjoyed by most people, the broader sense of community that has been created, and the ending of the old, bitterly competitive scramble for a bare existence."[46]

The modernizing communist regime advocates remained somewhat more ambivalent than the concerned scholars toward the Cultural Revolution. The violence dismayed them, since unlike their younger colleagues they had no ideological justification for it, and they preferred to minimize it wherever possible. Nor could they accept the revolutionary socialist thesis that it had originated in a deliberate effort by Chairman Mao to temper the youth and reinvigorate the bureaucracy, although they conceded that principled differences of policy, and not a power struggle, had divided Mao from his enemies. Finally, they were bothered by the politicization of higher education and the absence of intellectual freedom that the Cultural Revolution had brought, although Professors Fairbank, Terrill, and others argued that improvements in literacy, rural life, and the general welfare more than offset these losses.[47]

In their assessment of the achievements of the Cultural Revolution, the modernizing communist China scholars were more guarded than their radical colleagues but were still positive. Michael Frolic, a Canadian China-watcher, found during his 1971 revisit that "compared to 1965, it appears that the Chinese are better off economically, with enough food and an increasing variety of goods available to them. While cereals, cotton, and edible vegetable oils [that is, food and clothing] are still rationed, it would seem that individual Chinese can get enough of these to satisfy their daily needs. . . . We [China-watchers] generally concluded that most of the goals of the Cultural Revolution were unworkable and would negatively affect China's development. Yet it appears that the reverse is occurring: China's standard of living has not declined; many of the 'impractical' radical innovations of the Cultural Revolution are actually being attempted; China 'put the pieces together' a lot more quickly than we ever could have predicted."[48]

Like the revolutionary socialists, they saved their rancor for colleagues to *their* right: those who insisted that the Cultural Revolution had originated in Mao's efforts to destroy his rivals and reassert control over the party and state, and who saw the Red Guards—however idealistic they were at the outset—as quickly degenerating into rat packs of young thugs. When Ivan and Miriam London and Ta-ling Lee published their classic account of Red Guard terrorism, "The Making of a Red Guard," in the *New York Times Magazine* in early 1970, it elicited a curious—and revealing—response from a keeper of the modernizing China paradigm, the Harvard University Professor Ezra Vogel, and his student Martin Whyte.[49]

After a deft feint toward the concerned scholars (they called "The

Making of a Red Guard" "a needed antidote to the effort of some American radicals to see Red Guards only as the sweet personification of idealism and democracy"), Vogel and Whyte come to grips with their real antagonists, whose work was "equally one-sided":

> In our interviewing of refugees we have not encountered any cases which involved this much violence. . . . Like other articles on the Cultural Revolution which come from Taiwan sources, it stresses only violence. Being printed at a time when there are signs of a beginning of a minor thaw in Sino-American relationships, it helps convey the Taiwan Government's image of China as a country of violence toward decent citizens. This article ignores the problems which the Cultural Revolution was designed to correct, the idealism of many Red Guards and the key issues of the Cultural Revolution.[50]

In this attack on the explanation of the Cultural Revolution in "The Making of a Red Guard," Vogel and Whyte exposed the assumptions of their own paradigm:

1. *Violence was limited.* Dr. London responded: "Concerning evidence of considerable violence, it is, frankly, difficult for me to see how Messrs. Vogel and Whyte could have missed this unless their interviewing data were extremely fragmentary for the years 1966 and 1967. And what do they imagine was taking place during the armed factional clashes of 1967—an exchange of valentines?"[51]

2. *Those who suggest otherwise were toeing the Taiwan line.* Dr. London responded: "We are concerned with research, not image-building. The source of this article is an American, academically based research project under my direction. Our interviews have been conducted in both Hong Kong and Taiwan; if we could not be assured in Taiwan of field conditions guaranteeing all the requirements for objective research, we would not operate there."[52]

3. *The Cultural Revolution was designed to correct real problems in society and government, and many Red Guards were motivated by idealism.* To this Dr. London replied that "The purpose of our research . . . is to present as minutely, accurately and vividly as possible the events of recent Chinese history *as they were perceived* by Chinese who themselves participated in its creation."[53]

Such assumptions illustrate the extent to which otherwise sensible academics had come under the sway of the Maoist rhetoric that abounded during those years. For them the persecution, even unto death, of entire classes of people was easily abstracted into bloodless jargon ("class warfare") and cloaked in proletarian virtue ("Maoist equality"). When the Londons and Ta-ling Lee went on to publish *Revenge of Heaven*, a case study of the Red Guard leader Ken Ling written in the form of an autobiographical narrative, Ling's vivid descriptions of torture and violence were criticized, this time by none other than the "dean" of Sinology himself. "We have little reason to doubt that China's turmoil saw this kind of personal savagery," Professor Fairbank intoned in his review, "but when the Maoist rationale is strained out, it becomes merely violence for its own sake or, as the Soviets say, 'hooliganism,' instead of *violence in the name of virtue;* which others report as typical of the Cultural Revolution."[54]

As Kuo and Myers point out, "Some American scholars argued that ideals—or even utopian impulses—motivated the Maoist policies of the period; they were, however, unable to make balanced assessments of the destructive effects these policies had on the fabric of Chinese society."[55] Yet within a few years after the death of Mao, even the Chinese Communist party had reversed itself on the once-vaunted "achievements" of his last decade of rule. On 1 October 1979 one of Communist China's top leaders, Ye Jianying, pronounced the party's new verdict: "The 'Cultural Revolution' forced the country to endure an entire decade of oppression, tyranny, and bloodshed."[56]

One did not have to wait until the Chinese Communist party stood Mao on his head to learn this, of course. Peggy Durdin, who had long since recovered from her early fascination with Zhou Enlai, provided a historically accurate perspective in an article entitled "The Bitter Tea of Mao's Red Guards," which appeared in early 1969. The Red Guards had just been sent down to the countryside by order of Chairman Mao, there to languish on army farms and communes. Disillusioned and disheartened, they began slipping back to the cities and across the border to Hong Kong. Durdin's account, like those of the ex–Red Guards, was free of the infatuation with Maoist thought that would beguile academics for years to come. Her conclusion is worth quoting in full:

In the final analysis, and in practical terms, it is not very important how many young Chinese had or developed sophisticated political ideals during the Cultural Revolution. What matters is that tens of thousands of Red Guards and rebels enjoyed, for the first time in their lives, a high degree of physical mobility, personal freedom—including the freedom to make mistakes—and political and social authority. Even when, as time went on, they were criticized for their obvious and inevitable failings, they did not dream that they would be firmly and abruptly put back into the old scheme of things, where they could not make decisions about their own lives, much less about the affairs of the nation. The sudden gift of power, freedom, participation and responsibility in 1966 and its brusque withdrawal in 1968 cannot be anything but psychologically harmful and even devastating. As far as politics is concerned, this kind of treatment produces not the new Maoist man but the sullen cynic.

Mao Zedong has indeed sold Chinese youth down the river. For a short time and for his own ends he used and manipulated—and heartened— a whole generation, then imposed on it all the old bureaucratic and dictatorial fetters. The resulting alienation of Chinese young people, who Mao himself says are the leaders of the future—successors to *his* revolution—may make it not more difficult but easier for some form of revisionism to develop in the China of tomorrow.[57]

When I lived in China ten years later, I found that this attitude of cynical disillusionment was characteristic of virtually all who had actively participated in the Cultural Revolution. By then, as Deng Xiaoping sought to steer China on a new course, it was becoming politically permissible to talk about Mao as if he were something less than the incarnation of political wisdom. Many no longer bothered to hide their opposition to his now-abandoned policies. Deng is often given credit for slaying the dragon of Maoism, but it was Mao himself who had many years before perpetrated this act of intellectual infanticide—killing his own brainchild in the persons of millions of Red Guards. Maoism had been dead in China since the early phases of the Cultural Revolution, though many years would pass before its decomposition began to be noticed by its foreign disciples and hangers-on. Indeed, Nixon's visit would give it new life abroad.

7

The Selling of China: Nixon's Visit

Nixon was there to trilaterize the tensions among the three superpowers; to make sure that the Chinese would feel that there was an alternative to rapprochement with the Soviet Union. He attempted this at great psychological cost; undermining American opinion that Communist revolutions affected by totalitarian means are odious.

—William F. Buckley
"Nixon to China"

Concerned Asian students and their mentors would have recoiled in horror at the thought that they were instruments of President Richard Nixon's rapprochement with China. But if none of them were involved in the actual overture to Beijing—the decision seems to have been Nixon's own—they had been actively advocating a new China policy for years. There is slight hyperbole in the lament of a disgruntled Soviet official that "most U.S. scholars on the Soviet Union oppose improvement of relations with the U.S.S.R., while all American specialists on China are for improved relations with the People's Republic."[1] Indeed, in one respect their assistance was critical. American academics provided Nixon with a ready-made image of the New China, stamped with the scholarly seal of approval, which he in turn could sell to the American people.

It would be a tough sell, since American opinion in the late sixties was decisively hostile to Communist China, but Nixon had no alternative. If he wanted to play geopolitical poker with Communist

China, he first had to convince his fellow citizens that there was no shame in gambling with the likes of Mao Zedong and Zhou Enlai. "[P]ublic sentiment is everything," noted Abraham Lincoln, a president of no small acquaintance with politically parlous ventures. "With public sentiment, nothing can fail; without it, nothing can succeed. Consequently, he who molds public sentiment goes deeper than he who enacts statutes or pronounces decisions. He makes statutes and decisions possible or impossible to be executed."[2] Unless popular opinion could be changed, Nixon knew that his China venture would go nowhere.

In short, Nixon and his national security advisor Henry Kissinger, later secretary of state, found themselves facing the same difficulty as the American correspondents discussed in chapter 4, only multiplied: an American public that was not only anti-Communist but anti–*Chinese* Communist. And like the correspondents, they had resort to various fictions about the Communist Chinese.

The first step taken by Nixon was to stop calling them Communists. In official press releases and public statements the word *China* was now prefaced by "People's Republic of" and not "Communist," "Red," or even "Mainland." Mao Zedong and Zhou Enlai were now China's Chairman and Premier, respectively, and not Chinese Communist leaders. In part this was a diplomatic semaphore, the use of proper titles by Nixon to alert Beijing to his change of heart. But this is not the whole story; otherwise how does one explain that in these official press releases and statements Mao Zedong is never called by his proper title—Chairman of the Chinese Communist party—instead of the abbreviated "Chairman"? Or the absence of any reference to the fact that the People's Republic of China was run by the Chinese Communist party? Or the fact that in the State Department's official compendium of presidential statements, toasts, and press conferences surrounding the China trip, the word *communism* appears not once?[3] Clearly the word was taboo, and not because it would have upset Maoist sensibilities. It was American sensibilities that such ellipses were intended to soothe.

Nixon's second fiction concerned the character of the Chinese leaders with whom he would be meeting. It would not do for him to be seen toasting a pack of ruthless villains, which is roughly what most Americans thought of Mao Zedong, Zhou Enlai, and other Chinese leaders at the time. Nixon ordered China-watchers in the State Department and Central Intelligence Agency to refrain from public discussion of the bitter infighting underway within the Communist party. When stories about Lin Biao's failed coup attempt against Mao and subsequent death appeared in American newspapers in late 1971, Nixon's aides were furious. Stanley Karnow reports that they seriously considered giving lie-detector tests to those officials suspected of having leaked the information.[4]

Henry Kissinger, who seems to have been enchanted with the urbane, witty Zhou Enlai, personally took charge of his rehabilitation campaign.[5] Returning from his visit to China in July 1971, he held a seemingly endless series of briefings of the press, Congress, and administration officials at which he described in superlatives his meetings with the Chinese premier. The pleasant convergence between the demands of *realpolitik* and his own affection for Zhou made it possible for him to speak with special conviction. His reception in China had been "enormously gracious and polite." The negotiations with Zhou had been "very businesslike, very precise, no rhetoric on either side." Overall, he had been treated "extraordinarily well" by his Chinese hosts. As Marvin and Bernard Kalb remark about Kissinger's public relations effort, "Clearly, China was no longer to be regarded as a 'threat,' nor Zhou as a remote and ambiguous figure."[6] Isaacs's prediction, made after the Red Terror and the Korean War, that Zhou's charm would never again be mistaken for a quality of inner virtue had proven overly optimistic. Henry Kissinger for one had lost his head over Zhou and endeavored to convince Americans that his newfound friend was not the barbaric Red they had heard so much about.

Nixon's third fiction was that China's "system," or "philosophy," was its own affair and that differences between the United States and China should not be allowed to impede relations. Moral neutrality in matters of popular sovereignty is an unfamiliar position for most Americans, who will not long tolerate the embrace of a regime perceived to be tyrannical. One could not suggest to an American audience that China's government was legitimate, as Nixon frequently did, without also implying that it was at least well-intentioned.

This problem was compounded by Nixon's propensity to utter the kind of fine, capacious, and understanding remarks that were tailor-made for misapprehension. Take, for instance, Nixon's assertion that China's leaders had impressed him above all with "their total belief, their total dedication, to their system of government. That is their right, just as it is the right of any country to choose the kind of government it wants."[7] What Nixon means, of course, is that it is all right by him that Mao Zedong and Zhou Enlai are committed Communists. But since he must speak in code, he sounds both inane and duplicitous—inane because dictators, Communist or otherwise, are rarely less than "totally dedicated" to their continued governance, duplicitous because the Chinese people have never "chosen" to be governed by the Chinese Communist party, which conquered the country by force of arms decades before and which has yet to hold a free election.

William F. Buckley believed that it was Nixon's "excessive moral energy" that led him "to transubstantiate purely diplomatic relationships into sacramental necessities."[8] Whatever the reason, Nixon's public utterances lent a democratic flavor to a despotic regime. Although the onetime cold warrior stopped short of fully endorsing the view held by Fairbank and other academics that communism had been good for China, all could see that he had abandoned his old position that China was a totalitarian regime. He also imposed a straitjacket on the government, ordering the U.S. Information Agency not to produce, publish, or broadcast reports that were critical of China.

Foreign leaders took their cue from Washington, and the new view of China spread from the United States to Europe. Writing in November 1971 for *Successo*, Galeazzo Santini described how "China is now the fashion around the world, and in no uncertain terms. Everywhere politicians of the most conservative and bourgeois kind are attempting to rebuild for themselves a compromised career by singing the praises of Mao Zedong."[9]

When a clear-eyed Richard Nixon swore, on the eve of his departure for Beijing, that he was going "without illusions," he may be taken at his word.[10] There is no evidence that he was personally in thrall to the new view of China that his visit was so painstakingly arranged to reinforce. During his week in China the old image of the People's Republic as a brutal dictatorship implacably hostile to America dissolved abruptly in a series of extraordinary *tableaux vivants*:

Nixon applauding a Revolutionary Opera ("certainly the equal of any ballet I have seen"); Nixon at the Great Wall ("This is a Great Wall"); Nixon offering a toast to Chairman Mao and the brilliant, handsome, and witty Premier Zhou ("let us start a new Long March together").

With the president displaying a sympathy and affection for the Beijing regime and its leaders beyond the demands of protocol, how could Americans continue to react to China with their accustomed antagonism? It was anti-Communists who most keenly felt the incongruity of their position. For decades they had maintained an unremitting hostility toward Communist China, never letting themselves or their fellow citizens forget the millions of lives claimed by the Red Terror, the Great Leap Forward, and the ongoing Cultural Revolution. Now here was one of their own, whom they had elected to the highest office in the land, betraying everything they had stood for. No wonder that the sight of Nixon raising his glass to Chairman Mao struck them dumb. Even William F. Buckley, who fought a long and eloquent battle against this bizarre communion, seemed less certain of his opposition to Chinese communism in the immediate wake of this visit, regretting only that Mr. Nixon chose himself instead of an assistant secretary of state to celebrate it. Later, of course, he was to express the opinion that Nixon's fatuous and dissembling remarks on China were good training for his future statements on Watergate.[11]

Anti-Communist liberals, whose Wilsonian crusade for democracy in Vietnam had ended in a quagmire, embraced Nixon's China like a drowning man thrown a life preserver. "Long overdue" was their instant assessment of the U.S.-China rapprochement, which they hoped would provide an honorable way out of America's prolonged agony. It was with relief that they shed the now-burdensome image of Chinese Communists as fanatical aggressors; perhaps the reasonable comrades in Beijing would agree to cut the aid or twist the arms of the unreasonable comrades in Hanoi. They were also quick to accept the optimistic assessments of the unity and progress China had made under socialism; perhaps they had been mistaken to think that South Vietnam—and Laos and Cambodia—would suffer at the hands of Communists. Like the "liberal opinion" of the 1930s, which in the name of a formless and mindless "anti-Fascism" accepted a body of fictitious images relating to China, Spain, and Russia, so did the "liberal opinion" of the 1970s, in the name of a formless and mindless "anti-imperialism," seek to pave America's retreat from South Vietnam in particular and Asia in general with comfortable illusions about life in China and North Vietnam. Although they were not above denouncing the timing of the visit as a reelection ploy, or its presentation as a media circus stage-managed for maximum domestic political impact, they were glad Nixon had gone.

The New Left wished Nixon had stayed home. Self-styled Maoists were as outraged by the sight of their mythic leader toasting the despised Richard M. Nixon as Buckley had been at the sight of his president toasting the detested Mao Zedong. They went madly riffling through their Little Red Books in search of some explanation for this defilement of the purity of the world revolutionary movement—and came up gnashing their teeth. "Ironically, among the most vocal critics of China at present are members of the leftist Committee of Concerned Asian Scholars," wrote Stanley Karnow, "who have been disappointed by the Chinese rapprochement with Richard Nixon in much the same way that the Old Left became disenchanted with the Kremlin following the Molotov-Ribbentrop pact in 1939."[12] Yet even those who felt that Chairman Mao had betrayed his revolutionary vision by receiving Richard Nixon still believed that same vision had brought incalculable benefits to China. As David Kolodney, seeking to bolster the spirits of the disenchanted, wrote in the pages of *Ramparts:* "The transformation of Chinese society in the last 20 years remains an unparalleled vindication of the revolutionary process, of the power of a liberating idea, of unity and action, of the creative energy released as people discover in themselves the determination and the capacity to make their own history. To look at the Chinese revolution . . . reveals to us the dimensions of the revolutionary opportunity that lies ahead."[13]

GULLIBLE TRAVELERS

On the surface it was an unlikely proposition: that American journalists could maneuver through a non-Western society from which they had been barred for a score of years, and around which an unlikely coalition of anti-Communist Administration officials and radical Maoists had planted a bamboo thicket of myth, exaggeration, and half-truths. Not surprisingly, they lost their bearings.

The press proved a willing accomplice in Nixon's remaking of China. The *New York Times,* for better or worse the pacesetter of American journalism, was the first to discover the New China of immaculate cities, prosperous, well-fed peasants, and officials who served the people. No longer did it malign the Chinese government, as it had in 1959, as "the most totalitarian regime of the 20th century." Instead it endorsed Seymour Topping's view of Chairman Mao's doctrines as having "propelled China into a continuing revolution that is producing a new society and a new 'Maoist Man.' "[14] Topping's account of a brief visit to the "typical" Chinese-Vietnamese Friendship People's Commune[15] could have been filed by Harrison Forman from Yenan: "[T]he villages of the commune have considerable economic independence and enjoy communal democracy in management of their local affairs."[16] Other more down-to-earth but equally arresting generalizations published by the *Times* concerned sanitation. "The People's Republic of China is faultlessly clean," Audrey Topping announced after traveling by train from the Hong Kong border to Canton. "Dirt is a dirty word."[17] In the aftermath of a winter storm, Max Frankel was delighted to discover that hundreds of thousands of "volunteers" had taken to the streets of Beijing to sweep, scrape, and shovel the snow and ice away. "What power can turn out the masses?" he wonders. His answer: the selflessness and community spirit learned in the Cultural Revolution.[18]

The views of the *New York Times* columnist James Reston underwent a transformation similar to his newspaper's, and with considerably more justification. Shortly after arriving in China in July 1971 Reston fell ill with acute appendicitis. Zhou Enlai personally summoned physicians, who recommended an emergency appendectomy. The operation went off without a hitch with only minor postoperative discomfort (relieved not by painkillers but Maoist acupuncture). Reston, attended throughout by a phalanx of solicitous doctors and nurses, made a prompt and full recovery. Such an experience could not fail to evoke in the columnist a stronger sense of obligation than any number of lavish banquets in his honor or exclusive interviews with Zhou Enlai. A grateful Reston left the hospital believing that

145

"Maoism itself has obviously become an infectious disease, even among many of the well-educated urban citizens who had a hard time during the Cultural Revolution."[19] No more would he assert, as he had in the early sixties, that the Chinese had "made . . . a ghastly mess of their revolution." Now he compared the revolution to an old-time "cooperative barn-raising" that ought to make Americans "outrageously nostalgic and even sentimental."[20] China was "one vast school of moral philosophy," Reston advised Eric Severeid. "I'm a Scotch Calvinist. I believe in redemption of the human spirit and the improvement of man. Maybe it's because I believe that . . . that I was struck by the tremendous effort to bring out what is best in man, what makes them good, what makes them cooperate with one another and be considerate and not beastly to one another."[21]

During Nixon's visit, the art of barbarian management was practiced with sophistication and subtlety on correspondents who had dropped their defensive cynicism and skepticism for the occasion. When the columnist Joseph Kraft was offhandedly introduced by President Nixon as a "Soviet expert" to Premier Zhou Enlai at the end of a long reception, he later found himself questioned by a young man from the Ministry of Foreign Affairs on Soviet affairs. From this little acorn of information about the efficiency of Chinese translators, Kraft grows a giant oak tree of eidetic powers of mythic proportions: "With scores of people jabbering incoherently of cabbages and kings, Zhou Enlai had caught every word. Whatever else may be said about the Chinese, they have undoubted powers of concentration."[22]

Kraft, who was allowed to stay on in China for several weeks after Nixon's departure, in the end grew faintly suspicious of lines like "literature is a spare part of the revolution." His sole attempt to fathom the murky depths of China's political crisis, however, was hardly worthy of a seasoned correspondent: he requested to meet alone with an English-speaking Chinese intellectual, without a translator or any other official present. He was closeted with Jian Weizhang, a high-ranking official in the Chinese nuclear program, who politely scolded him for asking too many questions about Lin Biao and tensions in the leadership. "I must tell you that you will never learn anything by such questions," Dr. Jian told him. "Who's Who counts for nothing in China. You have to ask which is the right road, which is the wrong road. . . . We don't pay much attention to who is up and who is down. Those kinds of changes are not important."[23] Kraft swallowed this incredible assertion without remonstrance. Like his colleagues, he had come to treat the Chinese officials he encountered with delicacy, as if the worst offenses against the truth were not worth upsetting their sensibilities. He got nothing for his small cleverness in requesting a private meeting except a repetition of the same official cant he had been hearing all along. Did he think that his Chinese handlers would let him meet with a dissident? Or that a dissident would dare to contradict the official line to a visiting correspondent, knowing that his comments would appear in an American newspaper column?

The Walter Duranty prize for the most imaginative reporting from the New China must be awarded to Harrison Salisbury, one of the *New York Times'* most seasoned and prolific foreign correspondents. Salisbury presents his visit to China as a quest for the New Maoist Man, "a new being born out of chaos, and endowed with moral qualities such as had never been seen before."[24]

Salisbury first sighted his elusive quarry at the so-called May-seventh cadre "schools"—actually quasi-penal labor reeducation camps—in the person of a middle-aged party official who had just completed a two-year stint of ideological retooling and manual labor. "It was a wonderful experience," this official told him. "It was the great experience of my life." Salisbury commented that he knew that the man was speaking the truth "from the emotion in his voice, from the reverence with which he spoke."[25] He was also greatly stirred by the songs and dances of the students, which included such Maoist favorites as "Chairman Mao Has Sent Us Revolutionary Seed," "The Song of the Pig Breeders," and "Happy is He Who Drives the Night-soil Cart." He likened the May-seventh "schools" to a "combination of a YMCA camp and a Catholic retreat," a comment strikingly similar to John Service's description of Yenan's ambience as close to that of a "religious summer conference."[26]

Visiting cities, factories, and schools across China, Salisbury everywhere encountered New Men (and New Women) of "remarkable moral qualities." He was even able to sleuth out the secret recipe for their "creation." It consisted of one part liberation mixed with one part anarchism, tempered in the red heat of labor reeducation. The first transformed "subservient, slave-like peasants and workers into self-sufficient men and women"; the second "administer[ed] a social shock to the whole body politic," especially "the Chinese white collar class"; the third "exposed [them] to an evangelical campaign to reorder their thinking."[27]

Only the residents of the China-Cuba Friendship Commune were a disappointment. The small stores of grain they kept in their home struck Salisbury as a manifestation of "greed," the pleasure they took in their spare primitive furniture as "pride in possession," and their new black silk blouses and pants as an insidious "tendency toward *embourgeoisement.*" The villagers, all spruced up in their holiday best for the visit of the wealthy and influential American correspondent, succeeded only in rousing him to a fury: "But had they piled up those precious jars of grain for the good of the state?" Salisbury wrote accusingly. "Had they bought their mahogany furniture, their elaborate clocks and their stocks of wool and silk because of some new revolutionary urge? Were they constantly thinking of their neighbors and how they could do them good? I doubted that. I thought the gleam of the old devil shone in the[ir] eyes."[28] It wasn't the villagers' fault that they had offended Salisbury, of course. How could these simple people have known that he was on a *spiritual* quest and would only be put off by material distractions.

A few reprobates aside, however, the New Maoist Man was alive and well in the New China. Salisbury considered this new creation "the miracle of the modern world." "I think that it is a great achievement to put a man on the moon," he told Zhou Enlai. "But to put a man on the earth—that is even more."[29]

Salisbury ends his quest by quoting some of Mao's purloined poetry:

> So many deeds cry out to be done, and always urgently;
> The world rolls on, time presses.
> Ten thousand years are too long,
> Seize the day, seize the hour!
> The Four Seas boil, clouds and waters rage,
> The Five continents rock in the wind and roaring thunder.
> Away with all pests;
> Our force is irresistible.

"That, I thought, was China today," writes Salisbury with unconscious irony.[30] "That was the strength of its spirit after the *luan* [chaos] of the Cultural Revolution. But where was that of America?" Decadent Americans, not forged in the crucible of Maoist revolution, had little hope of answering the spiritual challenge of the "New Maoist Man": "When would the New American Man and the New American Woman walk the earth, proud and confident, making the oceans boil and the continents shake?"[31]

It is perhaps also fair to ask, in paraphrase of Max Frankel, what power could turn the press into such a pack of ninnies? I submit that it wasn't merely the techniques of the guided tour, which most of the reporters quoted here had experienced before. Nor was it primarily the press piling on a popular theme, although there was an element of this. Rather, China was an extraordinarily rewarding place for a correspondent or columnist to visit. Virtually everything they chose to scribble about was published—often on the front page and to great acclaim, authenticated solely by its dateline. It was with good professional reason that Max Frankel exulted: "This country is still virgin territory as far as reporting is concerned. Every time you turn around there's something fresh and different and new."[32]

But was there? China had certainly changed from the 1930s and 1940s (Theodore White argued that it had changed "completely"); twenty-three years of peace, if nothing else, would have ensured some progress. The Old China/New China dichotomy, however, which the correspondents tripped over themselves describing, begged the real question: had China changed since the fifties and sixties? For if China was not virgin territory at all but that much-trodden terrain of totalitarianism, or even the bounded and known field of "modernizing Communism," then there was *nothing to write home about*. The "Chinese government" reverts to the "Red Regime," Mao metamorphosizes from a "poetic ideologue" back into a "Communist dictator," and Zhou Enlai degenerates from *Time* magazine's "brilliant, subtle, ruthless and endlessly flexible statesman" to *Life*'s bluntly unflattering "political thug and professional assassin.[33] Americans had heard it all before. Frankel and the other correspondents *assumed* what they needed to prove—that is, that the revolutionary socialist paradigm, not its predecessors, unlocked the truth about China. Without a new paradigm there would have been no New

China—no Maoist Man, no startling advances in education and acupuncture, no cheerful peasants busily sculpting the countryside—to describe to the gaping yokels back home.

Harrison Salisbury was making the same point, though in a slightly different way, when he drew a parallel between himself and the political pilgrims of an earlier age. "In 1919 Lincoln Steffens had gone to the new-born Soviet Union and, returning, proclaimed to Bernard Baruch: 'I have been over into the Future—and it works.' Could it possibly be that China was the Future of our generation?"[34] The People's Republic was neither the Future nor, as America was later to discover, did it even work very well, but one could write whole books on the pretense of exploring the possibility. Whatever role ideological bias played in the ready adoption of the revolutionary socialist paradigm by many visiting American correspondents, it was a perspective that served them well—after the fashion of a full-employment act.

Worse than the correspondents' fear of being struck dumb, which was not always conscious, was their dread of losing their visa privileges. For Stanley Karnow, this explained why "most American newsmen visiting China these days are reluctant to pose tough questions. . . . For example, we [a delegation of visiting journalists] hesitated to ask about China's defense establishment and its advanced weapons program, and we made no attempt to seek out dissenters opposed to the regime, as reporters invariably do in the Soviet Union. Nor did we complain when the Chinese refused to show us such innocuous places as a newspaper office or a television station. Hard as it is to admit, I think that our mildness was partly motivated by the opportunistic concern that we might be blackballed from getting back to China if we raised a fuss."[35]

Perhaps the most surprising convert to the Maoist cause was Joseph Alsop, and his rationale for this change of heart more closely resembled Henry Kissinger's than Harrison Salisbury's. The nationally syndicated columnist had long been one of Communist China's most vociferous critics. In 1959, for example, Alsop saw the "ruthless" collectivization of the countryside as an extension of the Communist policy of "forced labor," asserting that Mao had "chosen to out-Stalin Stalin." A few months after the "fearful" and "hideous" communes were set up, he wrote, "Refugees . . . began to report bare tables in the communal mess halls." In 1961 at the height of the post–Great Leap Forward famine, he was blunt: "The population of China is starving. The starvation is methodical and rationed, but it is not even slow starvation." He estimated that the Chinese diet was averaging only six hundred calories a day, and that the population was in decline. Indeed, he went so far as to speculate that this "methodical and rationed" starvation was being orchestrated by Beijing in order to ease pressure on food supplies.[36]

During a month-long visit to China in December 1972, in which he was treated with the deference due a prince of the print media, Alsop did a spectacular about-face. His columns were suddenly filled with a sense of wonder at what he now called "the new China," and its flourishing communes, thriving cities, and efficient factories. He speaks of the "prosperous affairs" of a commune of "comparative wealth," and compares it to the "management of one of our large American industrial farms." He estimates Chinese peasants to be among the richest in Asia. "Everything in China has changed," he concludes, "except the endlessly resilient, hard-working and clever Chinese people. The quality of life has changed, vastly for the worse for the ancient ruling class but for the better for everyone else."[37]

Alsop did have occasional spasms of doubt, admitting in one column that he kept "thinking nervously of all the woolly minded Westerners who made such fools of themselves in Russia in the cruel thirties," and saying on another occasion that "I may think [the Chinese system] works better than it does work." But he denied allegations that he was viewing China through rose-tinted glasses. He, Joseph Alsop, had not changed; China had.[38]

This was the New China's most important victory, though it was won not by the assiduous efforts of official guides, nor by a desire for professional advancement on the part of one of America's most successful columnists, nor by a fear of being denied reentry, nor even by the nostalgia of an old man for a country and a people he had loved in his youth. Alsop, an early advocate of containment and a hawk on Vietnam, was coming from a different quarter. In interviews he spoke of "a significant, even a strong, community of interests between the United States and China from the moment the Soviet threat [to China] began to be serious. Given the consequences of a successful Soviet attack [against China], I'm convinced that if the danger becomes much more serious, we ought to do everything in our power, which is limited, to go to China's aid."[39]

Alsop may have romanticized China, but underneath his ecstasy he was practicing his own brand of *realpolitik*. He was an early advocate of what would become known as playing the China card. In their eagerness to enlist China into their struggle against the Soviet Union, moderates and even conservatives like Alsop found themselves vigorously applauding the revolutionary opera produced by Beijing for their benefit, while ignoring the unpleasant goings-on backstage.

Although it came to dominate in the prestige press, the revolutionary socialist paradigm did not completely sweep the field. *U.S. News & World Report* soberly headlined an article about China's economy, "A Second-Rate Power—With a Long Way to Go."[40] Robert P. Martin's "China Revisited," appearing in that same magazine, was a more balanced piece of reporting than what most "Old China Hands" turned out. (Martin asked one of the "students" at a May-seventh labor reeducation camp whether he had volunteered. "Yes," the man replied, "we volunteer in rotation.")[41] And of course there were William F. Buckley's columns.

Even those correspondents who were best disposed toward the New China could not overlook the personality cult of Chairman Mao, the regimentation of education, and the persecution of intellectuals. Such Stalinoid features were too prominent and too reminiscent of recent events in the Soviet Union to pass entirely without mention. But the media's description of these features often assumed a tone of studied ambiguity. "[B]y assuming the role of China's Dr. Spock, its John Dewey and, indeed, its Gloria Steinem," *Newsweek* magazine commented, "the Chairman has radically altered the Chinese way of life." One might reasonably conclude from this description that Mao was merely a kindly, if slightly radical, old physician bent on curing the ills of the Chinese body politic.[42] *Time*'s Hugh Sidey is struck by the regimentation at a model school: "The students sit like robots," Sidey writes, "[and] recite like soldiers, turning to their books and back again on command, as if executing close-order drill." But he closes on a less exacting note. "It is like a machine, but the harshness of the moment is softened by the kids' faces. They are kind, eager, respectful, cheerful, warm. There is the scent of life about the place."[43]

CHINA CRAZE

President Nixon's Chinese initiative ignited enormous interest in China, especially among U.S. intellectuals, and made it possible for those who were neither as well-connected as Snow nor as politically reliable as Lynd and Hayden to obtain visas from the Beijing regime. Mainstream political commentators flocked to Red China to learn about the societal virtues of a "New" China that they had never dreamed existed. Praise of the Maoist revolution in China, hitherto limited to radical left circles, could now be found in the *New Republic,* the *Atlantic Monthly,* and *Foreign Affairs.*

Enrollment in courses about China rose spectacularly on many campuses, doubling and even tripling at places like Stanford, Berkeley, and Cornell. Viewing China through optical lenses ground in the Vietnam conflict and polished during visits to China in the early seventies, they marveled at China's advances, exalting the Maoist miracles they believed they had seen. The list of such innocents was endless and included such celebrated figures as John Kenneth Galbraith, Barbara Tuchman, David Rockefeller, and Shirley MacLaine.

Harvard professor Galbraith, impressed by the "easy, affable, and sensitive manners of the Chinese," wrote in 1973 that "one transfers [one's] reaction to [these manners] to the society. Dissidents are brought firmly into line in China but, one suspects, with great politeness. It is a firmly authoritarian society in which those in charge smile and say please."[44] Galbraith did not know that during his visit, China's prisons were still full of victims of the Cultural Revolution, among them Nien Cheng, who describes in her bestseller *Life and Death in Shanghai* how her Maoist captors repeatedly tortured, starved, and abused her during the six-year incarceration.[45]

The historian Barbara Tuchman wrote in the *New York Times,* "The elimination of these conditions [graft] in China is so striking that negative aspects of the new rule fade in relative importance." (To which Buckley offered the barbed rejoinder, "Thus the loss of every known freedom was then defined, in the glory years after the demarche with Mao Zedong's China, as a mere 'negative aspect.' ")[46]

China-watcher Orville Schell, observing children performing martial arts exercises at Dazhai, a model commune in the backward Shanxi province, spins a wonderful yarn: "The evenness of talent is astonishing, reflecting the concern of the Chinese with developing the backward as well as the advanced. This has been one of Mao's obsessions: all-around equal development of every sector of Chinese life. It is for this reason that he first called attention to this once-impoverished desolate village, which has now succeeded in such a dramatic way. It was a village with no unique talents and no lucky breaks. Yet it transformed itself."[47] The main thing Dazhai had going for it, as was later revealed by Beijing, was the patronage of Mao Zedong, who was indeed obsessed with proving to foreigners and the Chinese that his commune system was not a costly failure.

David Rockefeller, the chairman of the board of Chase Manhattan Bank, toted up the balance sheet in 1973 and found the Chinese Revolution well in the black: "Whatever the price of the Chinese Revolution, it has obviously succeeded not only in producing more efficient and dedicated administration, but also in fostering high morale and community of purpose. . . . The social experiment in China under Chairman Mao's leadership is one of the most important and successful in human history."[48] A more sober opinion of Mao's leadership was offered by one of his successors. Then–general secretary Hu Yaobang, on the occasion of the Chinese Communist Party's sixty-fifth anniversary, remarked that "an aging and confused Mao Zedong brought catastrophe to China by launching the 1966–76 Cultural Revolution."

The wave of literary chinoiserie soon reached such overblown proportions that virtually anything written on China could be published, provided it contained the obligatory elements of the genre: The border crossing into China, the wonderful service in Chinese hotels, the miraculous acupuncture operation, the visit to the model factory, school, and clinic, and the pilgrimages to Dazhai and Yenan, "the birthplace of the revolution." The bland sameness of these accounts is further enhanced by their simplicity of style and, in a fundamental sense, their naïveté about China. Their authors took their experience in China altogether too seriously, and wrote about it with the subtlety and nuance of a comic book.

The pinnacle of the genre is perhaps represented by the work of Charlotte Salisbury, who was able to publish, to rave reviews, her unexpurgated diaries of her China experience.[49] Charlotte Salisbury, it is important to note, is the wife of Harrison. In his introduction to his wife's book, the *New York Times* correspondent informs the literary public that they will want to read *China Diary* because it is illuminated by the pure touch of woman's inspiration, which "is as sensitive as a dragonfly's wing and as penetrating as a laser beam."[50]

Laserlike, the distaff Salisbury penetrates to the heart of her problem on the second page of her book when she asks, "Will we react as most of the other visitors have, with enthusiasm and admiration for this country that in twenty short years has transformed itself, its government, society, and some say, even its people, in a complete rebirth?" The perceptive reader may well wonder how it would be possible to react with other than enthusiasm and admiration for any country which, in the span of two short decades, had "transformed itself, its government, society, and some say, even its people, in a complete rebirth."[51]

And indeed, within minutes of crossing into China from Hong Kong, Salisbury alighted upon proof-positive of socialism's superiority in the ladies' room in the waiting room for foreigners at the Shenzhen station. Unlike the ladies' room in the Hong Kong station, which was "smelly and disgusting," here she was delighted to find "a regular toilet in an airy room, clean and spotless." Her sensitivity took wing, and she soared to the conclusion that "there can be no doubt about the better system."[52]

Whether the Chinese have created a New Maoist Man is an issue Salisbury explores more sedately. She defers a definitive answer until Day Three but drops unmistakable hints along the way, reassuring the reader that she is not questioning this important revolutionary achievement. On Day One, after emerging from the ladies' room, she exclaims that "never have I seen such polite, civilized people, friendly and so attractive." A little later she reports that her fellow travelers are of like mind: "They feel that the Chinese really have created a new man, a man who knows what he wants and is peaceful and kind." And before she goes to bed that night, she reflects that, "there is a dignity about each person that I have seen, a self-respect that is very evident."[53]

The remaining pages of her diary she devotes to descriptions of her round of visits to model schools, factories, clinics, communes, and so on. Each visit provides yet another opportunity for her to engage in wild flights of fancy on the successes of the revolution.

After seeing a propaganda film on reforestation, for instance, she concluded that "it seems as if China had no trees, was one big desert before Liberation." After visiting a university, she implies that China is morally superior to the United States, where "the rich get richer and the poor get poorer as they increase in number, while here in China, no one is rich. And while many are poor by our standards, they have work, food, shelter and care, every one of them." After visiting the Red Flag Canal, another monument to the Revolution, she writes that "to be a native here now, compared to life under the feudal landlords before Liberation, and before the dams and canals, must be heaven—no matter how dirty, dusty and poor everything may look to me."[54]

As the trip goes on, some of the incongruities of China's socialist system begin to impinge ever so slightly on her consciousness. Not being a reflective person, however, Salisbury quickly dismisses incidents that might cause doubt and uncertainty about Mao's successes in others. On one occasion, she discussed "the art and music of today's China" over dinner with some "Chinese friends." These good fellows, party apparatchiks all, not surprisingly averred that all Chinese artists follow Mao's dictum and serve the people—writing, composing, and producing nothing that is not relevant to the worker, the peasant, and the soldier. They made a believer out of their listener, though she is bewildered by the absence of artists and writers. "I wonder where the artists and writers are," Salisbury writes. "We have still to meet one."[55]

Her request to travel to Tibet, Inner Mongolia, and Xinjiang is turned down by her hosts because, they tell her, "The Cultural Revolution is still going on in these places." Piqued by this rebuff, she writes that "it is interesting that this 'new man,' peaceful and full of good will, is a product of such upheaval." But she offers no insights on this contradiction and merely concludes that "I guess that is what revolution means."[56]

A flicker of awareness that all may not be as it seems follows an evening with John Fraser, a Canadian diplomat who tells her of the isolation in which all resident foreigners are kept, and of the often violent suppression of dissent prescribed by the "leader whose heart is in the right place." "There must be another way to create a decent, healthy, secure society without stifling what we cherish as our most precious possession—freedom of speech and choice," Salisbury writes, coming perilously close to discovering the distinction between democracy and tyranny. At the last moment she draws back, however, extricating herself from her conundrum by turning the question around so that it points like a dagger at her own heart. "But when I think of the wretchedness of some people in my country," she remarks sadly, "why should I be free to choose and talk when so many others have no real freedom of anything?"[57]

EXPORTING MAOISM

Many of the visitors returned with a missionary zeal to bring their message and newfound vision to the American people and to help them appreciate the greatness and worth of Chinese communism. Like an earlier generation of Sinophiles, they were converted to Beijing's cause as much by their affection for the Chinese as by the ideals and programs of the Communists.

In the view of liberation theologians and others, Third World countries in particular could profit by slipstreaming in China's wake. Al Imfeld, in his *China as a Model of Development*, held up Mao's China as the revolution incarnate, the solution to capitalist exploitation, international dependency, and rural poverty.[58] Gustavo Gutierrez regarded the Cultural Revolution as the answer to the prayers of the rural poor for economic salvation.[59] Even Pope Paul VI described Maoist doctrine as "a moral socialism of thought and conduct," and said that China "looks toward the mystique of disinterested work for others, to inspiration to justice, to exaltation of a simple and frugal life, to rehabilitation of the rural masses, and to a mixing of social classes." Professor Gurley, from whose book this quote comes, offers the observation that "while this is not a completely accurate account of Mao's goals, it does very nicely catch the spirit of Maoism."[60]

Within the United States the New Maoist Man, already a considerable figure in the minds of American intellectuals, had achieved truly mythic dimensions. There was an aspect of this chimera for everyone. Those to the left of center extolled his egalitarian virtues in the hope that these would soon be replicated in a New American Man who would, in Salisbury's unforgettable formula, make the oceans boil and the continents shake. Containment theorists hailed the New Maoist Man's militancy, now that his ideological wrath had been at least partly redirected toward the Soviet Union. And all those eager for a negotiated peace in Vietnam saw in him a force for accommodation in that conflict. After the dark age of hostility through which he had passed, the New Chinese Man and the new society he had helped to create entered upon an enchanted existence as the answer to many of America's societal and foreign policy needs.

In the early seventies, at the high tide of the China fervor, a group of American academics (of whom concerned scholars were a minority) held a major symposium to study the Chinese experience in national development in terms of its usefulness to the United States. As the United States had generously assisted in the recovery of war-torn Europe through the Marshall plan, perhaps the People's Republic—acting through its local interpreters—would graciously consent to help solve the terrible problems facing the United States.

In the introductory essay, "On Learning from China," Michel Oksenberg opens with a "dreary list of domestic problems: racism, bureaucratism, urban decay, pollution of the environment, depletion of natural resources, inflation and unemployment, inadequate medical care for the poor, the increasing use of narcotics, and the accompanying rise in crime. . . . [I]s America doomed to decay until radical, even revolutionary, change fundamentally alters the institutions and values?" he asks. Fortunately for us, there is an alternative: We can borrow ideas and solutions from "peoples in many lands [who] appear more relaxed, secure, and foresighted."[61]

"Of all the nations from which we might borrow," Oksenberg continues, "one is particularly intriguing—China. After all, that nation faced a seemingly insurmountable set of problems twenty-three years ago: civil war, hyperinflation, foreign domination, periodic famine, illiteracy, and superstition. Within a generation, most of these obstacles to development have been removed. The nation appears to have regenerated itself and to be making economic and social progress. Moreover, the Chinese have undertaken bold experiments in a number of areas that are of direct concern to us, such as bureaucratic practice [e.g., the arrest of officials by young thugs], education [closing the universities], the patterns of urbanization [keeping the peasants out of the cities], penology [labor reeducation camps], public health [barefoot doctors], factory management [worker committees], and civil-military relations [armed occupation of the cities]. . . . Beyond this, the Chinese Revolution is an optimistic statement about the capacity of man to solve his problems. Perhaps, given the mood of pessimism in the United States, the nation needs such inspiration. The Chinese dedication to building a more decent, just society might also spur us."[62]

This symposium must surely stand as the high-water mark reached by the new secular religion of Maoism as it flooded through the halls of academe. And it cannot be dismissed as an esoteric polemic against the United States by a small coterie of alienated academics. Not only were they themselves *perfectly serious*, they were accepted as such by the majority of their fellow China-watchers. Fairbank spoke for many of his colleagues when he argued that America could learn much from the Cultural Revolution: "Americans may find in China's collective life today an ingredient of personal moral concern for one's neighbor that has a lesson for us all." This, he added admiringly, was the result of "a far-reaching moral crusade to change the very human Chinese personality in the direction of self-sacrifice and serving others."[63]

HOOK, LINE, AND SINKER

Bankrolled by a motley alliance of academics, leftists, and corrrespondents, Nixon had placed his bet on the People's Republic—and won. A Gallup Poll taken a few days after his return from Beijing revealed that the public now had a "far more favorable image" of the Chinese Communists than it had in 1966. Favorable terms like "hard-working," "practical," "intelligent," "artistic," and "progressive" were selected over negative terms by more than 3 to 1. American perceptions of China had once again flipflopped. The once ignorant and antlike masses had taken upon themselves the endearing characteristics of Pearl Buck's hardworking and practical peasants. The "sly" and "treacherous" Zhou Enlai and the "warlike" Mao Zedong stood gloriously revealed as intelligent, artistic, and progressive mandarins in the Marco Polo mold.[64]

In the end, Americans had grown so euphoric over the New China that even the Chinese officials responsible for crafting these illusions in the first place were shaking their heads over American credulity. Zhou Enlai, who had devoted much of his life to convincing visiting foreigners of the virtues of the Chinese revolution, somersaulted in July 1971 and began to mention its vices. When American enthusiasts gushed over China's progress, he would observe that China was still a poor, weak country. Praise of the Cultural Revolution elicited a thoughtful remark on the serious economic losses caused by the unrest. When a group of Concerned Asian Scholars sought to extol China's many achievements, Zhou cut them short by saying that much remained to be accomplished.[65] Yet his listeners usually dismissed his demurrals as mere modesty.

Zhou Enlai and other officials were driven to the extreme of publicly criticizing the U.S. media for its excessively upbeat view of their country. Zhou complained to a group of American scholars that the coverage of Nixon's visit on American television was biased because the camera crews "only took pictures of beautiful things" and ignored less attractive sights. The print media was guilty of similar distortions, according to Qiao Guanhua, the deputy foreign minister. "American journalists are not critical enough," Qiao objected. "They used to write that everything in China was wrong. Now they write that everything in China is right."[66] This must surely rank as one of the wonders of the global village: Beijing's master image-makers giving lessons in balance and objectivity to American journalists.

Initially, Zhou, Qiao and others must have been pleased when images of the New China that they had planted took such sturdy root in the soil of American ignorance, spreading runners into academic, government, and media circles, ultimately coming to flourish in the public at large. But the fruit it produced—an infatuation with the Cultural Revolution—must have seemed to them a mockery. No one knew better than they the malaise, the emptiness, and the fear that gripped their country. However lush and delicious radical Maoism appeared to outsiders, they understood that it was all bitter rind and no pulp.

8

The Age of Disillusionment

꽈꽈꽈

When China entered its enchanted phase in the early seventies, it became unfashionable and injudicious, at least for China-watchers, to point out that the glistening armor of the tall Maoist prince concealed a squat toad of repression. In the great proletarian mythology through which so many Americans rediscovered China after 1971, there was little tolerance for the notion that the country's leaders might be less principled than power hungry, or that the masses might be less revolutionary than running scared. The party's reputation for ruthlessness, acquired during the political campaigns of the fifties and sixties, was allowed to expire unremarked. Even the voices of the Right, ever wary of Communists and their machinations, were largely muted for a time. The few scholars who took aim at the fuzzy, romantic images that then passed for fact were themselves, like Prometheus, raked by the claws of China's outraged defenders.

Before 1960 the husband-and-wife research team of Ivan and Miriam London dedicated themselves to the study of the USSR. They were Sovietologists skilled at decoding the country that Churchill had once called "a riddle wrapped in a mystery inside an enigma." With Khrushchev's denunciation of Stalin's crimes at the Twentieth Party Congress and the relative openness that characterized the early years of his rule, it seemed that the riddle was unwrapping itself. Thinking that it was only a matter of time before most of the remaining barriers to understanding the Soviet Union would come down, the Londons felt drawn to a new challenge, the People's Republic of China. They spent several years in careful preparation for field work, sifting through published materials in Sinology. Then in 1963 they traveled from their academic base at Brooklyn College to first Taiwan and then Hong Kong to interview recent refugees from the mainland. It was a journey they would repeat twelve times in as many years.[1]

Coming to the study of China outside of normal Sinological channels, with almost no contacts in the field, the Londons had few preconceived ideas about what they would find. They applied methods and insights developed from their work during the 1950s on Soviet society, including an intensive, open-ended interviewing technique. Informants were allowed, indeed encouraged, to recount their lives in detail, and to elaborate on key events and happenings. In short, they relied on the Chinese themselves, not their Sinological colleagues, for their understanding of life in the PRC. It is a testament to the meticulousness of their research and their caution in drawing conclusions that they spent years immersing themselves in a growing volume of interview data before publishing their results. Their first article did not appear until 1970.

The former Red Guards, peasants, and workers that the Londons interviewed did not, as they put it, "converse in *People's Daily* platitudes." Former Red Guard Ken Ling recounted the Cultural Revolution as an endlessly vicious period of bullying and betrayal. A member of the landlord class matter-of-factly told the Londons how he was forced to kneel each day before a photograph of Chairman Mao and confess that "I have done so many bad things that I have lost human semblance and turned into a heap of dog dung." A poor peasant from Guangdong recalled how his mother was terrorized into suicide by the local village security officer. And informants from all parts of China returned again and again to the topic of malnutrition and famine. The pall of hunger still hung over the villages.[2]

Like the Red Guards, peasants, and workers they interviewed, the Londons recounted all this in a colorful, forceful prose that was faithful to the existential truth of life in the People's Republic.[3] For this reason alone their writing was disconcerting to those academics who prefer to keep reality at arm's length. Books and articles such as *The Revenge of Heaven* and "The Making of a Red Guard," with their grisly tales of murder, suicide, and rape, were painfully difficult for heads accustomed to soaring effortlessly through an empyrean realm of abstract ideals and bloodless generalizations. The reason that other researchers encountered less violence in their interviews with former Red Guards may well be that they subtly discouraged their informants from dilating on the macabre. The Londons let their informants tell their own stories.

To those infatuated with the New China, the rapidly accumulating London *oeuvre* was more than just a fly in the Maoist ointment. It was a solvent that threatened to dissolve the shimmering image of the People's Republic as an egalitarian, just, and unselfish society. Not that the Londons intended to do more than convey accurately the insider's experience of Chinese reality, with the rich nuances and telling detail usually filtered out by conventional academic treatments. But they soon found themselves colliding head-on with fantasy. How could their informants' tales of official corruption or concupiscence be squared with the Maoist dictum, "Serve the People?" Or stories peopled in part with thieves, pickpockets, prostitutes, and other holdovers from the bad old days be reconciled with Maoist claims to societal perfection? The truth embodied in such particulars was that vice and virtue continued their uneasy coexistence in China and that vice might well be gaining the upper hand.

By 1976 the Londons felt themselves ready to address the central myth of Revolutionary China, the widely accepted premise that "the famine-ravaged land of the past is gone. After centuries of recurrent misery the problem of feeding the myriad descendants of the Middle Kingdom—at whatever cost—has been solved." In a three-part series published in *Worldview,* they sharply challenged beliefs that China was producing more than enough food for its population, that food was distributed equitably to all—especially to areas suffering from flood or drought—and that beggars no longer existed.[4]

To say that the Londons were bucking the tide would be an understatement. They were trying to make headway against a raging torrent of contrary views. George Bush, then-director of the CIA, expressed "surprise" at reports of malnutrition, suggesting instead that Beijing was providing "a basic level of nutrition for the entire population."[5] Typical of the experts' enthusiastic depictions of China's agricultural prowess was Leo Orleans's *The Role of Science and Technology in China's Population/Food Balance.*[6] Orleans argued that there were lessons for the developing world in China's creation of new fields through *corvée* labor, excellent pest control, and a "diversified" national diet. Indeed, he offered the truly novel observation that China's agricultural productivity had been systematically underestimated by Western experts because they focused exclusively on grain production, neglecting the many other foods that the Chinese had incorporated into their diet. He suggested that such delicacies as roots, grasses, berries, insects, snakes, birds, seaweed, sea urchins, snails, birds' nests, and camels' humps were not inconsequential sources of nutrition.

Now no one would deny that the Chinese have an enormous and inventive cuisine, the result of periodic famines that have punctuated China's long history to the present day. Or that when they face starvation, they are more than capable of wresting from nature every possible bite of provender. But in normal times there are many "foods" that they prefer not to consume—insects and grasses, for instance. In retrospect, it seems incredible that anyone would seriously suggest counting famine foods as part of China's "agricultural productivity." Yet Orleans's proposal did not seem in the least outrageous to his colleagues, many of whom were gripped by the same enthusiasm whenever the question of China's food situation was raised.[7]

There was no way to reconcile the bright and colorful image of China prevailing in academe with the Londons' darkly shaded monochrome. Either China was "almost unique in Asia as a land free of widespread hunger, malnutrition, and famine" or it was not.[8] Either China had "largely solved the food distribution problem" or it had not.[9] Either China had "no beggars [to be] seen" or it did.[10] The Londons understood better than anyone how far out of step they were with the discipline. "The irreconcilability of these images is astonishing," they wrote at the time. Still, they were surprised by the angry and irrational reaction of some of their colleagues to their reports. "It is now possible for scholars to write realistically about the Soviet Union without arousing the sort of passion that true believers vent on infidels," the Londons wrote, more in sorrow than anger. "Eventually the same will be true of the China field."[11]

Their prediction would be borne out perhaps sooner than they had imagined. With Chairman Mao's death at the end of 1976 and the arrest of his wife, Jiang Qing, and her closest associates, the climate of opinion in the United States began once again to shift. It would be several years before the Beijing regime admitted that up to 200 million peasants were living in semistarvation and that the country-side continued to be afflicted, as it had been for centuries, by periodic provincial famines—admissions that confirmed the Londons' findings. But even by early 1977 the China-watchers were beginning to offer a respectful hearing to more critical views.

CHINESE SHADOWS

The first book to benefit from the new mood that followed Mao's passing was written by a Belgian art historian named Pierre Ryckmans. He had observed the early stages of the Cultural Revolution from the vantage point of Hong Kong. Despite his own commitment to socialism, he found little to admire in the anarchy that resulted in China, or in Mao's machinations. Later, as the cultural attaché of the Belgian Embassy in 1972, he went to China to survey firsthand the damage that had been wrought on the Chinese people and on their cultural heritage. Writing under the pseudonym Simon Leys, he had the good fortune to have his book *Chinese Shadows*, originally published in French as *Ombres Chinoises* (1974), appear in English translation in 1977.[12] The time was ripe for Maoism to be demystified.

Cracks had started to appear in the Maoist facade of harmony and stability the year before. Zhou Enlai died early in April 1976, and the residents of Beijing seized the occasion to protest Maoist despotism. More than a hundred thousand people gathered on Tiananmen Square on 5 April. That night, in a bloody preview of the Tiananmen massacre of 1989, paramilitary troops were ordered to clear the square. Blame for the demonstration was placed on Deng Xiaoping, who was immediately sent into internal exile. The *New York Times* was initially bewildered by this breach of China's surface calm, editorializing that "China had seemed to be so orderly, so completely controlled in recent years."[13] Later that year the newspaper began running a series of highly critical dispatches by Ross Munro, the Beijing correspondent for the Toronto *Globe and Mail*.

On 26 July 1976, for example, under the title "Hints of Unease and Indiscipline are Discerned in China" the *Times'* readers learned from Munro that "last year one listened skeptically when someone said that there were still beggars in China. This year one sees a couple of beggars who are bold enough to operate even when foreigners are around."[14] Subsequent articles written by Munro and carried by the *Times* mentioned labor camps and other deficiencies in human rights in China, and led to his expulsion.

Following Mao's death on 9 September the cracks rapidly widened into chasms. Both Jiang Qing and Hua Guofeng, who had become premier following Zhou Enlai's death, claimed to have been anointed by Mao to continue the revolution. Jiang Qing quoted a poem that she said Mao had written to her during his final days: "You have been wronged. I have tried to reach the peak of revolution but I was not successful. But you could reach the top." Hua Guofeng countered with a scrap of paper on which Mao had written, "With you in charge, I am at ease." Hua, who was also the commander of Beijing's security forces, won the argument by having "the Empress" and her closest associates arrested on 6 October.[15] With the imprisonment of the Gang of Four, as they were thereafter known, the intense factional fighting surrounding the dying dictator was revealed to the world.

By early 1977 angry crowds of Beijing residents were marching through the streets carrying posters that read "Cut Jiang Qing into Ten Thousand Pieces" and "Boil the Gang in Oil." Incredible stories of Jiang Qing's addiction to pornographic films, chauffered limousines, and handsome young athletes circulated throughout the country—and rocked China's overseas' admirers. The ravages of the Cultural Revolution—the millions of deaths, murders and suicides, the disintegration of the educational system, the ruination of China's traditional culture—were blamed on the Gang of Four. In these denunciations the Chinese were encouraged, even directed, by their new ruler. But the uninhibited glee with which ordinary people celebrated the downfall of "the Empress" made it clear to foreign observers that this was more than just another propaganda compaign. No one had told the Chinese to hold up five fingers when they discussed the outrages of the "Gang of Four" and thus point a finger at the late Chairman Mao.

A fog of unresolved contradictions had descended upon previously sharp and fixed images of Mao's China, blurring and shifting them into unrecognizable shapes. There was, China's many admirers promptly discovered, no way to cut through this fog without damaging those enveloped images. If the attacks on Jiang Qing and her followers were true, then the radical egalitarianism of the Cultural Revolution had been less than universally welcomed—or practiced. On the other hand, if the attacks on Mao's wife were false, then the flesh-and-blood China still fell short of the limpid vision that had inspired them. For they had long believed that China's top leaders were, in John K. Fairbank's phrase, "honest revolutionaries," who conducted their policy debates on a higher and more principled plane than did grasping and greedy democratic politicians. Those who had lived for and by such images of revolutionary purity, installing them as sacred icons in a central sanctuary of their minds, resisted as long as they could the encroachments of reality. Two weeks after the arrest of the Gang of Four, for instance, Fairbank was still arguing that "Ford vs. Carter is a more naked power struggle than anything going on in Beijing. . . . By calling the conflict between Beijing policy factions a 'power struggle,' we . . . cut down dedicated revolutionaries and personal aggrandizement to the size of ambitious individualists of a type we know well—Zhang Chunqiao [one of the Gang of Four], for instance, is implied to be no more than John Connally with chopsticks."[16] The forcible uprooting of such revolutionary icons in the late seventies was a painfully disorienting experience for Western Maoists.

Much of what Leys had to say about China was not, strictly speaking, news. Even those China-watchers who had succumbed to the euphoria of the early 1970s were beginning to come down to earth. And there were others, especially those who paid careful attention to detail, who had always been partly immune to the romanticism that had crept into the broad ethnographic descriptions or sweeping historical comparisons of some scholars. John Kenneth Galbraith, writing out of his specialty of Western economics, might claim that "clearly there is very little difference between rich and poor."[17] But the careful research of sociologist Martin King Whyte of the University of Michigan, published in 1975, revealed a very different picture: "Officials and employees in the state bureaucracy were ranked from level 1 (top national leaders) to level 30 . . . and the differential between the highest and lowest levels was about 28:1. . . . In regard to income differentials, then, one can say that the existing situation is quite different from the impression that the egalitarian rhetoric of the Cultural Revolution or the uniformity of dress of the population may convey."[18] Liberation theologians like Al Imfeld might hail China as a model of development for Third World countries, but Professor Donald Zagoria pointed out in 1975 that there is less to Mao's economic accomplishments than meets the eye. "According to the latest World Bank figures," Zagoria wrote, "the per capita growth rate for China [2.9 percent for the period 1952–1971] is less than the average growth rate in Central and South America from 1960–1970, which was 4.3 percent per year, and it is less that the *average* growth rate in the same period for all Asian and Middle Eastern countries excluding Japan, i.e., 4.2 percent."[19]

It is one thing to publish such views cautiously inside an academic journal of limited circulation and quite another to write a tone poem of two hundred–odd pages for the public at large. Although a scholar, Leys chose not to couch his indictment of the regime in dry, academic jargon. His book *Chinese Shadows* is a frontal assault on the New China as a high-minded, egalitarian, and purposeful society. Leys is not content merely to infiltrate this once glorious castle, with its claims to societal perfection rising like lofty towers from behind impregnable walls of isolation. He sets about dismantling the regime's pretensions one by one, leaving a barren and rocky landscape where once an imposing structure had stood. This despoliation is accomplished almost gleefully, with a wit that is brilliant, lively, and devastatingly thorough. What Leys later wrote about Solzhenitsyn applies equally well to his own work: "Solzhenitsyn's unique contribution lies in the volume and precision of his catalogue of atrocities—but basically *he revealed nothing new*."[20]

Leys's book was widely applauded, at least outside the academic community, for taking the reader behind the shadowplay that had misled so many earlier visitors. Where most Westerners were bedazzled by surface manifestations of equality, he pointed out that:

The Cultural Revolution has hypocritically masked some of the most obvious forms of class divisions, without changing their substance. In

168

trains, for instance, first, second, and third classes have disappeared *in name*, but now you have "sitting hard" (ying tso), "sleeping hard" (ying wo), and "sleeping soft" (juan wo), which are exactly the same classes as before and with the fares, as before, ranging from single to triple prices. External insignia have nearly completely disappeared in the army; they have been replaced by a loose jacket with four pockets for officers, two pockets for privates. . . . In cities one can still distinguish between four-pocket men in jeeps, four-pocket men in black limousines with curtains, and four-pocket men who have black limousines with curtains and a jeep in front.[21]

It was not just the happy timing of its appearance that garnered for Leys the publication of lengthy excerpts from his book in the *New York Review of Books,* or largely positive reviews in every major paper in the United States. *Chinese Shadows* is a gem of a book, alternately lively, amusing, and poignant, that ranks as one of the most moving jeremiads of this century. Attracted to the study of China by her art, history, and architecture, Leys was a cultural connoisseur. Like that of Candide, his shock when confronted with the wholesale destruction of that country's cultural legacy was both real and apparent. For pages at a time his account becomes a lament as he describes how temples, monasteries, and city walls that had survived centuries of turbulent Chinese history were destroyed in a few days by bands of young philistines, or by the Beijing regime itself:

"The panic that seized me when I could not find the [Beijing city] gates is not easy to describe. Everyone who has known them must naively believe, as I did, that they were immortal, and they will understand my state of mind that day in May 1972, as I rushed breathlessly from Zhongwen men . . . all the way to Xizhi men, finding only, in place of each gate, the dull flatness of an abnormally wide and empty boulevard. For a while, I tried to tell myself that I had gotten lost. . . . This could only be an absurd nightmare. . . . Finally, at Xizhi men, dead-beat after rushing around madly for a whole afternoon, I could not deny the evidence: this obscene stump among the rubble, which the workmen were beating down with their picks, this was all that remained of Beijing's last gate."[22]

In the course of surveying the ruins of China's traditional culture, he dispatched along the way countless numbers of Maoist fictions, often with a single well-aimed blow:

To those like Claire Sterling, who wrote in the *Washington Post* that "it may come as a shock to some of us in the West to learn that Mao Zedong takes better care of the environment than we do. . . . Unlike the opulent West, China does not abound in the more profligate kinds of waste: plastic containers, tin cans, old cars and castoff refrigerators," Leys is caustic.[23] Celebrating the absence of pollution, waste, and traffic problems in China, he pointed out, was like "prais[ing] an amputee because his feet aren't dirty."[24]

To those who thought that the "people" (as in "People's Republic of China") was more than just a convenient fiction, Leys recounts an anecdote: "A Western country was planning a big industrial exhibit in Beijing. The Maoist authorities were most cooperative. They asked the organizer, 'How many visitors would you like to have?'

" 'Eh?' asked the other, somewhat taken aback by the bluntness of the question.

" 'Twenty thousand? Forty thousand? Sixty thousand visitors?'

" 'We-ell, I think, I dunno, but sixty thousand would be nice.'

"His exhibit had precisely sixty thousand visitors."[25]

To those like Orville Schell who took the Maoist injunction "Learn from Dazhai!" seriously enough to spend three weeks working at "the most renowned work brigade in China," Leys recounts his own visit: "The village headman . . . came in with his head wrapped in a carefully knotted towel, which in the fields under a glaring sun would be useful for wiping the sweat away but at an official gathering or other social occasions becomes something like the feathered headdress of an Apache chief selling souvenirs to tourists. . . . The lodging house at Dazhai had subtle rustic touches: international capitalists and other tourists who 'do' China are like Marie Antoinette playing at being a shepherdess; the meals are no less delicious or less abundant than in the Beijing, Guangzhou or Shanghai palaces for foreigners, but here they are touched with a well-studied primitivism, a shrewd naivete. In the usual vast array of dishes, some dissonant notes are skillfully struck—a dozen hardboiled eggs on a tin plate here, a bowl of gruel there—and added to the usual choice of wines, beers, soft drinks and alcohol is a fearful local spirit. The gourmet brave enough to taste it is suddenly drenched in sweat, giving him the virile and exalting sense that he is somehow communing with the hard task of building socialism."[26]

To Ross Terrill, "who visited China on one of those standard six-week tours . . . [and] wrote a book of a fairly impressive size, which he had the guts to subtitle *The Real China*," Leys wryly suggests that his own *Chinese Shadows* "could be entitled *The Unreal China*. Unreal in two senses: first, because it deals in part with stage settings artificially created in China for the use of foreign visitors, second, because like most other books on the People's Republic it focuses not on the real life of real people (to which, alas! we have no access) but on the puppet theater of the Maoist gerontocrats, those wretched lead-and-cardboard bureaucrats who are mistaken for China's driving forces when they merely weigh on it as its fetters."[27]

Only the material pretensions of the PRC escaped Leys's wrecking ball. "We must acknowledge the considerable material improvements in many areas of Chinese life since 1948," he wrote in the preface to *Chinese Shadows*—not that this made him tolerant of Maoist tyranny. Leys reserved real rancor for those who downplayed the crimes of Mao as unfortunate accidents of an otherwise commendable movement. "Yet I feel that however considerable the achievements of the present regime," he remarked, "we should not forget, if we have any respect for the Chinese and their culture, what price the people have paid for those accomplishments. . . . [I]t is a fantastic imposture to present the regime as socialist and revolutionary when in fact it is essentially totalitarian and feudal-bureaucratic."[28]

The American public, under the sway of experts on the Chinese economy who found that Maoism had solved the food problem and guaranteed everyone subsistence, held a roughly similar view. The Chinese had made a difficult tradeoff between bread and freedom. Bread was now more abundant and more equitably shared. Freedom was a scarce commodity, not available to those the regime considered its enemies. They did not subscribe, as did China's admirers, to the belief that this state of affairs was either historically inevitable or transient. At the same time, it seemed reasonable to many that Chinese peasants, who for centuries had lived in fear of famine, might choose freedom from hunger over the freedom to starve. Those like

William Safire of the *New York Times* who suggested that the cost in terms of human freedom had been too high were brought up short by Chinese officials. "We were free before 1948," one told Safire with heavy sarcasm, "free to starve, and free to be jailed and killed by the Kuomintang."[29] It was an argument that was hard for outsiders to refute.

James Michener, an amalgam of tourist and correspondent, best expressed the ambivalence with which Americans in general, as opposed to China-watchers in particular, regarded China in the early and mid-seventies. "As I prepared to leave China, I was filled with conflicting sentiments. I had learned much. Unless I had gone there, I would not have understood, for example, that China is a young nation run by old men. If one judges from the extreme violence of the Cultural Revolution, China should anticipate trouble when Mao and Zhou depart. On the other hand, I find no reason to think that the Chinese people are now dissatisfied. Things are better than before Mao took over; there is food; there is an orderly state. But I cannot dispel my lasting impression of contemporary China as a dreadfully dull place, cowed by dictatorship and obsessed by puritanism. . . . The job of China today is to find a way to retain order while permitting some kind of liberty."[30]

A Gallup Poll in September 1976 revealed deep differences among Americans concerning China—divisions that at one level reflected the relative importance the interviewees assigned to Michener's question of order versus liberty, and that at another level reflected the paradigms themselves. Asked to rate several nations on a scale of +5 to −5, the responses for "Communist China" were widely scattered:

Plus 5	1%
Plus 4	2
Plus 3	4
Plus 2	4
Plus 1	9
Minus 1	11
Minus 2	7
Minus 3	10
Minus 4	9

Minus 5	36
Don't Know	7

A substantial majority of those interviewed, 73 percent, on the whole viewed China negatively, presumably because they held the blessings of liberty to be more important than the benefits of order. Of these, nearly half thought that there was nothing good to be said on Communist China's behalf, a response that may be taken as a crude definition of the totalitarian paradigm. Less than one in five held positive opinions of China, presumably because they believed that China's new order, with its equitable provision of food to all, counted for more than liberty. The "revolutionary socialist China" and the "modernizing Communist China" paradigms were clearly less successful among the public at large than they were in their intellectual and academic strongholds.[31]

It is one thing to argue that the Chinese people have paid dearly for improvements in their material well-being, chiefly a guaranteed supply of food, clothing, and shelter. It is quite another to suggest, as the Londons did, that these improvements are mostly illusory. If Leys's book had contended that Marxism had brought only misery to China, *Chinese Shadows* would have been roundly attacked, if not ignored. The central myths of the Chinese Revolution would take many more years to delegitimize.

THE END OF THE AGE OF MIRACLES

During the Cultural Revolution the practice of offering morning and evening devotions to Mao Zedong became a fixture of life in China. With the death of its central figure, China's new secular religion quickly lost its intensity. Many rituals ceased to be observed almost immediately as soon as the artificial prop of the Great Helmsman disappeared from the scene, which was well before the post-Mao leadership began to attack the late Chairman's excesses. As a result, some Maoist rituals were never debunked, either by foreigners or by the Chinese. Acupuncture operations, which one wide-eyed foreigner called "the Miracle of the Thousand Needles," are a case in point.

173

Most of the socialist wonders that China displayed to the world were minted in the standard coin of the Communist realm. Model communes (or state farms) swarming with smiling peasants, steel mills belching black smoke, canals bringing moisture to parched lands—all these could be seen in a dozen countries. But there was one miracle that was unique to China: acupuncture. During the Cultural Revolution it was claimed that the proper application of tiny needles to the human body could cure the deaf, heal the sick, and anesthetize the suffering for major operations.

An acupuncture operation was *de rigueur* for visiting foreigners in the early seventies. It followed a script as precise and calculated as a manual of arms. The patient would already be a human pincushion by the time the foreign guests were ushered in to witness the removal of, say, an ovarian tumor. As the doctors sliced and snipped their way into the patient, a nurse would put a series of questions to her. These questions and her answers would be interpreted for the benefit of the wide-eyed foreigners. No, she was in no pain. No, she really couldn't feel anything except a slight pulling and stretching. Yes, she would like something to eat. This last answer caused a plate of orange slices to be brought out. The sight of the patient calmly swallowing orange slices as her body disgorged a tumor as big as a softball was calculated to make a lasting impression on her stunned (and often queasy) audience.

Leaving to an assistant the task of sewing up, the attending surgeon would turn to his spellbound audience with a flourish as practiced as that of a magician completing a trick. The operation you have just witnessed was made possible by the diligent study and application of Chairman Mao's Thought, he would say, holding the Little Red Book aloft to underline the source of his inspiration. A few questions on acupuncture anesthesia and the show was at an end. The incautious, and there were many, hailed what they had seen as a miracle. Dr. John R. Hogness, president of the Institute of Medicine in the National Academy of Sciences in Washington, was so impressed with this and other Chinese medical techniques that he proposed an exchange program for American doctors to study them.[32] The *New York Times* columnist James Reston, whose acupuncture treatments followed his emergency appendectomy (done using standard anesthesia), let the whole world know how successfully the procedure relieved pain.

What no one remarked upon was the politics behind acupuncture anesthesia and other medical experiments of the time; nor did they mention the extreme measures taken by Chinese doctors to ensure that such demonstrations would be successful.

Acupuncture itself was as old as China. As early as the fifth century B.C., doctors discovered that headaches could be eased by applying pressure to the fleshy area between the thumb and forefinger. Experiments with slivers of stone revealed other points on the human body at which punctures produced a painkilling effect. Slender silver needles had replaced stone slivers by the year A.D. 220, when acupuncture was recognized in a dictionary of the time.

As time passed, its practitioners began making claims for their craft that went far beyond merely easing pain. The earliest surviving treatise on acupuncture, dating between A.D. 265 and 429, lists an elaborate network of 649 puncture points, connected by "meridians." Everything from pneumonia to tumors could be treated, the treatise claimed, simply by stimulating the proper combination of points. A later work published during the Ming Dynasty further expanded the list of afflictions for which the silver needles provided a cure. The acupuncturists had overreached themselves, and an aura of quackery grew up around this ancient practice. Acupuncture was outlawed in 1822 by the Ching Dynasty. Western-trained Chinese doctors looked down on acupuncture as unscientific hodgepodge, similar to such folk remedies as the art of cupping, or moxibustion, the use of ground deer antlers to cure impotency, the imbibing of ginseng as a general restorative, and the thousand and one herbal concoctions contained in the great pharmacopia of traditional Chinese medicine, the "Yellow Emperor's Classic." Still, acupuncture continued to be popular among the peasants, who appreciated its simplicity and economy. Chiang Kai-shek found it necessary in 1929 to remind Chinese doctors to concentrate on Western medicine.

Acupuncture enjoyed a brief revival during the civil war, when Mao Zedong commanded his backwoods Red Army doctors: "Give both Chinese and Western treatment." The needles were first used only for their traditional purpose, to relieve pain. Later, in 1958,

Mao began urging the Western-trained Chinese medical establishment to investigate other claims made on behalf of traditional Chinese medicine. As Stalin had promoted Lysenko and his theory that acquired characteristics could be inherited, so Mao promoted the cause of acupuncture with its claims of wondrous cures. His statements were paid little more than lip service until the onset of the Cultural Revolution, when it became dangerous to appear to take lightly any pronouncement of the Great Helmsman. With Western medicine under attack as a foreign import, hastily designed research programs in acupuncture were mounted at a dozen hospitals and universities.

Most of these experiments went nowhere. The deaf were not made to hear, nor the blind to see. But researchers at the Number One People's Hospital in Shanghai, a metropolis that was a center of the Cultural Revolution, found that in certain patients the painkilling effect of acupuncture was powerful enough to allow major surgery to be performed with no other anesthesia. Other hospitals in Shanghai and elsewhere quickly added acupuncturists to their surgical teams, and the practice spread throughout China. Properly administered to a suitably susceptible patient, the needles provided a powerful analgesic, allowing operations from caesarean sections to brain surgery to be performed.

For politically astute hospital administrators and doctors, acupuncture anesthesia could not have arrived at a more propitious moment. It validated the power of indigenous medical practices. It was a practical example of how, following Chairman Mao's early teaching, Chinese and Western medicine could be combined. And best of all, at a time when many of their Western-trained colleagues were being attacked by the Red Guards, or hustled off to May-seventh cadre schools to be reeducated, it enabled them to stage repeated demonstrations of their loyalty to Mao's Thought.

Politically it was the perfect solution. Medically it was fraught with difficulties. But politics was in command. What did it matter that patients had to be carefully screened, in a wasteful, time-consuming procedure, to identify those who obtained sufficient analgesia from the needles to endure surgery? What did it matter that even with these few, acupuncture could only be used for operations that could be performed within the space of an hour or so, since the painkilling effects began to wear off fairly quickly? What did it matter if these operations had to be timed to coincide with the visits of high-ranking party, government, and military officials (or foreigners) to the hospital, rather than to the patients' needs? What did it matter that the patients were never asked whether they wanted this unpredictable form of anesthesia or, for that matter, to be laid open like laboratory animals before groups of gawking onlookers?

As soon as the artificial stimulus of Chairman Mao's personal interest was removed, the political necessity for such demonstrations ceased. It is safe to say that, within a year or two after the death of Mao, no further operations using acupuncture anesthesia were performed. The political winds had shifted and had blown this flimsy political construct down.

A BREACH IN THE WALL

It may not be an exaggeration of Zhou Enlai's central role in fashioning the PRC's revolutionary socialist image to date the beginning of its decay from his death in 1976. Not only did his death spark a massive popular riot that was widely reported outside of China, but his replacements were far less adroit in the art of barbarian management. Although Zhang Chunqiao may have been more than a John Connally with chopsticks, he and Hua Guofeng were poor seconds for Zhou. Left in the hands of those less skilled in the Chinese code of courtesy, Chinese manners became less charming, Chinese amenities less attractive, and visits to Beijing less pleasantly memorable. Following Zhou's death even Henry Kissinger was heard to ruefully remark that China had changed.

Following the arrest of the Gang of Four, several circumstances combined to encourage more accurate reporting. Visas became easier to obtain, more cities were opened to foreigners, and conversations with ordinary Chinese became possible. Government officials now seemed to delight in unmasking past unpleasantness, at least that which could be blamed on the Gang of Four.

During the early seventies, one had to be a well-known journalist, a sympathetic Sinologist, or a member of a radical organization to travel to China. This process of preselection, in conjunction with the desire of the Chosen for a return visit, virtually guaranteed a preponderance of favorable notices. Journalists wary of "breaking their cooking pots and sinking their ships," as the Chinese say, carefully refrained from offending the authorities in their dispatches. It was this self-censorship that Edward Luttwak was referring to in 1976 when he remarked, "[I]t is only the rare newspaperman who makes his own prior decision that he will seek no second visa who can be counted upon to serve us, and not the Chinese."[33]

This was doubly true of the handful of foreign correspondents who were already in Beijing, who had the example of John Burns, Ross Munro, and others before them. Nevertheless, it is customary for correspondents to dismiss the suggestion that they sometimes engage in self-censorship as a vicious slur on their professional integrity. Although they will sometimes privately admit to various political pressures bearing upon their work, they are sworn by an unwritten code of the journalistic profession to public silence on this point. Only occasionally, and under extreme duress, does a correspondent breach this code. In 1972 John Burns, then of the *Toronto Globe and Mail,* had tried to cable a story about a rift between China and North Vietnam, citing as evidence a secret, fractious meeting between Zhou Enlai and Pham Van Dong. It was intercepted by the Foreign Ministry, which formally accused Burns of abusing the friendship of the Chinese people and seeking to sow discord between them and the Vietnamese people. They demanded that he withdraw the cable. Burns agreed—and candidly admitted that he feared the *Globe and Mail* might lose its Beijing bureau, and he his position there, if his story appeared in print.[34] Although direct confrontations of this kind were rare, similar pressures were felt by all members of the Beijing press corps. It was not the frequency of such incidents but the awareness of their possibility that kept the correspondents writing with one eye to the authorities.

In 1977 the Chinese government began to relax its once stringent visa requirements, even for those not particularly well disposed to the regime. In this new political climate American correspondents based in Hong Kong and Japan found it possible to make regular visits. The threat of being denied access receded until it was a distant cloud on the correspondents' horizon. Though still not permitted to live in Beijing (this would not happen until the normalization of relations in 1979), such repeated forays into China marked the beginning of the end of parachute journalism. By the time correspondents had visited China for the fifth—or the fifteenth—time, they had become inured to the more obvious forms of manipulation. Indeed, the special amenities extended to correspondents and other foreigners—the separate-but-hardly-equal lifestyle that they were both encouraged and expected to enjoy—came to chafe on some. The gilding on the bars could not indefinitely distract them from the fact that these formed a cage.

Beijing's reluctant decision in 1977 to open up China to the tourist trade set off an avalanche of changes. To accommodate hundreds of thousands of wealthy and demanding foreigners, internal controls had to be relaxed, more cities placed on the open list, and dozens of tourist hotels and facilities built and staffed. The Chinese people, once denied any contact with foreigners, were now enlisted in large numbers to serve them. The authorities' efforts to continue some forms of segregation were unsuccessful. The tourists would not stay in Pandora's box; they themselves forced up the lid. One tourist with a Polaroid was a walking demonstration of the superiority of Western science; a group of tourists in full gawking gear—cameras, binoculars, sunglasses, visors—created a resplendent display of leisured opulence.

With the relaxation of political orthodoxy, ordinary Chinese no longer treated foreign visitors like the carriers of some loathsome disease. The same tour guides who once shielded visitors from the harsh realities of Chinese life could now occasionally be heard to criticize their country and its problems. It became possible to have conversations outside of official channels. Unflattering information about China began to trickle out of the country.

Milked by the Western press, this trickle soon grew to a torrent. "Revolutionary socialist China" had become the new orthodoxy, and it was "news" to debunk it. The fundamental dynamic of the news business came into play—the urge to plump the exotic, the unusual, and the exceptional—and there was no resisting it. The press, which had a short time earlier chorused its admiration for Mao's China, now obeyed its collective instincts and piled on in attack. The dog had fallen in the water, as the Chinese say, and it was opportune to beat it.

The sticks were provided by Beijing itself. It was the regime's thrashing of its recent past that gave Western correspondents much of the substance of their reports. Foreign correspondents and others, who for years had subsisted on a spare diet of official pap, now found the *People's Daily* and other official organs a daily feast of publishable information about past failings:

> The Communist Party newspaper [The *People's Daily*] . . . recently reported that of the $4 billion worth of farm machinery stored in China, one-third was unsalable because of low quality."[35]

> The most telling illustration of this failure [of China's] "socialist" agriculture is provided by the *People's Daily* itself which stated recently that 25% of non-cereal agricultural production sold to the state came from family plots which themselves constitute only 5% of all cultivated lands.[36]

> Official in Beijing Concedes 60's Moves Led to Catastrophe: Ye Describes Cultural Revolution as "Appalling."[37]

> China Says Its Rising Juvenile Crime Stems From Cultural Revolution.[38]

> China's meager forest resources have been badly depleted in recent years by indiscriminate and illegal logging. . . . The damage has been so great that some areas have had changes in climate, the Yellow River has become more silted than ever and agricultural output has suffered.[39]

Enterprising correspondents who ventured into the newly opened hinterlands filed reports confirming on the spot the violent excesses of past Maoist movements. Jay Mathews, visiting the isolated Southeast province of Fujian, reported: "The most vivid account of the Cultural Revolution is found in the book *The Revenge of Heaven*, published in 1972. A former Red Guard leader from Xiamen (Amoy) using the pseudonym Ken Ling describes [to Ivan and Miriam London] the persecutions and suicides at his middle school and bloody battles between Red Guard gangs whose principal weapons were machine guns and gang rapes. Teachers and former students from another middle school here, the Number One School in Fuzhou, narrated an almost identical account of persecutions at their school. Two teachers took their own lives and at least two students died in subsequent battles."[40]

The regime's piecemeal disowning of its own past was impossible for Western intellectuals to ignore. China's admirers could scoff at the Londons' report on hunger in China, but not at the well-informed communist Hong Kong monthly *Zheng Ming,* which wrote in May 1979 that "200 million peasants [were] . . . in a state of semi-starvation" during the so-called cultural revolutionary decade (1966–76). They could deride the Londons' reports of beggars, but not Beijing's *Guang Ming Daily,* which disclosed that throughout the same ten-year period, in one county of Henan province, about thirty thousand peasants—or every seventh inhabitant of this county alone—were forced every winter and spring to apply for permits to beg for a living elsewhere.

After years of projecting an image of virtual infallibility, Beijing was admitting that all had not been well in the world of Mao. These disclosures, in their vividness and specificity, had the ring of truth about them. Each injected a little paralyzing jet of poison into the rapidly dwindling ranks of Western Maoists. Their protests that these reports were false or exaggerated grew increasingly feeble. Adam Ulam's explanation of how intellectuals lost faith in the Soviet system following Stalin's death applies equally well to post-Mao China:

> An intellectual often finds a certain morbid fascination in the puritanic and repressive aspects of the Soviet regime and also in its enormous outward self-assurance, which contrasts so saliently with the apologetic, hesitant self-image of the democratic world. When this facade of self-assurance began to collapse, first after the revelations about Stalin in 1956, and then as a consequence of the split in the communist camp, many Western intellectuals began to shed their loyalty to the one-time idol, now certainly more humane than it had been under Stalin.[41]

It was not until the late 1970s that China's "facade of self-assurance" began to crumble, fatally undermined by the post-Mao leadership's attacks on the late Chairman himself. Mao had been "70 percent good, 30 percent bad," Deng Xiaoping was quoted as saying in November 1978, thereby opening a rancorous dispute in the upper ranks of the party on their former leader's merits and demerits. As the leadership conducted its largely secret debate over Mao's personal quotient of good and evil, ordinary Chinese were mulling over the fact that the infallible prophet-liberator of the continuing revolution had been officially pronounced capable of error. While it was a simple matter to dismantle the Maoist personality cult—razing statues, tearing down posters, and withdrawing Mao's works from bookstores— Mao's close identification with the party made it impossible to make a clean break with his past policies. Mao had been the party's principal actor, primary symbol, and undisputed ideological authority for so long that for this organization to bring charges against him was, as one of my Chinese friends tartly put it, "like slapping one's own face."

It was also like slapping the faces of Maoism's many foreign admirers. The process of de-Maoization required that the man long canonized as a "great teacher, great leader, great commander, and great helmsman" be severely criticized by name. Worse still, much that they had held inviolable was brought down with him—the achievements of the regime's three decades, the superiority of the socialist system, and the sacred revolutionary struggle itself. The Central Committee approved in 1982 a 27,000-word document that, though crediting Mao with the Communist victory, also held him responsible for many "practical mistakes" during his forty-one-year reign.

China-watchers like Orville Schell, who believed that Mao's "death could not erase the way in which he had almost become transubstantiated in his own people," must have been bewildered when "his people" abandoned the ideological legacy of Chairman Mao as fast as their thoughts could carry them.[42] Professor Terrill, who had spilled much ink in praise of such Maoist follies as the Great Leap Forward and the Cultural Revolution, must have been equally surprised to read on the front page of the *People's Daily* on the thirtieth anniversary of the People's Republic that Ye Jianying, one of Communist China's top leaders, had declared "the 'Cultural Revolution' forced the country to endure an entire decade of oppression, tyranny, and bloodshed."[43] And it must have confused Professor Oksenberg, who had put Mao Zedong in the same category of historical greats as Thomas Jefferson, Winston Churchill, Charles DeGaulle, and Franklin Roosevelt, to learn that Mao was to be held responsible for the Cultural Revolution, during which the party and the people "suffered the severest setbacks and the heaviest losses."[44] The public cataloging of Mao's failures, and the official correction of his misinformation (including a wholesale rewriting of China's agricultural statistics), was acutely embarrassing for those who had taken the earlier claims of the regime at face value.

To their credit, some China-watchers adopted a Maoist custom that they professed to admire: they wrote and published self-criticisms. Orville Schell, whose *In the People's Republic* ranks as one of the more fawning accounts of the early to mid-seventies, was by 1979 expressing some retrospective doubts about what he had seen on his 1976 visit. He now remembered "a profound sense of discomfort caused by the atmosphere of coldness and distrust which I felt around me. The message was too relentless, too absolutist, and finally too intimidating to win the heart as well as the mind. My predominant memory of the trip, aside from the friendly gentility of the peasantry and the hospitality of the common workers, was the way in which politically involved people were paralyzed, unable to speak their true feelings. . . . One felt constant pressure from the Chinese, as well as from certain American confreres, to toe the line, to prove one's political purity and stop being an ungrateful guest."[45] As to why this "predominant memory" had been so little in evidence in his earlier writing, Schell elaborated elsewhere: "A 'friend of China' felt constrained from disappointing his host by writing any-thing critical or unflattering. . . . All the special treatment and effort extended on one's behalf seemed to require repayment. . . . The 'friends' felt some fear of seeming impolite or ungrateful, or of en-dangering Chinese acquaintances. But one fear above all predomi-nated: the fear that if one uttered or wrote 'incorrect' thoughts one would never again be allowed back. And in one degree or another I think most of us who have written about China did capitulate to this fear. I remember all too well the dread that the Chinese would never let you back in again if, like an errant child, you disappointed them with your writing, if you betrayed their 'friendship' with a critical article or book."[46]

In 1983, in the pages of the *Atlantic Monthly*, Ross Terrill apol-ogized even more directly for his earlier defense of the Beijing regime and its policies. While in 1971 he had written that "in a magnificent way, [the New China] has healed the sick, fed the hungry and given security to the ordinary man," he now saw it differently: "for the billion who live there, as distinct from the foreign tourist, businessman, or journalist, China is first and foremost a repressive regime. The unchanging key to all Beijing's policies is that the nation is ruled by a Leninist dictatorship that intends to remain such."[47]

Many China-watchers, however, did not recognize an obligation to mourn publicly their past mistakes before proceeding to bury them. When, on occasion, these were exhumed by other witnesses, they desperately backed and filled in an effort to provide "context" for what they had written earlier. The political scientist Edward Friedman, an early member of the Committee of Concerned Asian Scholars, was by 1979 publishing articles detailing the excesses of Maoism. He wrote of academics "forced into endless, tortuous, vacuous confessions" and suicides, calling this "Marxist McCarthyism."[48] Only two years before, however, he published an article entitled "The Innovator," which was full of Mao-inspired fatuities like the following:

Mao was almost invariably responding in a uniquely creative and profoundly ethical way to deep political crises.

The Chinese path . . . was so popularly rooted that, virtually the antithesis of the Soviet story, its history was full of vibrant life void of purge and fear and murder.

Mao by the example of his struggle communicates the vigor of hope, the vitality of possibility, the vision of justice.[49]

When Paul Hollander cited the first of these statements in *Political Pilgrims,* as an example of how American intellectuals glorified Mao as a combination renaissance man and philosopher-king, Professor Friedman claimed he had been quoted out of context. He produced, as a character witness, none other than Arthur Schlesinger, who attested on the basis of documents provided by Friedman that he, Friedman, was a "sober and skeptical observer of China Communism."[50] Schlesinger argued that Friedman could not really be held accountable for his earlier observations because (1) he had not visited China at the time, and (2) he now takes a considerably different view of the Maoist era. These are odd pleas for an historian to make. For however painful the realization, concerned Asian scholars must be aware that their earlier infatuations form an important part of the historical record of American perceptions—and misperceptions—of China at the time.

Most interesting perhaps is that small coterie of Sinologists who, after the fashion of Lot's wife, were so mesmerized by their vision of Mao's City of Perfect Justice that their views seem to have crystallized for all time. As late as 1981 Professor Maurice Meisner, long an admirer of the Maoist revolution, could still opine in the pages of the *New York Times* that Deng Xiaoping could not denounce Mao Zedong as "a bloodthirsty tyrant," as Khrushchev had denounced Stalin, because "Mao remains something of a deity among the peasantry."[51] If Professor Meisner had interviewed Chinese villagers, he would have discovered that they, too, regarded Mao as a tyrant. Their hero was the former Head of State Liu Shaoqi, whom Mao disgraced and killed during the Cultural Revolution for his "revisionism." Liu's crime consisted of giving back to the peasants, in the form of private plots, a little of the land that Mao had taken away from them with his communes—an act that helped to end the post–Great Leap Forward famine.

By far the most important holdout, who continued to defend unabashedly the Beijing regime long after the revelation that its past policies had caused enormous suffering, was the Harvard Professor John K. Fairbank. In his 1982 autobiography, *Chinabound*, Fairbank describes himself as a "reverse missionary," and he does indeed fit Cressy's definition of the type: "[A]t home he is constantly changing the attitude of the millions of his constituency . . . bringing to them something of his new breadth of vision, and helping them to a larger appreciation of the greatness and worth of the civilization of the Far East."[52] Fairbank's central vision, of course, was that communism was good for China—a view that he consistently and enthusiastically promoted during his scholarly career.[53]

Even after his own students, including Fox Butterfield of the *New York Times*, began reporting from China on governmental corruption, inefficiency, and oppression, Fairbank continued to give the "New China" every benefit of the doubt. In a review of Butterfield's *Alive in the Bitter Sea,* a book unstintingly critical of the Beijing regime, Fairbank admits that the Chinese Communist party has "brought modernized indoctrination, surveillance and intimidation into every urban family." Lest this be taken as a criticism of the

Chinese human-rights situation, however, he adds that the American family faces a similar problem: The computer has invaded its privacy. Educated Chinese may be attracted to the concept of human rights, he writes, but they "have to put the collective interest ahead of individual rights. As in this country we try to defend ourselves against the computer, we can feel we have something in common with the Chinese."[54]

Most China-watchers were first drawn to the study of China by the romance of the Middle Kingdom, a great civilization of ancient wisdom. Yet there is some truth to the observation of George Kennan, the author of our postwar containment policy, that people who study the Soviet Union end up hating the Soviet Union; people who study China end up hating themselves. Those who were driven to their quest by a feeling of alienation from their own society, or by a contempt for democratic and free-market institutions, found much in Mao's China to reinforce these sentiments.[55]

Today such reverse missionaries, their numbers decimated by defections, cut pathetic figures. Their defense of the Beijing regime's human rights abuses is publicly criticized by members of China's democracy movement.[56] Their obeisances to a failed ideology and failing system are increasingly considered as irrelevant to the real, living China as a dead man's still-growing fingernails are to the state of his health.

9

The Age of Benevolence

[For many Americans] China was already a solved problem of communism; it was "going capitalist" and no longer a threat to the West, but, on the contrary, a useful ally against the Soviet Union.

—Miriam London
"China: The Romance of Realpolitik"

By the time the revelations about Maoist atrocities ended in 1981, reined in by Deng Xiaoping, even the most well-disposed of China-watchers were subdued. The calculated tradeoff between bread and freedom had been more costly than anyone had imagined. The entire ledger, indeed, might be said to be in the red. The communes and state-owned factories had produced not a bounty of food and economic development but famine and lingering backwardness. There had been not a temporary diminution of freedom, but a stark and decades-long oppression.

The tidal wave of disillusionment in the West reached its high-water mark and began to recede, taking with it the battered remnants of the revolutionary socialist and modernizing Communist China paradigms. Only the totalitarian redoubt weathered the flux, firmly anchored in the bedrock of Communist tyranny that was now, more than ever before, exposed to view.

The human mind abhors unstructured reality. Yet the totalitarian paradigm was still unacceptable to most China-watchers. So they set hastily to work, cobbling together a mental construct that bore little similarity to this or any other interpretation of the recent past. Its premises did, however, bear a striking family resemblance to China's newly unveiled blueprint for its future: the Four Modernizations. Once again, Americans found themselves gazing through a Chinese looking glass lovingly ground and polished to perfection by China-watchers—to Beijing's specifications.

Deng Xiaoping, twice purged by Mao Zedong and his fellow radicals, returned to power in 1978 to announce that China was to modernize. The egalitarian social policies of the past were to be cast aside and economics, not politics, placed in command. China was to undertake Four Modernizations—namely, the upgrading of agriculture, industry, science, and the army. The Chinese welcomed Deng's program, as pleased by the prospect of an end to brutal political campaigns as they were by the promise of a better material life.

The Western world was as taken by the Four Modernizations program as were the Chinese. After the voodoo economics of the Great Leap Forward and the trashing of China's culture in the ironically misnamed Cultural Revolution, here was a program of economic growth that made sense. When Beijing's propagandists called the program "The New Long March," the Western media was quick to exploit the hype. *Time* selected Deng as the Man of the Year for 1979, heralding him as the "Visionary of a New China." His project, a "Great Leap Outward," was termed "vast, daring, and unique in history."[1]

Americans in particular interpreted favorably the pronouncements and plans of the regime. When Deng visited an automobile factory and remarked, "We must emulate the United States and modernize China," thousands of American businessmen began to have heady visions of the potential profits in a market of nearly one billion people. When Deng seemed to promise more freedom of expression, bestowing his blessing on the Xidan Democracy Wall with an oracular "Xidan good," even Richard Nixon was heard to speculate that the PRC might one day abandon communism in favor of democratic socialism.

The new paradigm that emerged viewed the government of China as a benevolent dictatorship. The idea of the "authoritarian modernizing regime" contained the following basic propositions:

1. Mao Zedong's Cultural Revolution had been a political and economic disaster of the first magnitude. It was, along with overpopulation, responsible for China's continuing poverty.
2. The regime was no longer in the totalitarian mode of Mao Zedong, but had relaxed controls so that it was merely authoritarian. The prospects for eventual, if gradual, democratization were good.
3. The regime was committed to economic modernization rather than communist ideology, a process that would lead it down the capitalist road. It was thus as deserving of U.S. support as the government of any underdeveloped Third World nation; more so because it controlled a market that was vast and potentially important.
4. The regime was an important geopolitical player, especially useful to Washington as a counterweight against Moscow.

It is testament to a wonderfully expedient convergence of motives on the part of scholars, diplomats, businessmen, journalists, and others with interests in China that this paradigm immediately found a large and appreciative audience. *Time* invoked the paradigm when it wrote that "the Chinese, their primitive economy threadbare and their morale exhausted by the years of Mao Zedong's disastrous Cultural Revolution, hope to have arrived by the year 2000 at a state of relative modernity, and become a world economic and military power. . . . The normalization [of U.S.-China] relations opens potentially lucrative avenues of trade and new perspectives on world politics. . . . Deng and his backers have embarked on what sometimes looks suspiciously like a capitalist road."[2]

However radical China had seemed a few short years before, it was now, virtually everyone gravely agreed, going capitalist. Miriam London recounts the case of a Chinese emigré scholar who in the Orwellian year of 1984 attended an international conference on communism for conservatives: "[He] found that his presence was a meaningless formality. For the participants, China was already a solved problem of communism; it was 'going capitalist' and no longer a threat to the West, but, on the contrary, a useful ally against the Soviet Union."[3]

As always, what didn't fit into this super story was cast aside as irrelevant or, more likely, overlooked entirely. After years of full faith and confidence in Mao Zedong's every utterance some American observers now had trouble taking seriously Deng Xiaoping's political pronouncements, especially his repeated assertions that there were Four Absolutes. They simply could not believe that the "pragmatic reformer" behind the modernization program would insist on adherence to such outmoded concepts as the dictatorship of the proletariat, the leadership of the Communist party, Marxism-Leninism–Mao Zedong Thought, and the socialist road.

When reminded that Deng and his backers apparently *thought* they were still taking the socialist road, the response of some American analysts was to suggest that those old grey heads were in a grip of something akin to a false consciousness. As Zbigniew Brzezinski explained in this context, "Any large system of thought and practice lends itself to so many divergent interpretations that it is possible to be both a continuator and a dismantler of a certain ideological system at the same time. Trotsky and Stalin charged each other with being betrayers of Leninism, and each claimed to be the true inheritor of Leninism. In some respects, both were right in both instances."[4] While paying public respect to Marxism-Leninism–Mao Zedong Thought, the argument went, Deng was wreaking havoc upon its spirit. Without realizing what he was doing, China's paramount leader was modernizing the dictatorship of the proletariat out of existence.

Mentioning the *c* word in relation to China had long been in bad taste; now it became entirely taboo. This led commentators into innumerable awkward circumlocutions, and even into historical revisionism. They denied that the Chinese Communists had ever been real, committed, honest-to-goodness Communists. Philip Snow, for instance, in his 1988 book *Star Raft: China's Encounter with Africa*, writes that Mao and the Chinese Communist party were fighting "not so much for Communism as for China itself," and that their primary goal was to "driv[e] foreign influence forcibly from [Chinese] territory."[5] Never mind that Mao, after vanquishing the foreigners, spent the next twenty-five years in a bloody crusade for radical social change within China; this did not fit the new paradigm. Snow's claim would have undoubtedly generated the same response from Mao that American journalists of the forties heard from party officials at that time: "We call ourselves Communists because we are Communists."[6]

Stories of past government abuses had a place in the paradigm; reports of continuing brutalities did not. Thus *Life and Death in Shanghai,* Nien Cheng's autobiographical account of her long imprisonment and cruel mistreatment during the Cultural Revolution, was published to rave reviews and won hundreds of thousands of readers. Cheng's moving account did for Mao's Red Guards what Arthur Koestler's *Darkness at Noon* did for Stalin's minions—revealed them as the petty-minded, evil tyrants they were. Although *Darkness at Noon* is remembered today for its unmasking of institutionalized terrorism, Cheng's powerful drama is recognized only for its rendering of a personal story.[7] Few drew the larger conclusion that here were terrible institutions capable of committing appalling acts to preserve themselves.

Systematic violations of human rights were reported by Western correspondents in Beijing but were seldom analyzed in the Western press; they were documented by American scholars, when this was possible, but not with the attention to detail of abuses in countries where such abuses were *expected.* The list of stories given short shrift includes:

1. The suppression of the democracy movement from 1979 to 1981: No sooner had Deng wrested power from his rival Hua Guofeng in 1979 than he began a purge of the youthful activists who had aided his rise to power. From 1979 to 1981, while the Deng regime was busily wooing foreign businessmen to China, leaders of the Democracy movement were being arrested and sent to labor camps by administrative decree. Wei Jingsheng, the most famous of these youthful dissidents, was sentenced to fifteen years in prison for "counterrevolutionary activities" in a widely reported public trial— and promptly forgotten. In June 1986 during a press conference in Beijing, former President Jimmy Carter was asked about Wei, then serving his seventh year. "I'm not personally familiar with the case you described," said the President who had made human rights the centerpiece of his foreign policy.[8]

2. The repression of nearly six million Tibetans, which began when the Chinese Communists invaded their homeland in 1959 and slaugh-

tered 1.2 million of their countrymen, and which continued under Deng: Beijing's continued imperialism did not fit the paradigm and seldom interested the China watchers. The October 1987 anti-Chinese demonstrations, in which at least fourteen Tibetans were killed when security forces opened fire, received only a ripple of coverage.

3. The abuses of the population control campaign, in which millions of women in China have been forced to undergo abortions and sterilizations: Convinced that China's population (and not its political system) was the primary hindrance to that country's development, few in the West paid attention to this ongoing human tragedy.[9]

Even when a member of the Beijing press corps was the object of abuse, Western media and governmental circles have reacted mildly. In 1986 the Soviets' imprisonment and subsequent expulsion of Nicholas Daniloff, a Moscow correspondent for the *U.S. News and World Report,* was portrayed in the American media as a major international incident. Yet when John Burns, Beijing correspondent for the *New York Times,* was similarly treated by the Chinese, the story was not given major play.[10] "It is time for damage control," the Editor-in-Chief of the *New York Times* said matter-of-factly upon arriving in Beijing to bail out his imprisoned employee. The American media was clearly eager to put the episode behind it and get on with the real business of reporting on China's March to Progress. The Soviet behavior had reinforced stereotypes; the Chinese action had contradicted them.

THE MANY FACES OF BENEVOLENCE

This new vision of China had something for everyone. Liberals and conservatives, scholars and businessmen, diplomats and correspondents—all subscribed to it, though for different reasons, and with different emphases. For the first time since the fifties there was a consensus view of China, disputed only by a smattering of conservatives, radicals, and human rights advocates.

Many Americans accepted the necessity of cultivating good relations as the price of playing the China card. China was regarded as a natural partner in the struggle to contain the Soviet Union. Though conservatives, particularly, were not anxious to enter into an alliance with a regime they recognized as repressive, even they saw in the 4- (later 3-) million-man Chinese army a useful counterweight against the Soviet military machine. Richard Nixon wrote in 1982 that the fear of the Soviet Union that impelled him to seek reconciliation with China a decade before was even greater now that the USSR had "overtaken the United States in both strategic and theater land-based nuclear weapons; Vietnam, Cambodia and Laos have become Soviet satellites; and Soviet troops are in Afghanistan."[11] Even the Sino-Vietnamese War of 1980—when front-line units of the People's Liberation Army were badly mauled by the Vietnamese *border* militia— could not shake the belief in a powerful Chinese military. Many Americans also applauded China's willingness to allow the United States to set up three electronic monitoring stations near the Soviet border, replacing the ones lost to the Ayatollah in Iran, which provide telemetry data on Soviet missile launches to U.S. (and Chinese) intelligence agencies. Conservatives, especially, have tried to put the best face on Beijing's future prospects for fear of jeopardizing this strategic relationship in general and our intelligence-gathering capabilities in particular.

Businesspeople embraced China, and its new image, in the hope that its new commitment to economic modernization and foreign trade would pay off. By the mid-eighties, American corporations had poured billions of dollars into China, lured by the promise of dirt-cheap labor and the prospect of a foot in the door of the economic powerhouse of tomorrow. Above all, the vision of a potential market in which one day tens of millions of Chinese would be shaving with Gillette razors, eating Beatrice food products, or driving AMC Jeeps persuaded the executives of these companies to set up operations in China. To question China's commitment to the capitalist road or its chances of successfully modernizing would have called into question the wisdom of these and other investments.

For professional China-watchers, the scholars and correspondents, the overriding question was one of access. By the 1970s, neither group was completely barred from China, as in the two previous decades.

Yet short visits on scholarly delegations could not compensate for the absence of opportunities for extended research and fieldwork in China. Neither was parachute journalism any substitute for residence in Beijing. Academics, especially, were ecstatic when the Deng regime signed a scholarly exchange agreement permitting them to carry out research projects on Chinese soil. The fifty American scholars, of whom I was one, who were chosen in 1979 to participate in the first year of the official U.S.-China scholarly exchange program congratulated themselves on their good fortune. Hundreds followed over the next ten years. The exchange scholars naturally tended to view the regime that had granted them this boon in a positive light and to refrain from publishing material that might jeopardize their future access to China.

Many China-watchers gravitated naturally from their earlier admiration of China to the new stance of respectful benevolence. Joined by former critics of the regime, they were convinced that by drawing China's leaders closer to the United States, encouraging economic reform, and peacefully exchanging goods and people, China would bloodlessly evolve away from a one-party state toward a more open and representative system. In this scenario, the Chinese Communist party would gradually reform itself—abandoning such practices as arbitrary arrest and imprisonment, mass political campaigns, and the persecution of intellectuals—until it came to resemble the socialist or liberal democratic parties of Western Europe. In the meantime, open criticism of Beijing was viewed as counterproductive because it would lead to a retreat from America's salubrious embrace. Convinced that the stability of Deng Xiaoping's regime was a precondition for economic and political progress, they refrained from endorsing rapid political change. Liang Heng and Judith Shapiro, who had earlier written *Son of the Revolution,* a highly critical account of the Cultural Revolution, returned from a 1985 visit to China to assert that this was a time of "relatively great freedom" in China. While the economic reforms had engendered problems of their own, they had led to changes that seemed "promising for the future of political participation."[12] Democratization was only a matter of time.

Only the Trotskyite Left, the staunchly anti-Communist Right, and human rights groups remained critical. Deng's effort to allow market forces a role in the economy suggested to the Left that he was retreating from his socialist responsibility to exercise direct control over the means of production. An odd collection of Trotskyite and Maoist groups shrilly charged China with "changing color," denouncing the new economic arrangements as fascist. "Ten years of Dengism have brought sharp class polarization, 30% inflation with no comparable rise in urban incomes, an end to the welfare state, and hunger," Doug Henwood wrote in the *Left Business Observer*. He went on to complain parenthetically that "official Chinese reports that up to 20 million people faced starvation last winter, true or not, received virtually no attention in the West."[13]

To the Right, Beijing was tarred with the same brush of tyranny as all Communist regimes. Communism could not be reformed—the idea was a contradiction in terms—but could only be overthrown. The notion that Deng Xiaoping would preside over the dissolution of the one-party dictatorship that he headed was dismissed as fantasy. His objective in relaxing economic controls and appealing for Western and Japanese aid and investment was to construct as rapidly as possible a powerful Communist state. China's future held not a "departure from communism," in the view of the German Sinologist Juergen Domes, "but the [pre-Gorbachev] political and organizational present of the Soviet Union."[14]

Human rights groups and activists published several studies on China in the eighties; all fell dead off the presses. With China "going our way," it was hard to interest the American public in troubling accounts of torture and ill treatment of "prisoners of conscience," including Roman Catholic priests, Tibetan nationalists, and democracy movement activists. With no organized domestic constituency determined to hold the Beijing regime accountable for its human rights transgressions (as exists in the case of Soviet Jews), China became the human rights exception.[15] The Chinese dissident Fang Lizhi complained bitterly in the pages of the *Washington Post* of Western politicians who have adopted a double standard by holding different attitudes toward human rights events in the Soviet Union and Eastern Europe on the one hand and China on the other. "When dealing with the former, they have openly expressed concern and have even made the issue a paramount condition in matters of their foreign policy. But, when dealing with the latter, they have said and done very little."[16]

RESURGENCE OF PATERNALISM

When Harold Isaacs interviewed Americans about their attitudes toward China, one phrase recurred over and over again. China was "a country we have always helped, a people to be helped."[17] Americans had regarded themselves as China's benefactors for a century, preserving China's territorial integrity and political independence. In their roles as the teachers, protectors, and saviors of the Chinese people, they had assumed, in Isaacs's words, "total responsibility for the minds, bodies, and immortal souls of the Chinese." This attitude of paternalism, long buried under layers of hostility, admiration, and infatuation, came back to life as the eighties began.

And how could it not? Thirty years before, Mao had announced that China was through kowtowing to the West ("China has stood up"), and slammed the Open Door shut in America's face. Now Deng had reversed his predecessor and had opened the Door wide, beckoning the United States to enter. This time, however, instead of assuming the "total responsibility" of a benevolent guardian, America's role was to be more limited. Americans were to teach English and the sciences, to invest in factories, and to help in other ways in the urgent task of modernizing China's science, industry, agriculture, and army. They were not to propagate their secular religion—democracy—or their transcendent one—Christianity, both of which Beijing was soon to brand "spiritual pollution." The scholarly and cultural exchange agreements that were drafted, the trade and investment protocols that were signed—all were couched in delicately balanced language to avoid any hint that the old paternalistic relationship was being revived.

Americans, grown more diffident about their role in the world after Vietnam, seemed to accept these conditions without hesitation. But few assumed that China had much to teach us. Before long the old missionary impulse reasserted itself, albeit with a twist. America, which had once set out to save China through transcendent religion, now seemed determined to rescue it through transcendent capitalism. The strength of this commitment engendered an almost irrational belief in its eventual realization, which was by no means limited to a particular band of the political spectrum. Just as in earlier years, when the Boxer indemnity was used to provide scholarships to

Chinese students so that they might "act as commercial missionaries," so many American colleges and universities have been generous to the new wave of Chinese who came to the United States in the eighties. China *would* be saved.

That Deng Xiaoping might have had very different plans for China did not occur to them. His repeated invocation of the Four Absolutes; his several campaigns against Western ideas of democracy and human rights ("Spiritual Pollution" and "Bourgeois Liberalization"); and even his threat to "spill the blood" of student demonstrators in December 1986—these pieces of the China puzzle could not be made to fit inside the framework of the modernizing authoritarian regime. Though large and obviously important, they were simply cast to one side. Deng seems to have understood, and been contemptuous of, the West's chronic inability to distinguish between his economic liberalism and his political orthodoxy. "We put Wei [Jingsheng] behind bars, didn't we?" he once asked with heavy sarcasm. "Did that damage China's reputation?" He had a better grasp of the West than it had of him.[18]

THE SCHOLARSHIP OF BENEVOLENCE

One China-watching academic who has reeducated himself according to the new paradigm is Harvard's Ezra Vogel. His *One Step Ahead in China: Guangdong under Reform* focuses on the economic reforms of the last decade as they have played out in the southern province of Guangdong.[19] Facts and statistics garnered from hundreds of interviews conducted with government officials throughout the province adorn every page. He provides much new information about Guangdong's cities and regions—the provincial and prefectural capitals, the wealthy counties of the Pearl River Delta, the impoverished mountain counties, the Hainan island. His book is carefully written and impressively researched, and with its publication he bids fair to inherit the mantle of Dean of Sinology from his retired colleague, John K. Fairbank.

One Step Ahead is a model of what might be called the scholarship of benevolence. Here are all the essential elements of the genre—the obligatory recounting of the horrors of the Cultural Revolution, the upbeat assessment of the modernization program's accomplishments and prospects, and the implicit belief that China's authoritarianism will gradually give way to a more open and democratic system. Vogel concludes his book with a typical display of missionary zeal, issuing a lengthy prescription designed to cure China's lingering ills. If China could just be made to take its economic medicine, the reader comes to understand, the symptoms of its chronic political crisis would take care of themselves.

As Vogel explains in his introduction, his research was carried out at the invitation of the provincial government, which specifically asked him to report on economic developments in Guangdong during the eighties. The first such foreign guests of the provincial government, he and his wife were treated as visiting dignitaries. They were lodged at well-appointed guest houses usually reserved for high-ranking party officials. Interviews were arranged by the Provincial Economic Commission, the powerful organization responsible for Guangdong's overall economic development. With the possible exception of the trusted Edgar Snow, who was given carte blanche by Premier Zhou Enlai in 1960 to travel in China, I can think of no foreigner who has enjoyed the special access granted to Vogel. Neither can Vogel. "I am not aware of other foreigners who have been given a comparable opportunity to study a Chinese province," he writes.[20]

Such enviable access, of course, does not come without certain obligations. Vogel avers that his biggest concern in accepting the invitation was maintaining academic standards of objectivity. He recounts how he explained to his official hosts that he "could not be like Edgar Snow, Rewi Alley, and other foreign observers who reported only the favorable side of China's developments."[21] They expansively responded that they no longer wanted blind followers and would not insist on reviewing what he wrote to see whether his conclusions were acceptable to them. Vogel seems to think that this understanding rendered the question of bias moot, and proceeded with his research. Yet the real dangers of accepting such largess are more subtle than overt censorship.

Although Vogel is no Edgar Snow, his view of the economic reforms is close to that of the senior Guangdong party officials who befriended him, and he is quick to offer explanations, even rationalizations, for party policies that entail gross violations of human rights. He concludes a discussion of economic corruption, for example, by pointing out that Guangdong's Communist party officials have not stood idly by while this unauthorized buying and selling occurred: "In 1982–83 alone, over a thousand people in the province were executed for economic crimes."[22] He argues that Chinese officialdom's fear of inflation is not irrational, since prices cannot be decontrolled before markets are fully developed, when in fact the main obstacle to the development of mature markets is the lack of a rational pricing structure.[23] He agrees with officials that "it would create too much disorder to allow the free movement of . . . people to the cities," suggesting instead that they be provided with "challenging opportunities within their home counties," without specifying how the peasants are to be kept down on the farm.[24] He remarks how "fortunate" China is to have "active urban neighborhood associations, which have played a key role in controlling crime and promoting family planning," without mentioning that these organizations are faithful servants of the Chinese Communist party and have proven particularly efficient in recent years in locating political dissidents and in imposing birth quotas on their resident populations.[25]

Vogel was never a Maoist in the Fairbank mold, promoting the Communist revolution as "on the whole the best thing that has happened to the Chinese people in many centuries." But he did flirt for a time with the notion that Chairman Mao and the Chinese Communist party had succeeded in creating a New Socialist Man. Friendship was on the wane in the People's Republic, he argued in 1965, replaced by the new social ethic of "comradeship." This he defined as "a universal morality in which all citizens are in important respects equal under the state, and gradations on the basis of status or of closeness cannot legitimately interfere with this equality." No doubt the Chinese masses would have been astonished to learn from Professor Vogel that they were the equal of "leading cadres" or that friendship no longer existed, yet in an article published in *China Quarterly*, this is what he maintained: "What is unique about Communist China is not the presence of a universalistic ethic governing personal relations, but the absence of a private ethic to supplement the public ethic and support the commitment of the individual to his friend."[26]

Nothing in *One Step Ahead* rings as self-evidently false as this claim, but Vogel's suggestion as to how the Chinese Communist party could in the future play "a more positive role" in society does give one pause. "As new interest groups and units develop in the modernizing economy," Vogel explains, "Communist Party organizations could be in a position to broker these interests. The Party has attracted people who are experienced in mediating between different interests, and, somewhat like traditional magistrates, Party leaders at each level, if they had a good understanding of the needs of modern society, could make decisions, balancing the claims of various groups." Vogel allows that this hopeful evolution of cadres into honest brokers "would require a new vision," but in fact it would require much more: an end to the Marxist-Leninist dictatorship that rules China in the name of the proletariat and an end to Marx-Lenin-Mao Thought as the reigning ideology—the end, in short, of the Socialist Road.[27] In its own way, Vogel's advice is as optimistic about the Chinese Communist party's willingness to yield its old role in Chinese society and adopt a new one as Leo Orleans's roots-and-berries calculation was about the party's ability to produce food. More likely, and desirable, is a recapitulation of the political evolution of Eastern Europe: the eventual dissolution of the CCP as a spent historical force.

As this example reveals, the central weakness of the scholarship of benevolence is its failure to attend to politics. Vogel and others are guided, perhaps unconsciously, by the Marxist premises of their paradigm. They believe that economic interactions are fundamental, with political and legal relations mere end products of such interactions. In this view, if economic reform is carried on long enough, and with sufficient intensity, it must inevitably result in a more pluralistic political system. In reality it is the political system, through the conscious exercise of political will, that largely determines the course of the economic.

Nowhere is the primacy of politics more evident than in the People's Republic, whose one-party dictatorship has swept the economy from Stalinoid stagnation to Maoist folly to market reforms (and partially back) in the last forty years. China's political volatility is certainly no secret, since its surface calm has been repeatedly punctured by explosive upheavals—the Great Leap Forward, the Cultural Revolution, the Beijing Spring democracy movement in 1979, the student demonstrations of 1986, and the Tiananmen uprising of 1989. Deng Xiaoping, who was once thought to have solved the succession problem, is now on his third designated successor, having sacked both of Jiang Zemin's immediate predecessors, Hu Yaobang and Zhao Zhiyang.

By ignoring this sorry history and the complaints of dissidents, by attending only to the optimistic projections of reform-minded officials, many Americans found it easy to be bullish on China. The "pragmatic," "flexible" Deng Xiaoping was selected as *Time*'s "Man of the Year" again in 1986. "There is no other leader in the world who is doing anything even remotely in Deng's league," the magazine quoted former assistant secretary of state Richard Holbrooke as saying.[28] The regime's decade-long dabbling in the free market was widely imagined to be irreversible; warnings that further economic reforms were tied to the fate of a particular party faction were ignored. Yet it would soon become painfully obvious that politics was still in command.

10

From American Illusions
to Chinese Reality

―――――――――― ⚇⚇⚇ ――――――――――

*Perhaps we should not be too harsh on these [China] experts: the fraternity
recently suffered a traumatic experience and is still in a state of shock.
Should fish suddenly start to talk, I suppose ichthyology would also have
to undergo a dramatic revision of its basic approach. A certain type of
"instant sinology" was indeed based on the assumption that the Chinese
were as different from us in their fundamental aspirations, and as unable
to communicate with us, as the inhabitants of the ocean depths; and when
they eventually rose to the surface and began to cry out sufficiently loudly
and clearly for their message to get through to the general public, there was
much consternation among the China pundits.*

Simon Leys
The Burning Forest

For seven weeks in the spring of 1989, the world was treated to a
spectacular show of defiance against the Chinese Communist regime
and its aging leaders. By the end of May, a million or more people
were surging through the streets of Beijing in protest of corruption,
bureaucracy, and dictatorship. Never before had so many people
gathered in the streets of Beijing—not even during the massive Red
Guard rallies of 1966. And while those events had been staged shows
of youthful support for Mao's policies, these were spontaneous demonstrations of disaffection from the Communist system that Mao had
midwifed.

On the night of 4 June, these peaceful, nonviolent protests were
answered with deadly force. As the West watched in horror, the

People's Liberation Army opened fire on unarmed demonstrators with automatic weapons and ran them down with tanks and Armored Personnel Carriers (APCs). We may never know exactly how many died that bloody night or how many more perished during the street fighting that raged for five days afterwards. Estimates of those killed outright run into the thousands, and many thousands more must have been wounded. By the standards of past political campaigns such numbers of victims are not large. What was different was the brutal manner of their execution before an international public. Beijing's stagecraft had utterly broken down.

The birth and death of the democracy movement was easily the most widely covered event in the PRC since Nixon's visit, and as before, this prolonged and intense reportage transformed American attitudes toward China. By the time Beijing had been pacified, the "modernizing authoritarian regime" paradigm lay in ruins. A new attitude had been locked in place toward a regime once more called—this time without equivocation or quotation marks—Communist.

The demonstrations began on 18 April, sparked by the death in mid-April of Hu Yaobang, a former party leader deposed by Deng and the orthodox Marxists for being too soft on democracy. As the marches came to include workers as well as students, and as their antigovernment tone became more pronounced, China's rising tide of unrest captured the attention of the American public. It was clear that the democracy movement was more than just the creature of a "tiny number" of malcontents, as the Beijing regime was later to claim. In fact, the students had tapped into a deep vein of popular discontent with Communist rule and had broad popular support through all segments of Chinese society.

Live reports from Beijing became a fixture on the evening news, while major newspapers devoted dozens of column-inches to the story each day. What television executive could resist footage of a hundred thousand Chinese shouting antigovernment slogans? And what American editor could resist a story about a small army of youth demanding democracy from their autocratic elders? Voice of America broadcasts in Chinese carried news of the students' activities back to other parts of China, along with messages of the outside world's encouragement, thus completing the circle.

A further element of drama was added when China's leaders began to threaten dire consequences if the students did not desist. A 26 April *People's Daily* editorial reacted to the formation of the Beijing University's Students' Autonomous United Association in late April by denouncing the students for a "conspiracy" to "poison people's minds, create national turmoil and sabotage the nation's political stability." "We must crack down on these students whatever the cost," Deng was reported to have told party leaders. "I had hoped that we wouldn't have to spill blood. But if we have to do so, then we will." Not to be cowed, more than one hundred thousand students responded the following day by breaking through police lines and marching ten miles to Tiananmen Square.[1]

The war of nerves continued for the rest of May. The students occupied Tiananmen Square, the symbolic heart of China, and vowed to remain there until their demands were met: an end to the widespread corruption in the government, a streamlining of the massive bureaucracy, and a more open political system. The Chinese leadership retaliated on 20 May by imposing martial law but found itself unable to enforce its decision. Two days later, in the largest spontaneous demonstration in the history of the PRC, an estimated one million persons peacefully paraded through the streets of Beijing in support of the students' demands. Columns of troops were sent marching into the city, only to become becalmed in huge seas of people who barricaded the streets with their bodies. The students were denounced as "counterrevolutionaries and hooligans" in an effort to place them beyond the pale, but it was too late. What had begun as a student protest had already assumed the character of a broad-based democracy movement. An Independent Federation of Workers was organized in Beijing, and demonstrations spread to other cities. Chinese in increasing numbers began to look beyond the present one-party dictatorship, whose misrule they had suffered for decades, to a Chinese government that would be respectful of their wishes.

By this time, the ranks of the resident foreign press corps had been reinforced by hundreds of correspondents from around the world. The majority had come to Beijing to cover two events that had been scheduled months before: the visit of Soviet leader Mikhail Gorbachev and a meeting of the Asian Development Bank (ADB). Both of these events were newsworthy in their own right. Gorbachev's visit was a first—no Soviet leader had ever before visited Beijing—and it promised closer Soviet-Chinese ties. The ADB meeting was also without precedent and was given added importance by the presence of an official delegation from the Republic of China on Taiwan—another first. Yet whatever their historical significance, these calm and orderly deliberations could not compete for the camera's eye or the reporter's notebook with the army of unruly, chanting youth outside. The arriving contingent of foreign journalists descended on Beijing's streets like a horde of hungry locusts, feasting on the drama they found unfolding there. The flurry of press reports about the demonstrations thickened into an unrelenting blizzard. By early June, the coverage of the *New York Times* and the *Washington Post* could be counted in whole pages, that of the network news programs in multiples of minutes.

While the increasingly tense confrontation between the students and the authorities had all the elements of a good story, this alone would not have generated such intense coverage by the U.S. media. In part, public enthusiasm for news of the demonstrations reflected America's long-standing romance with China. More important than this, however, was the students increasingly vocal commitment to democracy, especially American-style democracy. When on 13 May, about two thousand students began a hunger strike, they announced that they were prepared to die for democracy. Students avowed during interviews that they were avid listeners of the Voice of America. Banners appeared in demonstrations bearing quotations from Patrick Henry, Abraham Lincoln, and Thomas Jefferson. ("Give Me Liberty or Give Me Death" was a favorite.) As if to make the inspiration for their movement perfectly transparent, the students chose in the final days to erect a Statue of Liberty on Tiananmen Square. She went by the name of the Goddess of Democracy, to be sure, but no American who beheld that thirty-foot female figure holding high the torch of freedom could doubt her transpacific origins.

By such acts, the students sparked American interest into a blaze of sympathy. By appealing to freedom, equality, and those inalienable rights—the beliefs that constitute America's secular religion—they touched a deep, resonant chord in the American psyche. In the end, Americans came to see the students as living symbols of America's burgeoning influence in China. However quixotic the crusade of these

Chinese children for freedom may have appeared to some, however underdeveloped their notions of the democratic government they hoped one day to establish, Americans could not fail to wish them well. For the new creed to which they had sworn allegiance was our creed, and the new crusade on which they had embarked was our crusade.

It seemed almost too perfect a justification of the American political creed that China, in the person of her youth, was again appealing for instruction from her one-time (and self-appointed) guardian. It was easy to view China as the prodigal country, returning from its wastrel years of addiction to a hostile ideology, and to kill the fatted calf of benevolence. To be sure, America had already been invited back through the same Open Door from which she had once been ejected, but only on the limited basis of helping with the modernization program. At best, this opening was a partial vindication; China's democratization along American lines would render it complete.

PARADIGMS LOST

The "modernizing authoritarian regime" paradigm was severely battered by this ongoing tempest of protest. It had hypothesized gradual political change, not radical democratic movements. And it projected Deng Xiaoping as an enlightened pragmatist, not the kind of ideologue who would anathematize the students as "counterrevolutionaries" and threaten to spill their blood. Yet as long as the Beijing leadership avoided violent repression, it remained afloat. Once the bloodletting began, however, it sank quickly under the weight of an irreconcilable contradiction between its charitable reading of the Beijing regime and the brutal way that regime in fact dealt with dissent.

America's media representatives in Beijing were devastated by the People's Liberation Army's assault on the city.[2] Television correspondents reported in horrified voices on the mounting casualties, as they showed dark and forbidding footage of soldiers firing and shadows running. Writing in the sanctuary of their hotels, reporters without on-the-scene confirmation noted that Beijing's citizens had tried to stop oncoming tanks and troops with their massed bodies, only to be crushed under armored vehicles or shot by automatic weapon fire. News anchors in the United States spoke in tense and judgmental terms of a "bloodbath," a "massacre," a "slaughter." The killing would continue for several more days in the Chinese capital, as army units fought pitched battles with urban guerrillas armed with Molotov cocktails and captured weapons, but it did not take the media nearly that long to make up its mind. By the morning of 5 June they had concluded that this was a tyrannical and murderous regime, capable of any atrocity.

The best illustration of this sudden eagerness to believe the worst of Beijing was the wide circulation received by an unsubstantiated report of a massacre of students on Tiananmen Square proper. During the final stage of the assault on the Square, the rumor went, the army had surrounded thousands of students encamped near the Monument of Revolutionary Heroes and cut them down with machine-gun fire. Tanks had run back and forth over their tents to ensure that there were no survivors. The corpses had then been piled into mounds and burned under cover of darkness to destroy evidence of the slaughter. Stories along these lines ran in several major American newspapers, including the *Washington Post*. Correspondents continued to refer to this episode on the air and in print even after it was publicly disputed by Western eyewitnesses, such as Robin Munro of Asia Watch.[3] It was too perfect a demonstration of what Beijing was now believed capable of to be lightly abandoned.

The American media had switched sides; or rather, it had discovered there *was* another side. After years of treating dissidents as a sideshow, good for an occasional column but largely irrelevant to the Big Story of China's modernization, they were confronted with widespread discontent. After years of politely humoring Deng for his insistence on the Four Absolutes, they suddenly discovered just how deadly serious he was about enforcing the dictatorship of the proletariat. To express their new solidarity with the democratic movement, some in the media began referring to Deng's regime as "totalitarian" and even "Communist"—words that in recent years even the editors of the *National Review* had eschewed when talking about China. The *U.S. News & World Report,* reporting on the activities of the newly organized overseas democracy movement, regretted that "no organized resistance can operate today [in China] under the totalitarian thumb of China."[4] Others went even further. Reflecting on the lesson of Tiananmen, Meg Greenfield of the *Washington Post* declared that there was no reason why liberals and conservatives could not unite behind the banner of anticommunism.[5]

The events of 1989 also took the bloom off the rose for Chinawatchers. The guardians of the "modernizing authoritarian regime" paradigm were no better prepared than were the correspondents for millions of Beijing's residents to take to the streets. The *Washington Post*, reflecting this confusion, pronounced itself mystified by the sudden bursting forth of "a hunger for democracy which was unprecedented in China and which few people anywhere had anticipated."[6] And when the regime answered the demands of its citizens not with negotiations and concessions but with troops and tanks, the fraternity went into a collective shock. It was a humbled and contrite crew of China hands who analyzed this "unthinkable," "inconceivable" carnage in the nation's electronic and print media over the next few days. Michel Oksenberg, who had earlier dismissed the possibility of the regime's using deadly force to suppress the demonstrations, issued a personal *mea culpa* in the form of an essay—"Confessions of a China Watcher"—acknowledging that he and others had "sold short the resolve of the octogenarian leaders to defend their life's work."[7]

Ezra Vogel tried to put the Tiananmen massacre in historical perspective with the explanation that "throughout the country's long history countless emperors have tried to keep the Mandate of Heaven by annihilating those who threatened their rule."[8] But most Chinawatchers realized that the massacre and subsequent manhunt for democratic activists found more recent and obvious precedents in the numerous campaigns of terror launched by the Chinese Communist party against its real and imagined enemies. "Like the two faces of Janus, the China of Mao and Deng had been coexisting all along," wrote Professor Maria Chang. "Mao never really went away, after all."[9]

Among the few China-watchers who tried to defend Beijing's actions was Leo Orleans, who suggested that "the larger share of the responsibility for the tragedy that took place in China and for its aftermath . . . belongs to the students themselves, not to the government." The Chinese leadership, Orleans pointed out, had been "thoroughly humiliated" by "sneering" students who had "erect[ed] makeshift blockades and . . . prevented army troops from approaching Tiananmen Square . . . [and] ignored the imposition of martial law, which banned demonstrations." With the students unwilling to leave Tiananmen Square, the government had no choice but to react sternly.[10]

Orleans's apologia ignited a firestorm of criticism. "Leo Orleans's outrageous attack on the Chinese students [is] an isolated act of moral suicide," wrote Robert Zaller of Drexel University. "[W]ith sympathizers like Mr. Orleans, the Chinese do not lack for enemies," retorted Albert Yee of the Chinese University of Hong Kong. William Reid of the University of Texas took the editors of the *Chronicle of Higher Education* to task for printing the piece: "Leo Orleans's [article] is the most asinine you have published. . . . You have published garbage."[11]

The definitive rebuttal came from Professor Edward Friedman: "Where does Mr. Orleans get off besmirching the memory of martyrs? . . . Where does he get the idea that Deng Xiaoping—who cracked down hard in 1985 and 1986 on democrats . . . who is proud of the 15-year prison terms imposed on advocates of democracy, who brags about his willingness to shed the blood of democrats—would have made concessions to the democratic demonstrators if they had left Tiananmen Square earlier? Mr. Orleans is living in a fantasy world."[12]

That "fantasy world" had been home to a large and flourishing population of China-watchers before the massacre, all of whom shared Orleans's vision of Deng Xiaoping as pragmatic reformer. It was a wilderness in which Orleans now found himself wandering largely alone. The depth of revulsion felt by scholars led several of them to call for a complete boycott of the Beijing regime. "How could we possibly deal with a Government that murders its unarmed children?" wrote Karl Hutterer of the University of Michigan in the *New York Times*.[13]

Even the far Left, which is inclined to be apologetic about the occasional necessity of one-party dictatorships to liquidate their political opposition, saw defections. William Hinton, a Marxist China-watcher whose access to top leaders rivals that of the late Edgar Snow, left China in disgust on 23 June 1989, denouncing it as a "fascist government." He vowed not to return until the government condemned the assault on the demonstrators.[14]

The American public had not waited for either the instant judgments of the media or the belated soul-searching of the China pundits to reach conclusions about the regime and its opposition. Given the immediacy and vividness of the impressions carried into their living rooms, there was little room for the interposition of another "reality" between the viewer and the viewed. The stark reality of the camera's eye had told them all they needed to know. It required no great insight into China's cultural tradition to grasp the meaning of a student banner written in English demanding democracy. It required no deep understanding of political theory to decide that the slaughter of peaceful demonstrators was not the act of a benevolent dictatorship.

A Gallup Poll conducted six weeks after the June massacre and subsequent crackdown found that "the massacre in Tiananmen Square has badly damaged China's image in the U.S."[15] An overwhelming majority of the American public, some 87 percent, held that the PLA's action against the students was unjustified. American views of China, which had been moderately positive at the beginning of the student demonstrations, were mostly negative by the time the shooting stopped.[16]

The webs of wishful thinking spun by China's reformers and their foreign admirers had been swept away. Americans, who as late as February 1989 had held China in higher regard than Japan, the Soviet Union, South Korea, or Taiwan, now regarded it more unfavorably than all. Only 22 percent believed that a peaceful transition to a multiparty system was possible, while 68 percent now doubted that the Chinese Communist party would abandon its one-party dictatorship and thus allow the country to become more democratic.[17] Nien Cheng's post-Tiananmen evaluation was perfectly on the mark: "Americans . . . see the Chinese Communist government for what it really is: a repressive regime with complete disregard for its people and world opinion."[18]

DEFENDING DENG

During Richard Nixon's rapprochement with China, the media and the experts had assisted his efforts to refurbish Beijing's image. In 1989, the Bush administration and its allies tried to go it alone.[19]

For two and a half weeks after the demonstrations began on 18 April, President Bush ducked questions from the press on the events in China. When Bush finally allowed himself a public comment on 5 May, he may have made matters worse by implying that the heroic young student activists were merely unreasonable malcontents: "I have words of encouragement for freedom and democracy, wherever . . . [but] I wouldn't suggest that to any leadership, to any country, that they accept every demand by every group."[20]

Yet when an estimated one million persons peacefully paraded through the streets on 22 May in support of the students—proof positive that Chinese from all walks of life endorsed their reasonable demands—there were no words of encouragement from the Bush administration, much less criticism of the Beijing leadership for refusing to make concessions. On the contrary, Secretary of State James Baker's response made it clear that the desire of the Chinese people for democracy and freedom had to take a back seat to stability and the status quo: "I don't think that we should in any way be seen to be somehow inciting to riot. . . . I don't think it is in the best interests of the United States for us to see significant instability in China."[21]

Only after thousands had been wounded and killed did the Bush administration cautiously reverse course. It was late in the day of the massacre before Secretary of State Baker finally appeared before the press to make a brief statement. He deplored the outbreak of violence (without mentioning who was responsible) and called upon the two sides to settle their differences peacefully (without mentioning that one side was committed to the total destruction of the other).

Bush sounded the same note of moral equivalence in his 8 June press conference. He "deplored" the situation in China, but neither criticized the Beijing regime for the massacre nor held Deng and the other members of the leadership personally accountable. He announced the suspension of military cooperation with the PRC (in deference to the outraged reaction of the American public), but ruled out further diplomatic or economic sanctions as counterproductive. However much he might sympathize in the abstract with the tragic fate of the students, Bush made it clear that *realpolitik* demanded the preservation of a cooperative relationship between Washington and a stable Beijing regime.

No foreign policy expert did more to repair the damage caused by the massacre to the international image of the People's Republic than one of its original architects, former secretary of state Henry Kissinger. In articles and interviews Kissinger took the position of the Bush administration to its logical next step, criticizing the students' actions and defending Deng Xiaoping's response. Kissinger wrote on 1 August: "No government in the world would have tolerated having the main square of its capital occupied for eight weeks by tens of thousands of demonstrators, who blocked the authorities from approaching the area in front of the main government building. . . . [T]he caricature of Deng Xiaoping as a tyrant is unfair."[22] In an earlier article, published just six days after the massacre, he sympathetically explored Deng's reasons for ordering the assault: "To Deng Xiaoping the demonstrations recall[ed] the Cultural Revolution, when throngs of students sought to purify Communist ideology by means that led to loss of his liberty, made his son a paraplegic and disrupted the lives of tens of millions. In the end the Cultural Revolution produced so many diverse factions that China was at the edge of chaos."[23] Kissinger's parallel between the violent and destructive Red Guards called up by Mao and the peaceful and spontaneous legions of the democracy movement was unconvincing, even offensive, to many. But for those few who preferred to believe that Deng remained, at heart, a pragmatic modernizer, it provided a marginally satisfactory answer to the riddle of his barbaric action.

As though on cue, Nixon reappeared onstage in Beijing, lending credibility to a Communist regime that Americans had once again come to regard as odious. If his 1972 visit as president was understandable as *realpolitik,* then his 1989 tête-à-tête with Deng Xiaoping, undertaken as private citizen and political pariah, made sense only as sycophancy. His effort to replicate his foreign policy success of 1972—convincing Americans that the United States had much to gain by normalizing relations with the Beijing regime—was rejected as grotesque.[24]

Orville Schell noted in the aftermath of Tiananmen that "what has been most surprising about the official U.S. response to the pro-democracy events in China is its timidity. After waging 40 years of costly Cold War in defense of the 'free world,' American leaders seem to have lost their ardor now that the largest Communist country has spontaneously produced an extraordinary independent and nonviolent movement for freedom of expressions."[25] Yet this is less of an anomaly than it might appear.

As Miriam London has aptly written, "For our realpolitikers, the existence of a popular mood in China has always had a curious insubstantiality or, at least, irrelevance. For the Communist leadership, real people do not exist, except as a fiction called 'the masses.' When the non-existent dramatically asserted itself as a million individuals on Tiananmen Square, the result was not only consternation in the power center of Beijing, but surprise and discomfiture in Washington among those who had seen only a few Chinese Communist officials as solidly real."[26]

For twenty years, Nixon, Kissinger and other practitioners of *realpolitik* have by their moral neutrality taught Americans that the People's Republic of China was the exception to the rule that totalitarian methods are abhorrent. Is it surprising that their own views of China's leaders came to be marked by sentimentality and even fantasy, or that to the end of the democracy movement, they remained largely unresponsive to, and even ignorant of, the desire of the Chinese people for freedom?

It is, of course, precisely the professional China-watchers who should have been alert to the popular mood. Underneath the flat, misleading interpretations of official propagandists and foreign apologists, Chinese political life has developed an unruly richness and anarchic complexity in the eighties. For the first time since 1949 it was possible to hear the full range of China's authentic voices. Had more experts been listening to novelists, returned students, essayists, newspaper editors, and film directors, instead of a handful of superannuated leaders, they would not have been astonished by the stirrings of democracy. Equally important, had they borne in mind recent Chinese history, the willingness of those same leaders to "defend their life's work," or equivalently, to liquidate their political opposition, would not have come as such a shock.

FROM AMERICAN ILLUSIONS TO CHINESE REALITY

For the past two centuries, American perceptions of China have oscillated between the poles of love and hate. In brighter moments China was seen as the land of Marco Polo and Pearl Buck, peopled with wise, industrious, and courageous folk. But regularly, almost cyclically, the pendulum swung back, and the cruel and violent China of the Mongol hordes, the Boxer Rebellion, and the "human wave" attacks reasserted itself. The Chinese heroes of the anti-Japanese resistance became the totalitarian masses of the 1950s, the riotous young rebels of the 1960s, the public-spirited proletarians of the 1970s, and the poor but deserving folk of the 1980s. The Tiananmen massacre has once again tilted the balance, and the pendulum has swung to the other dark extreme.

Harold Isaacs, writing skeptically of Nixon's first overture to China, almost seems to suggest that these shifts in American public opinion occur independently of the Chinese reality: "It is like a turning column of mirrors with swiftly changing psychedelic lights hitting them from different angles."[27] But although these images may seem insubstantial, they are nevertheless reflections, however distorted and diffuse, of the hard strata of Chinese reality. The most that can be conceded is that America's intense and long-running emotional involvement with China—which some have described as a love-hate relationship—has exaggerated the swings between the "good" China and the "evil" China.

Yet there is a larger lesson in the ongoing struggle between the democracy movement and the government: it is that the unitarian view of China is incorrect. The Beijing regime no longer enjoys even the tacit consent of the governed and confronts active opposition in many quarters. By recognizing the distinction between the rulers and the ruled, we may, at last, reconcile our two sets of antipodal images.

The admirable people described by Marco Polo and Pearl Buck still exist. They remain a highly intelligent, persistently industrious, and cheerfully stoic people, many of them still silently coping with the adverse circumstances they have faced over the past two score and more years. Yet all too few Americans have been willing to listen to, if indeed they have been aware of, the swelling ranks of democratic activists who have taken up the struggle against state repression in China. In 1987 Fang Lizhi, China's Sakharov, told the one-time China correspondent Tiziano Terzani that his mission for China was democratization: "Without democracy there can be no development. Unless individual human rights are recognized there can be no true democracy. . . . Democracy that comes from above is no democracy, it is nothing but a relaxation of control. There will be a heavy fight. But it cannot be avoided."[28] For the few who were listening, Fang Lizhi's simple and courageous voice was prophetic. For the many who weren't, the massive demonstrations in Tiananmen Square were totally unexpected.

The cleavage between the Chinese people and their Communist rulers, purchased at such a price by the people, clarifies much. When the Communist party chief Jiang Zemin describes the conflict over democratization as "a serious class struggle that concerns the life and death of our party, state and nation," we recognize the class of democratic activists with whom his party struggles. When he voices optimism about the outcome and predicts a "bright Communist future for mankind," we are able to get a second opinion from Chinese dissidents.[29] And when he maintains that the socialist system is superior, and attributes China's continuing poverty solely to the size of its population, we recognize this for what it is: An attempt to blame the talented and industrious Chinese people for the failures of the party and system that he heads.

Jiang's claims, which in the recent past would have been taken seriously, can now be easily dismissed on the authority of Chinese dissidents, who regard Marxism as a nineteenth-century fallacy propounded by geriatric rulers supported by a sclerotic bureaucracy. In the view of Fang Lizhi, "Marxism belongs to a precise epoch of civilization which is over. It is like a worn dress that must be put aside. . . . [T]he only way open to China is that of reforms. Democracy, education, and intellectual freedom are its absolutely indispensable prerequisites."[30]

Asked to name the successes scored by the Communist party since "liberation," Fang's reply was blunt: "In China the Communist Party has never had any success. . . . Over the last thirty years it has produced no positive results." Fang's dismal view of the party's record was widely shared in China even before the Tiananmen massacre.

215

The hope expressed by Vogel and others that the Chinese Communist party can someday come to serve some more benign and socially useful purpose seems farfetched. Even if the party found the will to transform itself into a social democratic party along European lines, the Chinese people would surely vote it out of power during the free elections it would then be compelled to permit. The Chinese Communist party is often said to face a choice between adapting or perishing, but this understates its dilemma: to adapt *is* to perish.

If we in the West understand the People's Republic better today, our clearer vision does not come from academic China-watchers, foreign policy experts, or politicians, whose past portraits often have been misleading, self-serving, even false. It comes from the Chinese people, who have begun speaking to us directly about their aspirations for democracy, economic freedom, and human rights. A Fang Lizhi proclaiming the demise of Marxism requires no explanation; and there is no way to misinterpret a student waving this banner: "Give Me Liberty or Give Me Death."

Notes

Prologue
Nixon's Visit: The Chinese Shadow Game

1. Less than two years before, Chairman Mao had given an anti-American speech: "While massacring the people in other countries, U.S. imperialism is slaughtering the white and black people in its own country. Nixon's fascist atrocities have kindled the raging flames of the revolutionary mass movement in the United States. The Chinese people firmly support the revolutionary struggle of the American people." According to William F. Buckley, this speech was contained in a packet of material given to the American press corps. See *National Review,* 17 March 1972, p. 265.
2. *Department of State Bulletin,* 20 March 1972, p. 421.
3. *Chinese Shadows* (New York: Viking Press, 1977), p. 143.
4. *Department of State Bulletin,* 20 March 1972, pp. 422–23.
5. American pressmen present at the showing were more restrained in their praise. *Newsweek* (6 March 1972, p. 16) called it "a favorite Beijing potboiler," as if to suggest that Jiang Qing produced it because she was lacking the necessities of life.
6. *Newsweek,* 6 March 1972, p. 15.
7. Ibid., p. 16.
8. *Department of State Bulletin,* 20 March 1972, p. 432.
9. William F. Buckley, "Richard Nixon's Long March: Part II," *National Review,* 17 March 1972, p. 264.
10. Theodore H. White, "Journey Back to Another China," *Life,* 17 March 1972, p. 49.
11. Ibid., p. 49.

12. Ibid., p. 50.
13. Ibid., p. 50.
14. Ibid., p. 49.
15. Ibid., p. 50.
16. Buckley, "Nixon's Long March," p. 264.
17. Ibid., p. 265.
18. Ibid., p. 268.
19. White, "Another China," p. 50.
20. Buckley, "Nixon's Long March," p. 266.
21. Chen Jo-shi, "Nixon's Press Corps," in *The Execution of Mayor Yin* (Bloomington: Indiana University Press, 1978), pp. 210–11.
22. Ibid., p. 209.
23. *Newsweek*, 21 February 1972, p. 34.
24. The 1966 public opinion poll data is given in George H. Gallup, *The Gallup Poll: Public Opinion 1935–1971* (New York: Random House, 1972), p. 2015.
25. Buckley, "Mr. Nixon's Long March to China," *Inveighing We Will Go* (New York: G. P. Putnam's Sons, 1972), p. 79.

Chapter 1. Introduction: The Culture Brokers

1. Harold R. Isaacs, *Scratches on Our Minds: American Images of China and India* (New York: John Day, 1958), pp. 63–64.
2. Ibid., p. 71.
3. Reuven Frank, president of NBC News, informed his staff in 1963 that "every news story should, without any sacrifice of probity or responsibility, display the attributes of fiction, of drama. It should have structure and conflict, problem and denouement, rising action and falling action, a beginning, a middle, and an end." Cited in Jude Wanniski, ed., *The 1987 Media Guide* (New York: Harper & Row, 1987), p. 47.
4. Jan Myrdal, *Report From a Chinese Village* (New York: Random House, 1965) and Jan Myrdal and Gun Kessle, *China: The Revolution Continued* (New York: Random House, 1970), p. 192.
5. John Gurley, *China's Economy and the Maoist Strategy* (New York: Monthly Review Press, 1976), p. 13.
6. I recount this story in *Broken Earth: The Rural Chinese* (New York: The Free Press, 1983), pp. 302–6.
7. Ibid., p. 306.
8. Vera Schwarcz, *Long Road Home: A China Journal* (New Haven: Yale University Press, 1984), p. xx.

Chapter 2. Past Images of China

1. Herrlee Creel summarizes the activities and the influence of the Jesuits in China in *Confucius, The Man and The Myth* (New York: John Day, 1949), chap. 15.
2. Voltaire, "The Philosophy of History," in *Collected Works of Voltaire*, vol. 7 (New York: Walter J. Black, 1927), pp. 408–12. See also A. James Gregor, *The China Connection* (Stanford: Hoover Institution, 1986), pp. 1–3.
3. Quoted in Lewis M. Coser, *Men of Ideas: A Sociologist's View* (New York: Free Press, 1965), pp. 227–28.
4. Teng Ssu-yu, "Chinese Influence on the Western Examination System," *Harvard Journal of Asiatic Studies* 7 (1943): 267–312.
5. Arthur Christy, *The Orient in American Transcendentalism* (New York: Octagon, 1972; reprint of 1932 edition), pp. 6, 125. Cited in Isaacs, *Scratches on Our Minds: American Images of China and India* (New York: John Day, 1958), p. 96.
6. Isaacs, *Scratches on Our Minds*, p. 388.
7. Harley Fransworth MacNair, *The Real Conflict Between China and Japan: An Analysis of Opposing Ideologies* (Chicago: University of Chicago Press, 1938), pp. 26–27.
8. Jerome Ch'en, *China and the West* (Bloomington: Indiana University Press, 1979), p. 41.
9. Creel, *Confucius*, p. 263.
10. Kenneth Latourette, *The History of Early Relations Between China and the United States* (New Haven: Yale University Press, 1917), pp. 124–25.
11. Cited in Jerome Ch'en, *China and the West*, p. 41. For a brief summary of Fryer's numerous educational activities in China, see Paul A. Cohen, "Christian Missions and Their Impact to 1990," in *The Cambridge History of China*, Denis Twitchett and John K. Fairbank, vol. 10, Late Ch'ing, 1800–1911, Part 1, ed. John K. Fairbank (Cambridge, England: Cambridge University Press, 1978), pp. 579–80.
12. Ibid., p. 44.
13. Ibid., p. 41.
14. Arthur H. Smith, *Chinese Characteristics* (New York: Revell, 1894), and *Village Life in China* (New York: Revell, 1899; reprinted by Greenwood Press, New York, 1969).
15. Smith, *Village Life in China*, p. 5.
16. Paul A. Cohen, "Chinese Missions and Their Impact to 1900," in *The*

Cambridge History of China, vol. 10, Late Ch'ing, 1800–1911, Part 1, pp. 543–90.

17. John K. Fairbank, *The United States and China,* 3d. ed. (Cambridge: Harvard University Press, 1971), p. 298.

18. Earl Herbert Cressy, "Converting the Missionary," *Asia* (June 1919). Quoted in Isaacs, *Scratches on Our Minds,* p. 148.

19. Isaacs, Ibid., p. 164.

Chapter 3. The Age of Infatuation: American Journalists
in China During the 1930s and 1940s

1. A partial list of "adventurers" would include Tillman Durdin, Jack Belden, Albert Ravenholt, Harold Isaacs, and A. T. Steele.

2. Steven R. MacKinnon and Oris Friesen, eds., *China Reporting: An Oral History of American Journalism in the 1930s and 1940s* (Berkeley: University of California Press, 1987), p. 38.

3. The proceedings of this conference were published in 1987 as *China Reporting: An Oral History of American Journalism in the 1930s and 1940s,* edited by Stephen R. MacKinnon and Oris Friesen. It offers a unique historical retrospective into the mind set of the small coterie of correspondents who, more than any other group, were responsible for the way Americans came to view the contending forces in the Chinese Civil War. In the account that follows, I draw extensively on the comments recorded therein.

4. Ibid., p. 190.

5. See, for example, Theodore H. White and Annalee Jacoby's *Thunder Out of China* (New York: William Morrow, 1946), especially chap. 21, "Tentatively, Then . . ." (pp. 309–25).

6. MacKinnon and Friesen, *China Reporting,* p. 80.

7. John K. Emmerson. *The Japanese Thread: A Life in the U.S. Foreign Service* (New York: Holt, Rinehart and Winston, 1978), p. 207.

8. MacKinnon and Friesen, *China Reporting,* p. 85.

9. James Thompson, "Introduction," in MacKinnon and Friesen, *China Reporting,* p. 3.

10. Laszlo Ladany, *The Communist Party of China and Marxism, 1921–1985: A Self-Portrait* (Stanford: Hoover Institution Press, 1988), p. 209.

11. MacKinnon and Friesen, *China Reporting,* pp. 65, 81.

12. Ibid., p. 66.

13. Ibid., pp. 66–67. Zhou continued to seduce visiting foreigners—even

the most sophisticated—until the end of his life. Henry Kissinger, according to a close aide, "fell in love with the Zhou Enlai China. When Zhou went, it changed." Quoted in Richard Valeriani, *Travels With Henry* (Boston: Houghton Mifflin, 1979), p. 128.

14. MacKinnon and Friesen, *China Reporting,* pp. 81–82.
15. Raymond J. De Jaegher and Irene Corbally Kuhn, *The Enemy Within* (New York: Doubleday, 1952), pp. 213–14.
16. MacKinnon and Friesen, *China Reporting,* p. 40.
17. *New York Times,* 25 September 1944.
18. MacKinnon and Friesen, *China Reporting,* p. 80.
19. Ibid., p. 81.
20. Ibid., pp. 80–81.
21. Isaacs, *Scratches on Our Minds,* p. 163.
22. John Maxwell Hamilton, *Edgar Snow: A Biography* (Bloomington: Indiana University Press, 1988), p. 55.
23. Ibid., p. 131.
24. Ibid., p. 51.
25. Ibid., p. 52.
26. Ibid., p. 88.
27. Thompson in MacKinnon and Friesen, *China Reporting,* p. 4.
28. Emmerson, *The Japanese Thread,* pp. 181–82.
29. Quoted in E. J. Kahn, Jr., *The China Hands* (New York: Viking Press, 1975), p. 116.
30. Emmerson, *The Japanese Thread,* p. 183.
31. De Jaegher and Kuhn, *Enemy Within,* pp. 197–200.
32. *Christian Science Monitor,* 30 August 1944. This is a precursor of the "New Maoist Man" myth, which at this early stage had not yet become encrusted with the barnacles of Mao's personality cult.
33. *New York Times,* 26 November 1944.
34. *New York Herald Tribune,* 24 September 1944. His remarks about the nature of Chinese Communism are to be found on pages 178–80 of *Report From Red China* (New York: Holt, 1945).
35. Whittaker Chambers, *Witness* (reprint, Washington, D.C.: Regnery Gateway, 1980; originally published in 1952), pp. 497–98 of Regnery Gateway edition.
36. *New York Times,* 6, 13 August 1944. Epstein fails to mention the CCP practice of having its members agree in advance on a common position which, supported by a vocal and dedicated minority during the subsequent government meeting, would easily carry the day. Nor does he mention that every committee had several individuals who, though not

themselves members of the party, were sympathetic to its aims and were willing to follow its lead. What was a minority in theory became a majority in fact.

37. *Christian Science Monitor,* 25 July 1944.
38. William Tozer, "The Foreign Correspondents' Visit to Yenan in 1944: A Reassessment," *Pacific Historical Review* 41: 207–24. As evidence of Stein's sympathies, Tozer mentions his connection with the Sorge spy ring. See in this connection Chalmers Johnson's *An Instance of Treason* (Stanford: Stanford University Press, 1964), pp. 107–9.
39. *Christian Science Monitor,* 30 August 1944.
40. MacKinnon and Friesen, *China Reporting,* pp. 151–52.
41. Ibid., pp. 154–55.
42. Gunther Stein, *Christian Science Monitor,* 27 June 1944.
43. MacKinnon and Friesen, *China Reporting,* pp. 151–52.
44. Ibid., p. 130.
45. Mao Zedong, "The Role of the Chinese Communist Party in the National War," *Selected Works of Mao Tse-tung,* vol. 2 (Beijing: Foreign Languages Press, 1965), pp. 203–4.
46. MacKinnon and Friesen, *China Reporting,* p. 83.
47. Ibid., p. 190.
48. Chambers, *Witness,* p. 498.
49. MacKinnon and Friesen, *China Reporting,* p. 19. Hershey could be candid about his own political views. When Luce offered to bring him back to New York to train him for the managing editorship of *Time,* Hershey turned him down, arguing that he would be "a prickly choice, in view of [Luce's] bias in favor of the Republican party and the fact that I was a convinced Democrat." Here Hershey does not pretend that one's views are independent of the news; he is simply worried that the operant biases won't be his.
50. W. A. Swanberg, *Luce and His Empire* (New York: Scribner's, 1972), p. 225.

Chapter 4. The Age of Hostility

1. Mao Zedong, "On the People's Democratic Dictatorship," in *Selected Works of Mao Tse-tung,* vol. 4 (Beijing: Foreign Language Press, 1965), pp. 417–18.
2. Ibid. John K. Fairbank put the matter somewhat differently: "Since any individual could be transferred by a stroke of the pen to the category of reactionaries or enemies of the people, this framework was *completely flexible* as a basis for sifting out dissident members of the pop-

ulation," he wrote. "The power of class imputation remained with the Communist Party." (italics added) *The United States and China*, 3d. ed. (Cambridge: Harvard University Press, 1971), p. 328.

3. Fairbank later raised a dissenting voice, maintaining that the "people's democratic dictatorship" was a continuation of the united front that, in its particulars, "carried out the original idea of the New Democracy." But this was a minority view. *The United States and China*, 3d. ed., p. 328.

4. Father Ladany points out that in the *Xinhua Monthly,* a Beijing publication containing the month's major reports, articles on land reform were listed under politics, not under economy or agriculture, which he calls an "open admission of the true purpose and nature of the land reform." *The Communist Party of China and Marxism: A Self-Portrait, 1921–1985* (Stanford: Hoover Institution Press, 1988), p. 176.

5. *People's Daily,* 19 September 1951. Cited in Laszlo Ladany, *Communist Party of China and Marxism,* p. 178.

6. J. Clement Lapp, *Tensions in Communist China* prepared by the Legislative Reference Service for Senator Alexander Wiley (Washington, D.C.: Government Printing Office, 1960), p. 61.

7. Stephen Rosskamm Shalom, *Deaths in China Due to Communism,* Occasional Paper No. 15., Center for Asian Studies (Tempe: Arizona State University, 1984), p. 24.

8. Maurice Meisner, *Mao's China: A History of the People's Republic* (New York: The Free Press, 1977), p. 81.

9. Jacques Guillermaz, *La Chine populaire,* (Paris: Presses Universitaires de France, 1959), p. 47.

10. Jacques Guillermaz, *The Chinese Communist Party in Power, 1949–1976* (Boulder, Colo.: Westview Press, 1976), p. 24, n. 6.

11. Richard L. Walker, *The Human Cost of Communism in China,* (prepared for the Committee on the Judiciary of the United States Senate, 1971), p. 15.

12. For a fuller account of Bishop Ford's life—and death—see *The Pagoda and the Cross: The Life of Bishop Ford of Maryknoll* by John F. Donovan, M.M. (New York: Scribner's, 1967), especially chap. 7.

13. *New York Times,* 12 September 1952.

14. *Los Angeles Herald Examiner,* 12 September 1952.

15. The case of Bishop James E. Walsh of Shanghai is illustrative. In the spring of 1950 he was placed under house arrest for refusing to cooperate with Beijing's effort to create a schismatic "patriotic" Catholic church, and speaking out against the People's Republic. In 1958, he was convicted of espionage on behalf of the United States and sentenced

to twenty years imprisonment. Donovan, *Life of Bishop Ford of Maryknoll,* p. 182.

16. Isaacs, *Scratches on Our Minds: American Images of China and India* (New York: John Day, 1958), p. 212.

17. Seymour Topping, *Journey Between Two Chinas* (New York: Harper & Row, 1972), pp. 92–94.

18. As early as 1927, in one of his first published works, Mao had scorned the humanistic virtues of Confucian civilization as incompatible with revolution: "A revolution is not a dinner party, or writing an essay, or painting a picture, or doing embroidery, it cannot be so refined, so leisurely and gentle, so temperate, kind, courteous, restrained and magnanimous." This list of characteristics is not a casual compilation. Temperance, kindness, courteousness, restraint, and magnanimity were attributes ascribed to Confucius and his followers. See Mao Zedong, "Report on an Investigation of the Peasant Movement in Hunan," *Selected Works of Mao Tse-tung,* vol. 1 (Beijing: Foreign Language Press, 1965), p. 28.

19. *New York Times,* 10 October 1955.

20. Isaacs, *Scratches on Our Minds,* p. 223.

21. Stephen Rosskamm Shalom, *Deaths in China Due to Communism,* Occasional Paper no. 15, Center for Asian Studies (Tempe: Arizona State University, 1984), p. 25.

22. *New York Times,* 2 June 1959, "Editorial."

23. Mao Zedong, "On the People's Democratic Dictatorship," pp. 415–22.

24. Stuart R. Schram, *Mao Tse-tung* (Middlesex, Eng.: Penguin Books, 1966), p. 256.

25. Barry M. Richman, *Industrial Society in Communist China* (New York: Random House, 1969), pp. 405–6.

26. Isaacs, *Scratches on Our Minds,* p. 218.

27. See Robert Jay Lifton, *Thought Reform and the Psychology of Totalism: A Study of "Brainwashing" in China* (Middlesex, Eng.: Penguin Books, 1961).

28. "Statement Supporting the People of the Congo Against U.S. Aggression (28 November 1964)," *Quotations from Chairman Mao Tse-tung* (Beijing: Foreign Language Press, 1972), p. 82.

29. MacKinnon and Friesen, *China Reporting,* p. 84.

30. *Nun in Red China* (New York: McGraw-Hill, 1953); *Calvary In China* (New York: G.P. Putnam's, 1953); *Behind the Bamboo Curtain* (Washington, D.C.: Public Affairs Press, 1956).

31. Julian Schuman, *Assignment China* (New York: Whittier, 1956).

32. Liu Shau-tong, *Out of Red China*, trans. Jack Chia and Henry Walter (New York: Duell, Sloan & Pearce, 1953); Maria Yen, *The Umbrella Garden* (New York: Macmillan, 1954).

33. Frank Morae, *Report on Mao's China* (New York: Macmillan, 1953).

34. Isaacs, *Scratches on Our Minds*, pp. 214–15.

35. Lord Boyd Orr and Peter Townsend, *What's Happening in China?* (New York: Doubleday, 1959), p. 129.

36. George Stafford Gale, *No Flies in China* (New York: William Morrow, 1955), p. 184.

37. Cited in Gerald Clark, *Impatient Giant* (New York: David McKay, 1959), p. 142.

38. See, for instance, Kang Chao, *The Rate and Pattern of Industrial Growth in Communist China* (Ann Arbor: University of Michigan Press, 1965).

39. Walker, *Human Cost of Communism in China*, p. 6.

40. Clark, *Impatient Giant*, p. 143.

41. *Life*, 21 January 1957, p. 107.

42. Tai-chun Kuo and Ramon H. Myers, *Understanding Communist China: Communist China Studies in the United States and The Republic of China, 1949–1978* (Stanford: Hoover Institution Press, 1986), p. 10.

43. Benjamin Schwartz, "New Trends in Maoism?" *Problems of Communism* 4, no. 6 (July–August 1957): 7.

44. Richard L. Walker, *China Under Communism: The First Five Years* (New Haven: Yale University Press, 1955), p. 24.

45. Arthur F. Wright, "The Chinese Monolith, Past and Present," *Problems of Communism* 4, no. 4 (July–August 1955): 8.

46. Walter W. Rostow, *The Prospects for Communist China* (New York: John Wiley, 1954), p. 299.

47. John K. Fairbank, *The United States and China*, 2d. ed. (Cambridge: Harvard University Press, 1958), p. 314. Interestingly, the word *totalitarian* had been deleted from this passage in the Third Edition, which appeared in 1971. There the result of combining Communist theory and practice with traditional practices was merely "something quite new in Chinese experience." p. 327. Was Fairbank, too, reflecting changing perceptions of China, even though the Chinese reality of the 1950s and early 1960s had not changed?

48. In 1956 Carl Friedrich and Zbigniew Brzezinski identified the preconditions of a society that lead to a "totalitarian breakthrough." They contended that these features were common to both communist and fascist dictatorships in the twentieth century and included the following:

(1) an official, standard ideology; (2) a single mass party, typically led by one man; (3) a terroristic system of police control; (4) party control of mass communications; (5) party control of the army and of weapons; and (6) party control of the economy. *Totalitarian Dictatorship and Autocracy* (Cambridge: Harvard University Press, 1956), pp. 9–10.

49. Fairbank, 3d. ed., p. 326.

50. T. T., [pseudo.] "The Intellectual in the New China," *Problems of Communism* 2, no. 2 (1953): 4.

51. Lifton, *Thought Reform,* p. 420.

52. *Quotations from Chairman Mao Tse–tung* (Beijing, Foreign Language Press, 1972), p. 75.

53. *New York Times,* 22 February 1988. See also, the *Los Angeles Times,* 28 February 1988.

54. Isaacs, *Scratches on Our Minds,* p. 215.

55. Ta-chung Liu, "Quantitative Trends in the Economy," in Alexander Eckstein, Walter Galenson, and Ta-chung Liu, eds., *Economic Trends in Communist China* (Chicago: Aldine, 1968), pp. 143, 148.

56. Kuo and Myers, *Understanding Communist China,* p. 114.

57. Michael Croft, *Red Carpet to China* (New York: St. Martin's Press, 1959), p. vii.

Chapter 5. From Hostility to Second Admiration

1. Walker writes, "The term 'cultural diplomacy' probably represents a more accurate description of the Communist program than 'propaganda' or 'cultural relations,' because it calls attention to the fact that Sino-Soviet leaders utilize the exchange of information, ideas, persons, and culture as a systematic and unified arm of foreign policy. . . . Activities which for democratic societies are basically uncontrolled are within the Soviet-style framework an essential ingredient of foreign relations and the conduct of diplomacy." See "The Developing Role of Cultural Diplomacy in Asia," in *Issues and Conflicts,* ed. George L. Anderson (Lawrence, Kan.: University of Kansas Press, 1959), p. 45.

2. Earl Cressy, a well-known missionary educator, wrote in 1919 that home leave could be disconcerting for those who grew accustomed to Oriental courtesies. Rather than the expected sight of students quietly rising and bowing upon his entrance in American classrooms, he was greeted instead by a buzz of conversation that seemed uncivil. Compared with Chinese friends who bowed him out of the doors of their

homes, and even escorted him some distance down the street, American friends who saw him no farther than the apartment door and let him find his own way out of the building seemed lacking in courtesy. Earl Herbert Cressy, "Converting the Missionary," *Asia* (June 1919). Quoted in Isaacs, *Scratches on Our Minds,* p. 148.

3. One reason why foreigners found Zhou extraordinarily charming was that he, as the scion of an elite family, had early acquired first-rate skills in the art of Li.

4. Dennis Bloodworth, *The Messiah and the Mandarins: Mao Tsetung and the Ironies of Power* (New York: Atheneum, 1982), p. 154.

5. Robert Loh, "Setting the Stage for Foreigners," *Atlantic Monthly,* December 1959, p. 83.

6. Ibid., p. 83.

7. Ibid., p. 84.

8. Chermont de Brito, *Jornal Do Brasil* (7 November 1959, cited in William E. Ratliff, "Chinese Communist Cultural Diplomacy Toward Latin America, 1949–60," *The Hispanic American Historical Review* 49, no. 1 (February 1969): 77.

9. Ibid., p. 77.

10. The two were Frank Moraes' *Report on Mao's China* (1953), mentioned in the previous chapter, and Raja Hutheesing's *The Great Peace* (1953). Both were published in American editions.

11. Victor Alba, "The Chinese in Latin America," *China Quarterly* 5 (January–March 1961): 57.

12. Among the more sympathetic accounts were Basil Davidson's *Daybreak in China* (London: A.W. Bain, 1953), George Stafford Gale's *No Flies in China* (New York: William Morrow, 1955), and James Cameron's *Mandarin Red* (New York: Rinehart & Co., 1955). Julian Schuman's plainly pro-Communist *Assignment China* mentioned in the previous chapter falls in a different category, since he was later to become an employee of the regime.

13. Quoted in Ratliff, "Chinese Communist Cultural Diplomacy Toward Latin America, 1949–60," p. 60.

14. Simone de Beauvoir, *The Long March* (Cleveland: World Publishing Co., 1958), p. 10.

15. Hewlett Johnson, *China's New Creative Age* (London: Lawrence & Wisehart, 1953), pp. 110, 184.

16. Basil Davidson, *Daybreak in China* (London: Jonathan Cape, 1953), pp. 98, 134–35.

17. James M. Bertram, *Return to China* (London: Heineman, 1957), p. 37.

18. Scott Nearing, *The Making of a Radical* (New York: Harper & Row, 1972), pp. 247–48.

19. These quotations are taken from Felix Greene's book, *A Curtain of Ignorance* (Garden City, N.Y.: Doubleday & Co., 1964), pp. 159–60. The italics are in the original.

20. Ibid., pp. 161–62. The italics are in the original.

21. John K. Fairbank, *Chinabound: A Fifty-Year Memoir* (New York: Harper & Row, 1982), p. 338.

22. These charges were, in the view of some Sinologists, not without foundation. Professor Richard Thornton has recently written of Professor Fairbank that "[his] purpose was to help the Chinese Communists win the civil war against the Kuomintang. . . . as the raging Chinese civil war reached its critical stage, his views became less disingenuous and more strident. In "Can We Compete in China" his purpose was to bring about a U.S. military-aid cutoff from the Kuomintang and to demonstrate the indigenous roots of Chinese Communism." See "The King Has No Clothes," Unpublished manuscript in possession of the author, pp. 9, 12.

23. Walker, *Issues and Conflicts,* especially chap. 2.

24. Mary C. Wright, "Review of *China Under Communism,*" *The Far Eastern Quarterly* 15, no. 2 (February 1956): 274–76.

25. "China: Time for a Policy," *Atlantic Monthly,* April 1957, pp. 35–39.

26. Important elements of the KMT also had an animus toward traditional Confucian culture. Hu Shih, perhaps the leading Nationalist intellectual, was quoted as saying that "China has nothing worth preserving. If she has anything it will preserve itself. You foreigners who tell China that she has something worth preserving are doing a disservice for you are only adding to our pride. We must make a clean sweep and adopt Western culture and outlook." Quoted in E. Stanley Jones, "What I Saw in China," *Christian Century* 8 February 1933, p. 188. The only difference between this view and Mao's was that Hu Shih may have been content to let the old culture die a natural death. Mao wanted to practice cultural euthanasia.

27. Maurice Meisner, *Mao's China: A History of the People's Republic* (New York: The Free Press, 1977), p. 5.

28. Ping-ti Ho, "Salient Aspects of China's Heritage," in *China in Crisis: China's Heritage and the Communist Political System,* vol. 1, bk. 1, ed. Ping-ti Ho and Tang Tsou (Chicago: University of Chicago Press, 1968), p. 25.

29. In his "Comments" on Ho's article, Derk Bodde suggests that there is

a great difference between Confucian authoritarianism, and the Marxist-Leninist variety. Ibid., p. 58.

30. Thornton, "King Has No Clothes," p. 5.
31. Fairbank, *Chinabound,* pp. 317–18.
32. Ladany, *The Communist Party of China and Marxism: A Self-Portrait, 1921–1985* (Stanford: Hoover Institution Press, 1988), pp. 267–68. Mao's speech became public knowledge in the West only after it was published in 1969.
33. *Life,* 12 January 1959.
34. Ladany, *Communist Party of China,* p. 270.
35. Ibid., pp. 267–68.
36. Quoted in Dennis Bloodworth, *The Messiah and the Mandarins: Mao Tsetung and the Ironies of Power* (New York: Atheneum, 1982), p. 130.
37. In the section that follows, I draw heavily upon the work of Tai-chun Kuo and Ramon H. Myers, whose "modernizing communist regime" paradigm contains the following propositions: "[1] This regime sought to modernize China by means of competing visions, ideas, and policies that were either transformative or accommodative. [2] Because the regime primarily pursued transformative policies, economic policies fluctuated greatly when the leaders created new organizations and mobilized human and physical resources. These policies, however, did not seem to be associated with any long-run, serious dysfunctions in Chinese society. [3] The pattern of instability and mixed success at modernization owed much to the absence of traditional Chinese values and institutions, for which the leadership had not yet found appropriate substitutes." See Kuo and Myers, *Understanding Communist China: Communist China Studies in the United States and the Republic of China, 1949–78* (Stanford: Hoover Institution Press, 1986), pp. 21–29. This decriptive typology can be found on p. 22.
38. Benjamin Schwartz, "The First Decade," *China Quarterly* 1 (January–March 1960): 19–20.
39. Joseph R. Levenson, "Communist China in Time and Space: Roots and Rootlessness," *China Quarterly* 39 (July–September 1969): 10.
40. Victor H. Li, "The Role of Law in Communist China," *China Quarterly* 46 (April–June 1971): 66–111.
41. Kuo and Myers, *Understanding Communist China,* p. 25.
42. Alexander Eckstein, "Economic Growth and Change in China: A Twenty-Year Perspective," *China Quarterly* 54 (April–June 1973): 221. Cited in Kuo and Myers, p. 26.

43. Quoted in Felix Greene, *Awakened China: The Country Americans Don't Know* (Garden City, NY: Doubleday, 1961), pp. 102–3.
44. "Comments by Michel Oksenberg," *China in Crisis,* vol. 1, ed. Ping-ti Ho and Tang Tsou (Chicago: University of Chicago Press, 1968), p. 500.
45. Freda Utley, *China at War* (London: Faber & Faber, 1939), p. 74.
46. Edgar Snow, *The Other Side of the River: Red China Today* (New York: Random House, 1961), p. 122.
47. Ibid., pp. 106–7.
48. The Chinese premier may have been scarcely capable of more than pleasantries in English. "Zhou spoke poor English, so far as I could make out," Henry Lieberman of the *New York Times* recently recalled. "He had a trick that he'd pull . . . at some strategic point in the interview Zhou would stop the interpreter and say to him in English, 'No, not that word, this word.' " MacKinnon and Friesen, *China Reporting,* p. 81.
49. On famine see Snow, *Red China Today,* pp. 51–54, 147, 172–76, 280–81, 620–24.
50. In November 1932 Duranty reported vis-à-vis the Ukraine that "there is no famine or actual starvation nor is there likely to be." A year later he went even further, writing on 23 August 1933 that "any report of a famine in Russia is today an exaggeration or malignant propaganda." Cited in Robert Conquest, *Harvest of Sorrow* (New York: Oxford University Press, 1986), p. 319. Estimates of the number who died are given on p. 306.
51. Edward Friedman, "Maoism and the Liberation of the Poor," *World Politics* 39 (3): 408–28.
52. Felix Greene, *A Curtain of Ignorance: How the American Public has been Misinformed About China* (Garden City, N.Y.: Doubleday, 1964), pp. 98–99.
53. Ibid., pp. 93–94, 96.
54. Tracy Strong and Helen Keyssar, *Right in Her Soul: The Life of Anna Louise Strong* (New York: Random House, 1983), p. 318.
55. Third edition (Cambridge: Harvard University Press, 1971), p. 374. In the fourth edition, published in 1979, Fairbank's earlier judgment is unchanged despite additional information that had come to light in the meantime.
56. Harrison Salisbury, *To Peking and Beyond: A Report on the New Asia* (New York: Quadrangle, 1973).
57. Typical of this view is Professor Alexander Eckstein's letter to the *New*

York Times, which appeared on 5 May 1957: "The efficiency of food distribution has been greatly improved. As a result, the Chinese Communist regime is in a position to quickly alleviate or prevent local famines which have been traditional in China throughout history."

58. C. P. Fitzgerald, *Mao Tse-tung and China* (New York: Holmes & Meier, 1976), p. 119.

59. Meisner, *Mao's China,* p. 250.

60. Quoted in Reed J. Irvine, "Phantom Food in Communist China," *Asian Survey* 1, no. 1 (March 1961): 23.

61. Dr. George H. Gallup, *The Gallup Poll* (New York: Random House, 1972), pp. 1711, 1773. Despite their generally hostile attitude toward Communist China and its leaders, a majority of those polled answered in the affirmative in 1961, and a plurality in 1962 when it was asked again.

62. "Factionalism in the Central Committee," in *Party Leadership and Revolutionary Power in China,* ed. John Wilson Lewis (Cambridge: Harvard University Press, 1970), pp. 224–25. See also "A Chronicle of Events in the Life of Liu Shaoqi (1899–1967)," in *Current Background,* no. 834, 27 August 1967, pp. 20–21; and Dennis Bloodworth's *The Messiah and the Mandarins,* p. 182.

63. See J. Chester Cheng, ed., *The Politics of the Chinese Red Army* (Stanford: Hoover Institution Press, 1966).

64. Juergen Domes, *Internal Politics of China: 1949–72* (New York: Praeger, 1973), p. 115; see also his earlier estimate in *Von Der Volkscommune zur Kriese in China* (Studiengesellschaft zur Zeitprobleme, Bonn, 1964), p. 51.

65. Miriam London and Ivan D. London, "Hunger: Part 1–The Three Red Flags of Death," *The Other China* (New York: Council on Religion and International Affairs, 1977), pp. 4–11.

66. John S. Aird, personal communication, 12 July 1989.

67. Gallup, 1972, *The Gallup Poll,* pp. 1259, 1981. In answer to the question, Do you think Communist China should or should not be admitted as a member of the UN?, 79 percent answered in the negative in 1954 versus 67 percent in 1965.

68. Ibid., pp. 1881, 2325.

69. Ibid., p. 1931. Fifty-nine percent of the respondents thought that the Soviet Union would fight on the side of China; 18 percent, the United States.

70. Ibid., pp. 2104–5.

71. Ibid., p. 2015.

Chapter 6. The Second Age of Infatuation

1. Staughton Lynd and Tom Hayden, *The Other Side* (New York: New American Library, 1966), pp. 17–18.
2. Ibid., p. 40.
3. Ibid., p. 45.
4. Ibid., p. 46.
5. Ibid.
6. Ibid.
7. Robert Heilbroner, "Socialism and the Future," *Commentary*, 48, no. 8 (December, 1969): 36.
8. *Decision of the Central Committee of the Chinese Communist Party Concerning the Great Proletarian Cultural Revolution* (Beijing: Foreign Language Press, 1966), pp. 1–13.
9. Beijing Red Guards, "Long Live the Revolutionary Rebel Spirit of the Proletariat" (24 June 1966), in David Milton, Nancy Milton, and Franz Schurmann, eds., *People's China* (New York: Random House, 1974), pp. 284–85.
10. "Kwangsi Clashes Said to be Brutal: Losing Maoist Faction Says 50,000 Died on One Side," *New York Times*, 22 September 1968.
11. "U.S. Said to Lead in China Studies: Experts Believe Research is Dispelling Mystery," *New York Times*, 19 June 1966, p. 6.
12. "Purpose and Policy Statements," *Bulletin of Concerned Asian Scholars* 2, no. 1 (October 1969): 8–9.
13. Ibid., pp. 8–9.
14. James Peck, "The Roots of Rhetoric: The Professional Ideology of America's China Watchers," *Bulletin of Concerned Asian Scholars* 2, no. 1 (October 1969): 59–69.
15. Ibid., p. 65.
16. *Bulletin of Concerned Asian Scholars* 8, no. 2 (January–March 1976): 2.
17. I do not mean to suggest that the following descriptive typology encompasses the entire range of views of the Bulletin's Editorial Board, or among its authors and subscribers. However, most of those who sat on its Editorial Board and published in its pages from 1968 to about 1978 generally agreed with the typology's tenets.
18. In this section I again owe an intellectual debt to Kuo and Myers, who offer the following descriptive typology of the "revolutionary socialist regime: "[1] The Chinese revolutionary socialist regime, strongly influenced by Maoist thought and policies, initiated revolutionary strategies that greatly improved the welfare of the Chinese people and created a

more egalitarian society. [2] These developments were not associated with any severe difficulties for this new leadership and society." *Understanding Communist China: Communist China Studies in the United States and the Republic of China, 1949–1978* (Stanford: Hoover Institution Press, 1986), p. 29. I have appended to this the emphasis on "the revolutionary masses as a motive force in China's development" that frequently crops up in the writings of the concerned scholars.

19. John G. Gurley, *China's Economy and the Maoist Strategy* (New York: Monthly Review Press, 1976), p. 5. See also, "Capitalism and Maoist Economic Development," *Bulletin of Concerned Asian Scholars* 2, no. 3 (April–July 1970): 34–50.

20. Gurley, *China's Economy and the Maoist Strategy*, p. 11.

21. Carl Riskin, "China's Economic Growth: Leap or Creep?" *Bulletin of Concerned Asian Scholars* 2, no. 2 (January 1970): 22.

22. Committee of Concerned Scholars, *China! Inside the People's Republic* (New York: Bantam Books, 1972), p. 2.

23. Carl Riskin, "Maoism and Motivation: Work Incentives in China," *Bulletin of Concerned Asian Scholars* 5, no. 1 (July 1973): 11.

24. Stephen Andors, "The Dynamics of Mass Campaigns in Chinese Industry," *Bulletin of Concerned Asian Scholars* 8, no. 4 (October–December 1976): 38.

25. Phyllis Andors, "Social Revolution and Women's Emancipation: China during the Great Leap Forward." *Bulletin of Concerned Asian Scholars* 7, no. 1 (January–March 1975): 33–42.

26. Ibid., p. 37.

27. Benedict Stavis, "How China is Solving its Food Problem," *Bulletin of Concerned Asian Scholars* 7, no. 3 (July–September 1975): 22, 31. Stavis cites as his authority for these points the *Beijing Review*, a colorful English-language publication produced in Beijing for foreign consumption. He was not alone among the concerned scholars in accepting this publication as a serious source.

28. William F. Buckley's interview with the Harvard Professor Ross Terrill on the PBS talk show *Firing Line*, "The Meaning of China," (Transcript dated 12 March 1972, Southern Educational Communications Association) p. 8.

29. Gurley, *China's Economy and the Maoist Strategy*, p. 13.

30. Mark Selden, *The Yenan Way in Revolutionary China* (Cambridge: Harvard University Press, 1971), pp. vii–viii.

31. Gurley, *China's Economy and Maoist Strategy*, p. 16.

32. Richard D. Baum, "Ideology Redivivus," *Problems of Communism* 16, no. 3 (May–June 1967): 1.

33. Edward Friedman, "Cultural Limits of the Cultural Revolution," *Asian Survey* 9, no. 3 (March 1969): 188–201.

34. Soon after the bloodshed ended, the Chinese government began trying to minimize the armed conflict that had gripped the country, and especially the number of deaths. Professor Frolic, for instance, reported of his 1971 visit to China that "a number of Chinese criticized the Western press for 'grossly exaggerating' the violence that actually occurred in China between 1966 and 1970. Frequently Chinese officials, after a discussion at a commune or factory, would pointedly observe, 'As you can see, foreign friends, there was no violence here. The Cultural Revolution triumphed without bloodshed.' " B. Michael Frolic, "What the Cultural Revolution Was All About," *The New York Times Magazine*, 24 October 1971, p. 116.

35. Roland Berger, "Financial Aspects of Chinese Planning," *Bulletin of Concerned Asian Scholars* 6, no. 2 (April–August 1974): 16. Although a Frenchman, Berger is clearly operating within the revolutionary socialist paradigm.

36. Concerned Asian Scholars, *China!*, p. 112.

37. These propositions are not self-evidently false unless, of course, one has fixed notions of the nature of both human beings and communist systems. Casual visitors not so equipped had little reason not to conclude that peasant life was much improved, or be impressed by the spartan cleanliness of that city. The reader will find the evidence and a refutation in the next chapter.

38. See, for example, William F. Buckley's interview with "Harvard Professor and China expert" Terrill on the PBS talk show *Firing Line*, "The Meaning of China," p. 5.

39. Gurley, *China's Economy and the Maoist Strategy*, p. 13.

40. Heilbroner, "Socialism and the Future," p. 37.

41. James Peck, "The Roots of Rhetoric: The Professional Ideology of America's China Watchers," *Bulletin of Concerned Asian Scholars* 2, no. 1 (October 1969): 66.

42. See, for example, James Peck, "The Roots of Rhetoric: The Professional Ideology of America's China Watchers," *Bulletin of Concerned Asian Scholars* 2, no. 1 (October 1969): 59–69; John K. Fairbank and Jim Peck, "An Exchange," *Bulletin of Concerned Asian Scholars* 2, no. 3 (April–July 1970): 51–70.

43. This quote comes from Peck's response to Fairbank, "In Reply," pp. 56–57.

44. Richard M. Pfeffer, "Revolution and Rule: Where Do We Go From

Here?" *Bulletin of Concerned Asian Scholars* 2, no. 3 (April–July 1970): 89.

45. John K. Fairbank, "The New China and the American Connection," *Foreign Affairs* (October 1972): 31–36.

46. John S. Service, "Life in China is 'Obviously Better,' " *New York Times*, 26 January 1972, p. 37; "China's Very Unstarchy Army," *New York Times*, 27 January 1972, p. 37.

47. See, for example, W. F. Buckley's "The Meaning of China," *Firing Line*, p. 5.

48. B. Michael Frolic, "What the Cultural Revolution Was All About," *The New York Times Magazine*, 24 October 1971, pp. 119, 127.

49. Ivan and Miriam London and Ta-ling Lee, "The Making of a Red Guard," *The New York Times Magazine* 4 January 1970, pp. 8, 9, 56, 58, 60, 64, 66, 67, 68. This article became part of the first chapter of their later book, *Revenge of Heaven* (New York: G. P. Putnam's Sons, 1972), about the experiences of a Red Guard leader. Although in recent years a number of similar accounts have been published, it remains the best.

50. Ezra Vogel and Martin Whyte, "The Red Guards and China's Image," *The New York Times Magazine*, 1 February 1970, Letters Section, p. 20.

51. "The Red Guards and China's Image: Dr. London Replies," *The New York Times Magazine*, 1 February 1970, Letters Section, p. 20.

52. Ibid. It is revealing that the concerned scholars were never called to account by their mentors for their uncritical attitude toward, and excessive reliance on, Communist party and government sources, even though by their admission they treated such sources as unimpeachable.

53. Ibid.

54. John K. Fairbank, "A Review of 'Revenge of Heaven,' " *China Watch* (Cambridge: Harvard University Press, 1987), pp. 156–57. Italics added.

55. Kuo and Myers, *Understanding Communist China*, p. 108.

56. *Renmin Ribao*, 1 October 1979, p. 1.

57. "The Bitter Tea of Mao's Red Guards," *The New York Times Magazine*, 19 January 1969, p. 35.

Chapter 7. The Selling of China: Nixon's Visit

1. Allen S. Whiting, "SALT on the Dragon's Tail," *The New Republic*, 9 September 1972, p. 12.

2. *The Lincoln-Douglas Debates,* Edited by Robert W. Johannsen (New York: Oxford University Press, 1965), pp. 64–65.

3. "President Nixon's Visit to the People's Republic of China," *Department of State Bulletin* (Washington, D.C.: Government Printing Office, 20 March 1972), pp. 419–38.

4. Stanley Karnow, "China Through Rose-Tinted Glasses," *Atlantic Monthly* (October 1973), p. 74.

5. As correspondent Richard Valeriani wrote, "[I]t was apparent to anyone who traveled with Kissinger that Zhou was the one international figure he respected more than any other he dealt with—and he dealt with everybody in his time. For him, none of the others had the dazzling combination of intelligence, charm, sophistication, wit, and—to revive a once-popular word—charisma that Zhou possessed." *Travels With Henry* (Boston: Houghton Mifflin, 1979), pp. 94–95.

6. Marvin Kalb and Bernard Kalb, *Kissinger* (Boston: Little, Brown, 1974), p. 253. Kissinger, who could not even use chopsticks before he went to China, was fertile ground for the planting of a whole range of images. "Henry's knowledge—substantial knowledge and appreciation of nuances—about China was *zilch,*" one China specialist was reported to have remarked. (p. 216).

7. "President Nixon's Visit to the People's Republic of China," *Department of State Bulletin* (Washington, D.C.: Government Printing Office, 20 March 1972), p. 435.

8. See, for example, Buckley, "The Meaning of China," *Firing Line,* p. 9.

9. Galeazzo Santini, "A Great Wall of Philosophy," *Successo* 13, no. 11 (November 1971): 95–96. Quoted in Kuo and Myers, *Understanding Communist China,* p. ix.

10. Quoted in John Osborne, "Packing for Peking," *The New Republic* 19 February 1972, pp. 11–12.

11. William F. Buckley, "The Chinese Exhibitionists," Syndicated Column, *The Washington Star Syndicate,* December 14–15, 1974, p. 1.

12. Stanley Karnow, "China Through Rose-Tinted Glasses," p. 74.

13. David Kolodney, "Et tu China?" *Ramparts* (May 1972), p. 12.

14. Seymour Topping, "New Dogma, New Maoist Man," *Report from Red China* (New York: New York Times Co., 1971), p. 258.

15. Renamed in 1980, after the Sino-Vietnamese War.

16. Seymour Topping, "Rural China: Change and Continuity," *Report from Red China* (New York: New York Times Co., 1971), p. 153.

17. Audrey Topping, "Dirt is Now a Dirty Word," *Report from Red China* (New York: New York Times Co., 1971), p. 126.

18. Max Frankel, "A Reporter's Notebook," *New York Times,* 25 Feb-

ruary 1972. Frankel wrote the *Times'* lead story for each day of Nixon's trip.

19. James Reston, "Now, About My Operation in Peking," *Report from Red China* (New York: New York Times Co., 1971), p. 310.
20. James Reston, "China is Building a New Nation," *Report from Red China* (New York: New York Times Co., 1971), p. 246.
21. "Eric Severeid's Interview With James Reston," *Report from Red China* (New York: New York Times Co., 1971), pp. 338–89, 354–55.
22. Joseph Kraft, *The Chinese Difference* (New York: Saturday Review Press, 1972), pp. 6–7.
23. Ibid.
24. Harrison Salisbury, *To Peking—and Beyond* (New York: Quadrangle, 1973), p. 13.
25. Ibid., p. 61.
26. Ibid., p. 70.
27. Ibid., pp. 69–70.
28. Ibid., p. 81. An additional irony is that the goods so proudly displayed by the villagers were, in effect, purchased with the state subsidies that all model communes enjoyed.
29. Ibid., p. 301.
30. Much of Mao's later verse was actually the creation of a young Beijing poet and passed off as the Chairman's.
31. Ibid., p. 302.
32. "China Meets the Press," *Newsweek*, 6 March 1972, p. 26.
33. The first characterization appeared in "Zhou: The Man in Charge," *Time*, 21 February 1972, p. 30; the second in "By the Editors," *Life* 28 June 1954.
34. Salisbury, *To Peking*, p. 59.
35. Karnow, "China Through Rose-Tinted Glasses," p. 75.
36. Joseph Alsop, "On China's Descending Spiral," *China Quarterly* 11 (July–September 1962): 21–37. See also Joseph Alsop's column in the *New York Herald Tribune*, 13 September 1961, and David Shipler's article "New China Seen by Joseph Alsop," *New York Times*, 4 February 1973, p. 11.
37. Shipler, "New China," p. 11.
38. Ibid.
39. Ibid.
40. "A Second-Rate Power—With a Long Way to Go," *U.S. News & World Report*, 28 February 1972, pp. 16–17.
41. Robert P. Martin, "China Revisited," *U.S. News & World Report*, 12 March 1972, p. 29.

42. "Coming of Age in Communist China," *Newsweek,* 21 February 1972, p. 44.
43. "Excursions in Mao's China," *Time,* 6 March 1972, p. 17.
44. John Kenneth Galbraith, *A China Passage* (Boston: Houghton Mifflin, 1973), p. 137.
45. Nien Cheng, *Life and Death in Shanghai* (New York: Harper & Row, 1968).
46. William F. Buckley, "The New New China," Syndicated Column, Universal Press Syndicate, 9–10 July, 1983, p. 3.
47. Orville Schell, *In the People's Republic* (New York: Random House, 1977), p. 263.
48. David Rockefeller, "From a China Traveler," *New York Times,* 8 October 1973, p. 31.
49. Charlotte Salisbury, *China Diary* (New York: Walker, 1973).
50. Ibid., p. 2.
51. Ibid.
52. Ibid, p. 3.
53. Ibid., pp. 3–5.
54. Ibid., pp. 130, 137, 163.
55. Ibid., p. 51.
56. Ibid., p. 8.
57. Ibid., p. 201.
58. Al Imfeld, *China as a Model of Development* (Maryknoll, N.Y.: Orbis Books, 1976).
59. Gustavo Gutierrez, *A Theology of Liberation* (Maryknoll, N.Y.: Orbis Books, 1973), pp. 32, 91, 235, 237.
60. John G. Gurley, *Challengers to Capitalism* (New York: Norton, 1979), p. 182.
61. Michel Oksenberg, "On Learning from China," *China's Developmental Experience,* ed. Michel Oksenberg, Proceedings of the Academy of Political Science 31 (March 1973): 1–2.
62. Ibid., pp. 2, 16.
63. John K. Fairbank, "The New China and the American Connection," *Foreign Affairs* (October 1972).
64. "Mainland Chinese Have Risen in Favor of U.S., Poll Finds," *New York Times,* 13 March 1972, p. 5.
65. See, for example, John Osborne's "The Nixon Watch: Mission to China," *The New Republic* 4 March 1972, p. 8; or Harrison Salisbury's *To Peking—And Beyond,* p. 253.
66. The quotes are from Karnow, "China Through Rose-Tinted Glasses," p. 73.

Chapter 8. The Age of Disillusionment

1. Later, they were to benefit from the able assistance of history professor Ta-ling Lee, who became a research associate.

2. Ivan and Miriam London, "Three Stories from the Chinese Countryside," *China News Analysis* 960, 17 May 1974, p. 7.

3. As Dr. London explained, "Literary techniques were used in order to present the data in sufficient psychological and environmental context to suggest the living reality. As befits a research report, however, no liberties have been taken with the data." Ibid., p. 1.

4. Miriam and Ivan London, "The Other China, Hunger: Part I: The Three Red Flags of Death," "The Other China, Hunger: Part II: The Case of the Missing Beggars," and "The Other China: How Do We Know China? Let Us Count the Ways . . . ," *Worldview* (May, June, July, 1976). This series was later reprinted, along with letters received from supporters and critics, as a separate monograph, *The Other China* (New York: Council on Religion and International Affairs, 1977).

5. Bush's remarks came in response to a question from Senator Percy, who had received reports of a "great deal of malnutrition" in Tibet. Bush replied: "What you have said, sir, comes as a surprise to me. Maybe some of our experts can confirm it. Is anyone prepared to do that?" The CIA's China experts were silent.

   Later, at the conclusion of Bush's testimony, Senator Percy offers his own summary: "In other words, so far as we know, the claim that they have made that they are meeting the food problems of the country, and our own observations along that line, were accurate?"

   "Yes," Bush replied.

   "And I think they have been absolutely remarkable," Senator Percy added.

   Quoted in L. Navrozov, "What the CIA knows about Russia," *Commentary* (September, 1978), 66(3): 54.

6. Leo Orleans, *The Role of Science and Technology in China's Population/Food Balance* (Washington, D.C.: Congressional Research Service, 1977). *Science* magazine heralded the book as "a study of China's central accomplishment, her apparent ability to control population growth and keep her 850 million people adequately fed." See the "Role of Science in China's Development," *Science* 198: 1129.

7. The uniformity of such views was implied by one of the Londons' critics, who accused them of "ignoring the researched reports and studies of dozens of specialists from Japan, Europe, and North America." London and London, *The Other China*, p. 18.

8. Benedict Stavis, *Making Green Revolution: the Politics of Agricultural Development in China* (Ithaca, N.Y.: Cornell University, 1974).
9. Dwight Perkins, in *China: A Reassessment of the Economy,* papers submitted to the Joint Economic Committee of the U.S. Congress (Washington, D.C.: Government Printing Office, 10 July 1975), p. 353.
10. Donald E. MacInnis, "Letters to the Editor," London and London, *The Other China,* p. 25.
11. Ibid., "The Londons Respond."
12. Simon Leys, *Chinese Shadows* (New York: Viking Press, 1977).
13. *New York Times,* 7 April 1976.
14. *New York Times,* 26 July 1976. In 1977 Munro was informed by the Chinese Foreign Ministry that his visa would not be renewed.
15. Quoted in Ross Terrill, *The Future of China After Mao* (New York: Delacorte, 1978), p. 121.
16. *The New York Review of Books,* 14 October 1976, p. 3.
17. Galbraith, *A China Passage,* p. 120.
18. Martin King Whyte, "Inequality and Stratification in China," *China Quarterly* 64 (December 1975): 685, 692.
19. Donald S. Zagoria, "China by Daylight," *Dissent* (Spring 1975): 136.
20. Simon Leys, "Human Rights in China," *Quadrant* (November 1978): 74.
21. Leys, *Chinese Shadows,* p. 117.
22. Ibid., p. 56.
23. *Washington Post,* 20 March 1971. Cited in Alan Reynolds, "A Reader's Guide to Visitors' Reports," *National Review,* 3 March 1972, p. 211.
24. Leys, *Chinese Shadows,* p. 201.
25. Ibid., p. 184.
26. Orville Schell, *In The People's Republic* (New York: Random House, 1977), p. 208. Leys, *Chinese Shadows,* p. 75.
27. Leys, *Chinese Shadows,* p. xix.
28. Ibid., p. xi. Peter Kenez made the same point in an article recounting his 1973 trip to China: "I regarded China as a poor and backward nation that had made great strides in economic development at an enormous cost in freedom." ("Traveling in China," *The New Leader,* 26 November 1973, p. 6.)
29. William Safire, "The New Mysteries," *The New York Times Magazine,* 19 June 1977, p. 52.
30. James A. Michener, "China Diary," *Reader's Digest* (May 1972), pp. 284, 287.
31. George H. Gallup, *The Gallup Poll: Public Opinion 1972–1977,* vol. 2, 1976–1977 (Wilmington, Del.: Scholarly Resources, 1978), p. 915.

32. Frank Ching, "China: It's the Latest American Thing," *New York Times,* 16 February 1972, p. 14.

33. Edward N. Luttwak, "Seeing China Plain," *Commentary* (December 1976), p. 33.

34. A fuller account of this episode can be found in Jay Mathews and Linda Mathews, *One Billion: A China Chronicle* (New York: Random House, 1983), p. 24.

35. Malcolm W. Browne, "Visitor's Views of China's Gains Seen as Overstated," *New York Times,* 27 March 1979.

36. Claudie Broyelle and Jacques Broyelle, "Everyday Life in the People's Republic," *Quadrant* (November 1978), p. 16.

37. Fox Butterfield, *New York Times,* 30 September 1979.

38. James P. Sterba, *New York Times,* 12 February 1980.

39. Fox Butterfield, "Tree Loss in China Affecting Climate," *New York Times,* 18 April 1979.

40. Jay Mathews, "Scars of China's Cultural Revolution Linger in Province," *The Washington Post,* 11 April 1980, p. A36.

41. Adam Ulam, " 'The Essential Love' of Simone de Beauvoir," *Problems of Communism* 15 (March–April 1966): 63. Quoted in Paul Hollander, *Political Pilgrims* (New York: Harper & Row, 1981), p. 11.

42. Schell, *In the People's Republic,* pp. vii–viii.

43. *People's Daily,* 1 October 1979, p. 1.

44. Michel Oksenberg, "Mao's Policy Commitments, 1921–1976," *Problems of Communism* 24, no. 6 (November–December 1976): 19, 22.

45. "The Magic Filter," *New China* (Fall 1979): 51.

46. Orville Schell, "Friend of China," p. 10.

47. The first quote comes from *800,000,000: The Real China* (Boston: Little, Brown, 1971), p. 9; the second from "Beijing: Trying to Make China Work," *The Atlantic,* July 1983, p. 28.

48. Edward Friedman, "McCarthyism in China," *New York Times,* 21 February 1979.

49. Edward Friedman, "The Innovator," in *Mao Tse-tung in the Scales of History,* ed. Dick Wilson (New York, Cambridge, 1977), pp. 300, 302, 320.

50. Arthur Schlesinger, "Letter to the Editor," *The New York Times Book Review,* (13 December 1981).

51. Maurice Meisner, "Most of Maoism's Gone, But Mao's Shadow Isn't," *New York Times,* 5 July 1981, Op-Ed Page.

52. Quoted in Chapter 2, p. 45.

53. See John K. Fairbank, *Chinabound: A Fifty-Year Memoir* (New York: Harper & Row, 1982).

54. John K. Fairbank, *China Watch* (Cambridge: Harvard University Press, 1987), pp. 187, 194.

55. Paul Hollander has ably reviewed this phenomenon in his *Political Pilgrims: Travels of Western Intellectuals to the Soviet Union, China, and Cuba.* (New York: Harper & Row, 1981).

56. For example, Feng Shengping of Yale University dismisses as "racist condescension" the notion, which permeates Fairbank's writings, that "democracy and human rights are inappropriate to China's traditionally authoritarian and group-oriented society." Personal communication with the author, July 22, 1989.

Chapter 9. The Age of Benevolence

1. "Visionary of a New China," *Time,* 1 January 1979, p. 12.

2. Ibid., pp. 12–13.

3. Miriam London, "China: The Romance of Realpolitik," *Freedom at Issue,* no. 110 (September–October 1989): 11.

4. "Visionary of a New China," p. 20.

5. Philip Snow, *The Star Raft: China's Encounter with Africa* (New York: Weidenfeld and Nicolson, 1988), p. 69.

6. Seymour Topping, *Journey Between Two Chinas* (New York: Harper & Row, 1972), p. 2.

7. Yet she refrained from drawing larger conclusions about her lifetime of experience with the Chinese Communist party because, as she put it, "I was afraid that those who believed that the party had changed would simply ignore my entire experience. I wanted my story to reach and educate the American people." Personal communication with the author, July 1989.

8. Jim Mann, "U.S. Double Standard Seen on China Rights," *Los Angeles Times,* 23 November 1987. During his June 1986 visit to China, Carter also gave an interview to Chinese newspapers in which he commended Beijing for its praiseworthy treatment of the Tibetan people.

9. See, for example, Steven W. Mosher, " 'One Family, One Child': China's Brutal Birth Ban," *Washington Post,* 18 October 1987.

10. In 1987 two other foreign correspondents, representing the French news agency Agence France-Presse, and the Japanese agency Kyodo were expelled from China without major incident. See Mann, "U.S. Double Standard Seen on China Rights."

11. Richard Nixon, "America and China: The Next Ten Years," *New York Times,* 11 October 1982.

12. Judith Shapiro and Liang Heng, "China: How Much Freedom," *The New York Review of Books,* 24 October, 1985.
13. Doug Henwood, "China Crisis," *Left Business Observer,* 13 June 1989, p. 1.
14. Quoted in Miriam London, "China: the Romance of Realpolitik," p. 12.
15. See Roberta Cohen's "People's Republic of China: The Human Rights Exception," *Human Rights Quarterly* 9 (1987): 447–549 for a review of the reaction of American politicians and policy makers to human rights abuses in China.
16. Fang Lizhi, "Double Standard on Human Rights?" Translated by Orville Schell, *Washington Post,* 26 February 1989.
17. Harold Isaacs, *Scratches on Our Minds: American Images of China and India* (New York: John Day, 1958), p. 193.
18. Deng's remark has been widely reported. See, for example, Edward Friedman, "Letters to the Editor," *Chronicle of Higher Education,* 16 August 1989, p. B3.
19. Ezra Vogel, *One Step Ahead in China: Guangdong under Reform* (Cambridge: Harvard University Press, 1989).
20. Ibid., p. 5.
21. Ibid., p. 7.
22. Ibid., p. 413.
23. Ibid., p. 415.
24. Ibid., p. 419.
25. Ibid., p. 421.
26. Ezra F. Vogel, "From Friendship to Comradeship: The Change in Personal Relations in Communist China," *China Quarterly* 21 (January–March): 46.
27. Vogel, *One Step Ahead in China,* p. 421.
28. "China: Deng Xiaoping Leads a Far-Reaching, Audacious But Risky Second Revolution," *Time,* 6 January 1986, p. 28.

Chapter 10. From American Illusions to Chinese Reality

1. "China's Rising Tide of Unrest," *Newsweek,* 8 May 1989, p. 30.
2. Not everyone was surprised by the attack. On June 1, the *Central Daily News,* the official newspaper of the Nationalist Party of the Republic of China on Taiwan, published a news article asserting that an all-out assault on Beijing was imminent. Citing military intelligence sources, the report said that the Chinese leadership had ordered the army to retake Beijing at all costs and had authorized the use of deadly force

against students and other demonstrators. The assault came three days later, on the night of June 4.

3. Robin Munro was one of the Westerners with the final group of several thousand students occupying the Square. He reports that they evacuated the Square shortly before dawn on June 5 without loss of life. On the eighth he joined a BBC camera crew as an interpreter and was astonished to hear the BBC correspondent refer to the massacre of these students during the course of a broadcast as if it were an established fact. Robin Munro, personal communication with the author, 18 February 1990.

4. "Outside Agitators for Democracy: From the U.S., Chinese Students Fight On," *U.S. News & World Report*, 7 August 1989, p. 34.

5. Meg Greenfield, *Washington Post*, 8 June 1989.

6. Editorial, *Washington Post*, 5 June 1989.

7. Michel Oksenberg, "Confessions of a China Watcher: Why No One Predicted the Bloodbath in Beijing," *Newsweek*, 19 June 1989, p. 30.

8. Ezra Vogel, *One Step Ahead in China: Guangdong Under Reform* (Cambridge: Harvard University Press, 1989), p. vii.

9. Maria Chang, "Mao's Revenge: Totalitarianism Returns to China," *The Asia Column*, May–June 1989 (Montclair, Calif: The Claremont Institute, 1989), p. 2.

10. Leo Orleans, "Students Bear Much of the Responsibility for the Tragedy in China," *Chronicle of Higher Education*, 19 July 1989, p. A36.

11. Letters to the Editor, "Scholars Must Not Collaborate with China's Disgraced Regime," *Chronicle of Higher Education*, 16 August 1989, p. B3.

12. Ibid.

13. Karl Hutterer, "Chengdu had its Own Tiananmen Massacre," "Letters" section, *New York Times*, 23 June 1989.

14. James L. Tyson, "A Marxist Farmer Leaves China," *The Christian Science Monitor*, 28 June 1989. By way of contrast, the Marxist weekly, *The Workers World Party*, denounced the students "as counterrevolutionaries" and commended the army for "its decisive action." Cited in the *National Review*, 4 August 1989, p. 8.

15. The Gallup Organization, *Gallup Survey on American Attitudes Toward China in the Wake of the June, 1989 Crackdown: Summary of the Findings* (Princeton: The Gallup Organization, July 1989).

16. Ibid., pp. 11, 14.

17. Ibid., pp. 14, 18.

18. Nien Cheng, "Massacre in Beijing," *National Review*, 4 August 1989, p. 31.

19. The Chinese leadership was grateful for this assistance. A secret report published in the official journal, *Internal Reference Selections,* mentions Bush, Nixon, and Kissinger by name as working to repair Chinese-American relations. See "Strained U.S. Ties Reported in China: Secret Article Foresees More Conflicts but Says Bush Seeks to Cut Damage," *New York Times,* 5 October 1989, p. 19.
20. Steven Mosher, "The China Syndrome," *Reason,* October 1989, p. 23.
21. Ibid.
22. Henry Kissinger, "The Caricature of Deng as a Tyrant is Unfair," *Washington Post,* 1 August 1989.
23. Henry Kissinger, "The Drama in Beijing: When a Communist Country Tries to Make a REAL Great Leap Forward," *Washington Post,* 11 June 1989, p. C7.
24. David Holley, "Nixon Urges Beijing to Mend Fences," *Los Angeles Times,* 31 October 1989, p. A5.
25. Orville Schell, "Fang's Netherworld: Light a U.S. Candle," "Opinion" page, *International Herald Tribune,* 19 June 1989.
26. Miriam London, "China: The Romance of Realpolitik," *Freedom at Issue,* no. 110 (September–October 1989): 12.
27. Harold Isaacs, "Quarterback Nixon's Asian Game Plan," *The New Republic,* 19 February 1972, p. 22.
28. Tiziano Terzani interview with Fang Lizhi, "Farewell Marx and Mao; Your Party is Over," *Far Eastern Economic Review,* 22 October 1987, p. 52.
29. David Holley, "China's Party Chief Predicts a 'Bright Communist Future,' " *Los Angeles Times,* 30 September 1989.
30. Terzani, "Farewell Marx and Mao," pp. 53, 55.

List of Permissions

Material from "Richard Nixon's Long March: Part II" by William F. Buckley (*National Review*, March 17, 1972) copyright © by National Review, Inc., 150 East 35th Street, New York, NY 10016. Reprinted by permission.

Material from *The Enemy Within* by Raymond J. De Jaegher and Irene Corbally Kuhn (New York: Doubleday, 1952) reprinted by permission of Irene Corbally Kuhn.

Material from "The Red Guards and China's Image: Dr. London Replies," letter by Miriam London (*The New York Times Magazine*, February 1, 1970), copyright © 1970 by the New York Times Corporation. Reprinted by permission.

Material from *Chinese Shadows* by Simon Leys, English translation copyright © 1977 by Viking Penguin. Reprinted by permission of Viking Penguin, division of Penguin Books U.S.A., Inc.

Table from *The Gallup Poll: Public Opinion 1972–1977* by George H. Gallup (Wilmington: Scholarly Resources, 1978) reprinted by permission of the Gallup Organization.

Material from *Scratches on Our Minds: American Images of China and India* by Harold Isaacs. Copyright © 1958 by the Massachusetts Institute of Technology. Reprinted by permission of Harper & Row, Publishers, Inc.

Material from *China Reporting: An Oral History of American Journalism in the 1930s and 1940s* by Stephen MacKinnon and Oris Friesen, copyright © 1987 The Regents of the University of California. Reprinted by permission.

Index